Writing the Pandemic

Frameworks for Writing
Series Editor: Martha C. Pennington, Birkbeck University of London

The *Frameworks for Writing* series offers books focused on writing and the teaching and learning of writing in educational and real-life contexts. The hallmark of the series is the application of approaches and techniques to writing and the teaching of writing that go beyond those of English literature to draw on and integrate writing with other disciplines, areas of knowledge, and contexts of everyday life. The series entertains proposals for textbooks as well as books for teachers, teacher educators, parents, and the general public. The list includes teacher reference books and student textbooks focused on innovative pedagogy aiming to prepare teachers and students for the challenges of the 21st century.

Published:

Academic Writing Step by Step: A Research-based Approach
Christopher N Candlin, Peter Crompton, and Basil Hatim

Arting and Writing to Transform Education: An Integrated Approach for Culturally and Ecologically Responsive Pedagogy
Meleanna Aluli Meyer, Mikilani Hayes Maeshiro, and Anna Yoshie Sumida

Creativity and Discovery in the University Writing Class: A Teacher's Guide
Edited by Alice Chik, Tracey Costley, and Martha C. Pennington

Creativity and Writing Pedagogy: Linking Creative Writers, Researchers, and Teachers
Edited by Harriet Levin Millan and Martha C. Pennington

Digital L2 Writing Literacies: Directions for Classroom Practice
Ana Oskoz and Idoia Elola

English Composition Teacher's Guidebook: How to Survive (and Even Thrive) as an Adjunct or Part-time Instructor
Tom Mulder

Exploring College Writing: Reading, Writing, and Researching across the Curriculum
Dan Melzer

Investigative Creative Writing: Teaching and Practice
Mark Spitzer

Reflective Writing for Language Teachers
Thomas S. C. Farrell

Tend Your Garden: Nurturing Motivation in Young Adolescent Writers
Mary Anna Kruch

The "Backwards" Research Guide for Writers: Using Your Life for Reflection, Connection, and Inspiration
Sonya Huber

The College Writing Toolkit: Tried and Tested Ideas for Teaching College Writing
Edited by Martha C. Pennington and Pauline Burton

Understanding the Paragraph and Paragraphing
Iain McGee

Writing Poetry through the Eyes of Science: A Teacher's Guide to Scientific Literacy and Poetic Response
Nancy S. Gorrell, with Erin Colfax

Writing the Pandemic

An Instructor's Reflections on a New Era in Education

Tom Mulder

SHEFFIELD UK   BRISTOL CT

Published by Equinox Publishing Ltd.

UK: Office 415, The Workstation, 15 Paternoster Row, Sheffield, South Yorkshire S1 2BX
USA: ISD, 70 Enterprise Drive, Bristol, CT 06010

www.equinoxpub.com

First published 2023

British Library Cataloguing-in-Publication Data

A catalogue record for this book is available from the British Library.

ISBN 978 1 80050 342 7 (hardback)
      978 1 80050 343 4 (paperback)
      978 1 80050 344 1 (ePDF)
      978 1 80050 378 6 (ePub)

Library of Congress Cataloging-in-Publication Data

Names: Mulder, Tom (English teacher), author.
Title: Writing the pandemic : an instructor's reflections on a new era in
  education / Tom Mulder.
Description: Sheffield, South Yorkshire ; Bristol, CT : Equinox Publishing
  Ltd, 2023. | Series: Frameworks for writing | Includes bibliographical
  references and index. | Summary: "Writing the Pandemic addresses the
  many challenges that writing instructors and students have faced since
  the arrival of COVID-19 and their ramifications for teaching and
  learning. This book is intended for an audience of first-year college
  composition teachers and other English and language arts instructors at
  the postsecondary and secondary levels"-- Provided by publisher.
Identifiers: LCCN 2022058654 (print) | LCCN 2022058655 (ebook) | ISBN
  9781800503427 (hardback) | ISBN 9781800503434 (paperback) | ISBN
  9781800503441 (pdf) | ISBN 9781800503786 (epub)
Subjects: LCSH: English language--Rhetoric--Study and teaching (Higher) |
  English language--Rhetoric--Study and teaching (Secondary) | COVID-19
  Pandemic, 2020---Influence.
Classification: LCC PE1404 .M75 2023 (print) | LCC PE1404 (ebook) | DDC
  808/.0420711--dc23/eng/20230411
LC record available at https://lccn.loc.gov/2022058654
LC ebook record available at https://lccn.loc.gov/2022058655

Typeset by S.J.I. Services, New Delhi, India

Teaching is a radical act of hope.
It is an assertion of faith in a better future in an increasingly uncertain and fraught present.

—Kevin M. Gannon

Contents

Series Editor's Preface

Writing the Pandemic is written both for and to the multitudes of college English teachers who took on the monumentally challenging task of teaching first-year composition during the COVID pandemic. In so doing, these dedicated academics helped to issue in a new era in education defined by novel teaching and learning environments, which in turn created a need for new instructional contents and processes. Tom Mulder takes the reader on a journey through the COVID years and how he and his students participated in evolving these new instructional environments, contents, and processes in response to the many constraints and changes brought about by the pandemic. He draws attention to educational adjustments and innovations that are now well established and potentially permanent, and he speculates on what the post-pandemic future holds for the teaching of first-year writing and for education in general.

Through the lens of the pandemic, the author tackles many of the common themes and issues of first-year composition, including what to teach and how to teach, how to handle students' difficulties and competing demands, how to ensure a climate of fairness and social justice, and how to have positive and lasting impacts on those just starting in higher education. The book is philosophical as well as practical, including three essay assignments presented in detail, with student-ready Instruction Sheets for implementing and assessing every stage of the writing process and sample compositions for each assignment. It is written in a personal and reader-friendly style expressing the author's perceptive observations and insightful reflections in a voice that communicates his knowledge and experience, his beliefs and point of view, his creativity and flair for writing, and his commitment to students and dedication to teaching work.

For those who have been teaching during this same period, as well as for those new to teaching who have been students during the COVID years, much of what Mulder advises and proposes will sound familiar. Much of what might not be shared experience should nevertheless ring true, and readers should find the remainder of the author's reflections and recommendations, including his views on teaching post-pandemic, thought-provoking and enlightening.

Martha C. Pennington
Series Editor
Frameworks for Writing

Acknowledgements

A deeply heartfelt thank-you to my students, whose fortitude and perseverance in facing the pandemic and its numerous, attendant consequences continues to motivate and challenge me every day. Their indomitable pursuits of learning and success inspire me with hope, humility, and gratitude. And their insights help me refine and focus my attempts to make writing and learning ever more interactive, incremental, pragmatic, and democratic.

A special thanks to the students who graciously allowed me to include their exemplary writing in this book: David Austin, Sebastian Benavides, Justin Duhimbaze, Drew Gommesen, Denise Jones, Hadley Mueller, Ashtyn Stewart, and Holly Tovar, as well as many others who shared their COVID photos and granted me permission to include them in this book (some with and others without their names as they preferred).

Another big thank-you goes to Equinox Publisher Janet Joyce for agreeing to print this book in such an unsettled time and through delays caused by COVID-induced supply chain shortages. Thanks, too, to Reuben Israel for his textual design and typesetting, as well as to Mark Lee for his cover design including the youthful English Writing adjunct instructor from the cover of my *English Composition Teacher's Guidebook* (Equinox, 2000), now masked, on the cover of this book, and to Sarah Lee for her additional assistance.

Especially, I am grateful to Editor Martha Pennington, who accepted *Writing the Pandemic* for Equinox's Frameworks for Writing series and examined multiple drafts of the manuscript painstakingly, offering particularly helpful and insightful suggestions.

Finally, a huge thank-you goes to Cathy and my family for giving me up to these writing and teaching tasks for so many hours, days, weeks, months, and now years.

—Tom Mulder
Hudsonville, Michigan
Easter 2023

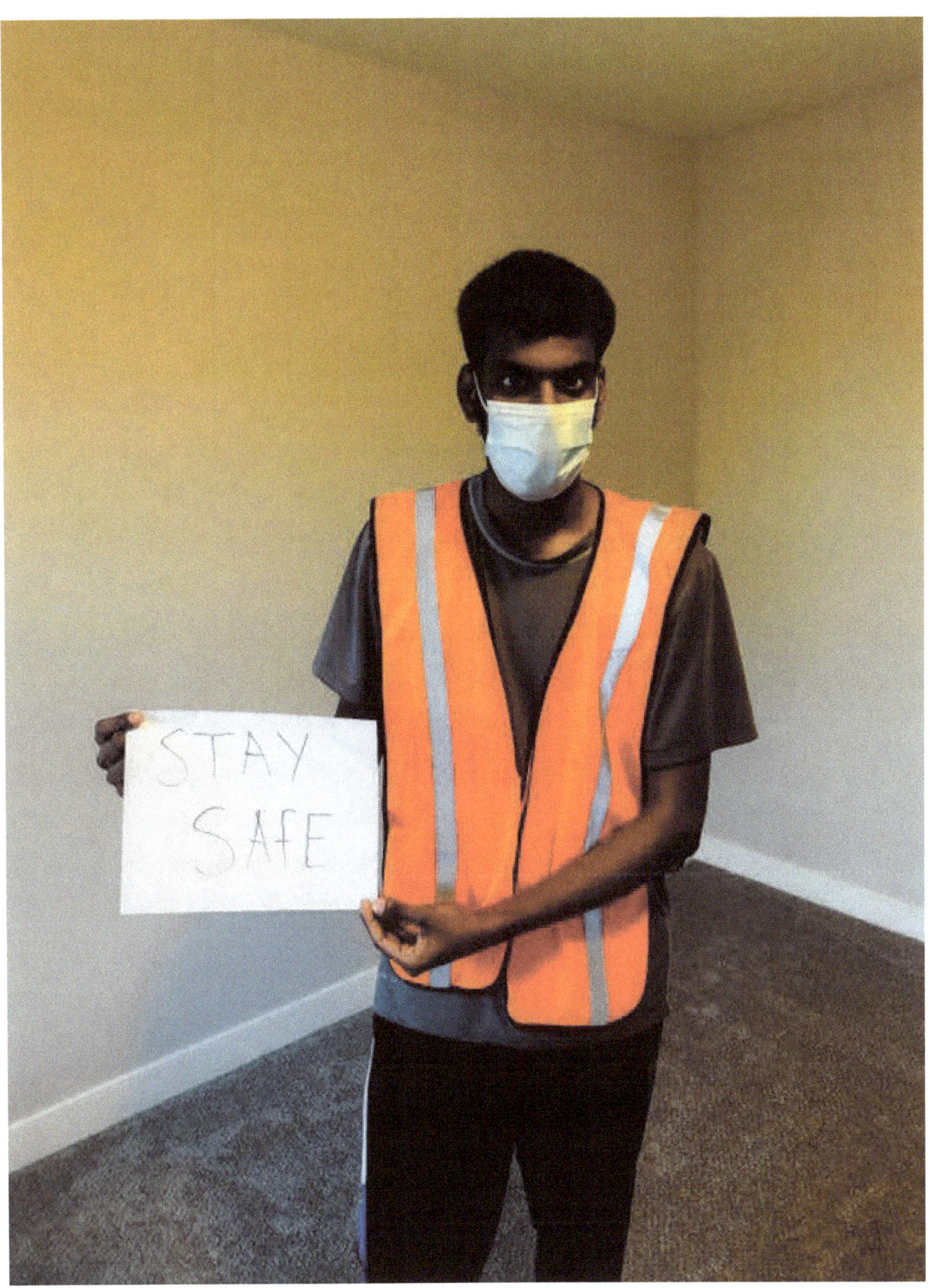

Figure 1. Stay safe. Photo Courtesy of Mayaran Mahadevan.

COVID Quote–2020

November 20—The U.S. Centers for Disease Control Warns Against Holiday Travel
The CDC urges Americans to stay home for Thanksgiving amid national spikes in COVID-19 cases and hospitalizations. The agency recommends that people avoid mingling with people who have not resided in their household for the last 14 days. As cases in the United States surpass 11 million, CDC officials worry that the situation could worsen during the holiday season.

—"A Timeline of COVID-19 Developments in 2020." American Journal of Managed Care, 20 November 2020, www.ajmc.com/view/a-timeline-of-covid19-developments-in-2020.

Figure 2. Doug Seelye exits 2020. Photo by Author.

Preface

Separation

When my in-person classes transitioned to remote instruction again the week before Thanksgiving Day during the fall term of 2020, I was not surprised, nor were my students. As they arrived at our last class on that Tuesday, no one admitted to anything other than a resigned acceptance of what we all agreed was inevitable. Most of them, after all, had given up the last three months of their senior season in high school, surrendering the pageantry and pomp of prom, graduation, class trips, and sports, as well as the fuss and tributes of open houses that hereabouts had grown into one-ring circuses with outdoor rental tents, catered smorgasbords, neighborhood signage, and bundles of balloons bobbing in graduates' commit-to college colors.

"Honestly, I'm surprised we lasted in person as long as we did. We did things right—washing hands, waiting our distance, and wearing masks—but my friends say [the local university] students still partied like ever: no safety precautions off campus."

"Actually, I thought we had a better chance of making it to Thanksgiving, maybe not Christmas, but at least to December. At least, I hoped so."

"Well, we came close, right?"

"I think we're further along into the semester than we got to last spring, aren't we?"

An adjunct English composition instructor, I taught first-year writing at a two-year community college one riverine valley north of Michigan's heel of the hand, positioned a couple blocks uphill from the Grand River, which cuts a lengthy lifeline across the state's peninsular palm westward, looping around Grand Rapids before dispensing into Lake Michigan at Grand Haven. The campus sits centered in the city, tucked between a sprawling, hyperactive hospital complex uphill to the east, many comparatively subdued government offices and courthouses northwards, and businesses, coffee shops, breweries, restaurants, hotels, an arena, and a convention center prevailing west-southwesterly, downhill along the river.

In the fall 2020 semester, besides my own students I rarely encountered anyone on campus except the two history adjuncts who shared my classroom at either end of my assigned times, a spattering of their history students, and the phalanx of custodians charged with cleansing the building's passages, classrooms, and restrooms before, between, and after classes. Most part-time and full-time instructors, in addition to the clerical staff and administrators, were home-bound, safely ensconced.

A commuting campus, ours experienced no one lingering for long beyond class times, especially that fall when fewer than 20% of the nearly 15,000 students attended classes on campus. Waived fees, financial incentives, a host of technological supports like mobile hotspots and laptop loaners, food bank aid, and mental and physical health advice encouraged students to enroll and study remotely that latter half of 2020. What normally is a bustling hive of students skateboarding and scootering, snacking and socializing around park tables, loitering at park benches and parking garages to text or check messages, and crowding at bus stops and curbs for carpools, pickups and drop-offs, and the odd Lyft or Uber, the campus commons often was mine alone to trek to/through as classes were assigned hither and beyond at staggered times to ensure individuals' distancing. Maintaining six feet was rarely a problem—outside of class, that is.

"Does everyone have working technology and online access at home?"

Almost all nodded, many closing their laptops. "Is the library going to stay open?"

I did not know. "Keep checking the website. Do you have a local library?" Already, I knew several county libraries that were restricting patrons to curbside pickups and parking lot wi-fi access, or closing altogether.

"There's always Starbucks and McDonald's," one chuckled, then sobered. "They won't close, will they?"

"Does IT offer remote wi-fi access? I live pretty far, and I can't get online at home. The town's library where I've been going to get online is already closed."

"Good question—Does anyone know?"

"No, I don't know that, but the college has wi-fi in its parking lot now if you don't mind working out of your car. I've tried it, and it's not so bad. But then I customized my Subaru…" the Automotive Tech student pushed down the accelerator and revved the engine.

"Yeah-yeah, boxer four-wheel drive, no mileage to speak of, and pristine body when you bought it for only fifteen grand down south somewhere, we know," another interrupted, chuckling behind her mask. We had all heard this mantra more than once.

"I'll see what I can learn about a remote wi-fi hotspot from the IT department. Could that benefit anyone else?"

A couple more hands raised and heads bobbed.

"Let me know if you encounter any problems, and what I don't know yet, I'll try to find out soon. Don't worry: We are going to make this work out for us all. Thanks for taking good care of yourselves and looking out for one another this semester. Keep up with the syllabus schedule, and I'll post every week's activities and assignments the Friday before, so you can get a preview on weekends. I'm going to check my email box twice a day, so send me your questions. Keep checking your emails, too: I'll be in touch. And one last time, please keep your distance as you exit. There's really no need to wipe down your worktables today. Be safe."

With that, class dismissed, my properly distanced students departing singly, obligingly waiting to file out the designated exit of our double-length classroom one by one, one final time.

Fortunately, we were flexible this second time, for we had almost all experienced this transition to remote learning before, albeit much more abruptly, back in March. That first time, sudden and jarring, caught my first-year composition students and me unprepared. This, although unwelcomed, disruptive, and discouraging, was not unexpected.

Contact

I think of teaching first-year composition as a contact game. Although it does not require blocking or passing, it involves plenty of conversations and interactions to plan, revise, and polish ideas and drafts. Often, the classroom hums with pods of students working together on group assignments, seeking consensus on a sentence-combining exercise, for instance, by sounding aloud their proffered suggestions to listen for clarity and cohesion within its context; or they may also be listening to one another read their introductions of essay drafts and share ideas to improve openings or thesis statements. Now and then, they may be interrupted by their instructor, who calls out from within a group, "Everyone, take a minute to finish what you're doing, so you can hear this amazing opener." While groups hurry to finish their conversations, the teacher asks softly, "Antony, would you like to read it to the class yourself, or would you rather I did?" Afterwards, there is a follow-up "Well, that deserves a hand!" And, following the applause, further encouragement to participate: "Who else tried something similar?"

Without tackling anyone, first-year writing instructors may catch a student who would benefit from a pep-talk to complete an essay or a reminder of an encroaching due date. They might run interference to prevent a group's insurrection against an individual who has not been contributing faithfully, possibly coping with undisclosed personal, family, or roommate struggles. Furthermore, instructors could stroll their classrooms to see what each student is penning or typing, eavesdrop or participate in groups' conversations or peer reviews, and redirect or refocus individuals' interactions as situations warrant. In the writing classroom, teachers can effectively guide learning and composing alongside individual students, writing partners, and discussion groups.

However approached, guiding students' writing cannot be accomplished nearly as efficiently or effectively when distanced. Most remote contacts, regardless of whether they are conducted individually or with groups, require dissociated, non-face-to-face text-only communication or on-screen, flattened-on-a-monitor interactions. Even projecting sample or collaborative documents does not confer the benefits of an instructor's physical positioning beside and among student writers. Lost is most of the in-class camaraderie, the implicit, "We are in this together, I am working beside you to assure your success, and I, too, struggle with these demands of writing." Nearly as challenging, *guiding alongside* is made difficult when masked and distanced, even when learning together inside the same classroom. Groups are less together when they need to be spaced out and individual members separated by six feet; and masks, particularly when all are seated at a distance from each other, obscure vocal, facial, and bodily expressions, making them all hard to interpret.

Most students had recently returned from their spring breaks when the two campuses where I work, the downtown community college and the local state university, closed for the semester in March 2020. For both colleges, spring break meant the midpoint of a semester, allowing students and staff a breather to refresh before the second half of the term kicked off. The clearing of campuses was abrupt, even jarring, and if so for us instructors, likely more so for our students, many of whom who had returned from spring vacations southward and were immediately required to vacate dorms and apartments to head for home. Most of them, planning for a brief "coronavacation," packed only the necessities for a two-week homestay, just enough for a virus to pass on before they expected to return to school and studies. Surges of 50 to 150 positive cases struck the nations of Italy and Iran. Then Latin America and North America each experienced their first diagnosed cases of COVID-19. No one knew what those early cases portended.

Closing classrooms and college campuses again at Thanksgiving initially felt like a relief. Already before the holiday, students and teachers alike worried aloud about what germs would be carried back onto campus and into dorms, cafeterias, classrooms, and laboratories by peers returning from their homes and travels. Without the campus and classroom safety protocols that colleges and universities had established back in September and maintained so assiduously throughout the fall, winter's resolve could suddenly crumble after the holiday as students and staff returned from regions that did not have mask mandates, distancing protocols, or contact-tracing practices. The risks of travel—inhaling the possibly infected exhalations of other passengers while sitting at length in the close quarters of a jet, train, bus, or car, or passing through hordes of travelers in airports, train stations, or bus depots—threatened a heightened spread of the coronavirus pandemic that for young and healthy students on campus lay mostly dormant but off-campus could ravage the elderly and the health-compromised. Post-holiday return journeys looked worrisome and even potentially lethal: only a few infected at a travel hub or family gathering could return on-campus and ignite a viral flare-up in a dormitory, classroom, athletic event, or other campus building or gathering.

The Howling 2020's
Begun during the holidays of Thanksgiving and Christmas 2020, *Writing the Pandemic* relates my experiences teaching first-year writing classes at two West Michigan schools, an urban community college and a rural state university, as the COVID-19 novel coronavirus took hold of our communities and institutions in that tumultuous year and then continued to affect us into a second and then a third year. My experiences, like those of many other first-year composition instructors, include transitions from teaching in-person, classroom-based, writing workshops to remote, online delivery in the spring semester of 2020; then on to the planning and teaching of a completely online first-year writing class that summer; and finally returning in the fall of that year to in-person, distanced classrooms, equipped with precautionary adaptations and periodically affected by interventions during the semester as knowledge of the virus itself developed—only to have the campuses and classrooms vacated again the week before Thanksgiving before a second spike of the virus. I later reflect on the second and then third years of the pandemic and what this might portend for the future of composition teaching and learning.

In every chapter, I note some observations about an apposite topic through which to compare the teaching of college composition before, during, and after the pandemic—or Before Pandemic (BP), During Pandemic (DP), and After Pandemic (AP). The changes writing instructors made to endure the extraordinary year of 2020 and its aftermath are sure to influence the teaching of composition for the foreseeable future; for what in 2020 seemed an anomaly now appears to be a perennial rite of returning to school as newer, more or less virulent variants of the virus spawn fresh outbreaks, as we learned in the holiday period at the end of 2021 and starting the new year of 2022, when the new omicron variant spread like wildfire. In each chapter I also pose a reflection question to ponder or spark a discussion with colleagues. Unfolding events during the virus's early spread in 2020–21 are posted throughout to recall the initial outbreaks and effects of SARS-CoV-2, the Severe Acute Respiratory Syndrome Coronavirus, in colleges and composition classes, and revisit the recurrences of the pandemic's successive waves and undercurrents.

I have also incorporated excerpts from some of my own blogs about the pandemic, along with several of my students' stories about their experiences contending with the COVID-19 pandemic. Posted irregularly as COVID-19 traveled around the globe, first flying from Asia to Europe and the Americas, next visiting my Michigan campuses, then lodging for extended stays nearby, I blogged observations and speculations while the virus moved and mutated. In addition, I invited my first-year writing students to record their own experiences with the virus, encouraging them to share their narratives. Many graciously granted me permission to include excerpts from their contributions as well as their personal photos, which are supplemented by some which I took. I have sometimes captioned these in a way which poses reflection questions related to the content of the chapter where they appear.

The book includes four complete and ready-to-use assignments, one in each of the even-numbered chapters, the first (in Chapter 2) a photo-based icebreaker. Reflecting my own experiences in a year of topsy turvy backs-and-forths in COVID responses, the three essay assignments (in Chapters 4, 6, and 8) incorporate step-by-step writing processes that I adapted to be able to pivot seamlessly whether teaching via an in-person classroom, a hybrid instructional format, or a wholly online remote mode. First is the (Virtual) Tour Essay, a place-based essay assignment that can be readily adapted by instructors for their own students to explore the town or area in which their institution is located, the environs and buildings of their campus, the student's hometown, or another chosen place of interest. Student writers may explore their city or campus in person as safety precautions and viral remediations allow, or they can map it online, taking care to note venues' openings and closings as well as any limited hours or restrictions related to health and other relevant conditions.

The Career Exploration Essay involves students' utilization of their educational institution's placement resources, selected websites, and opportunities for interviews if available, to research an occupation of their choice. Besides researching the job's duties, suggested education and preparation, starting and average salaries for their region and another area, students are asked to relate their own aptitudes and interests to the career as well as consider how it may benefit not only themselves and their own futures, but also their families, communities, and society.

Finally, the Unsung Hero/Ethnography Research Essay, particularly poignant in a season of pandemic and its demands of and tolls taken on essential workers, begins with an interview of an individual who may be often overlooked or underappreciated. After writing a descriptive profile of this Unsung Hero, students are asked to determine a background characteristic or interest of that person to research, normally using assigned resources from the institution's library, including an appropriate database. This is the aspect of the assignment in which they will be doing an ethnography of a group or people who share some characteristic(s) with their Unsung Hero—such as other people from the same ethnic group, people who do the same kind of work, or people who have the same hobby or interest.

For all of these assignments, I include a series of step-by-step processes to guide students through making an essay plan, generating a rough draft, crafting a revised draft, peer reviewing one another's revised drafts, then editing and formatting to complete a final draft, and finally reviewing and reflecting on what they have written. Each of these six steps is outlined on its own page, ready for projecting in a classroom, posting on a course's learning management system, or photocopying to hand out. Any of the steps can be readily adapted, combined, or omitted to best fit your own classroom needs and teaching practices. A sample student essay is included with each of the three essay assignments.

Besides the three essay assignments, a Photo Activity invites students to roam the campus or community, seeking a suitable spot to snap a selfie that reflects their educational aspirations. Camera in hand, they can arrange a pictorial composition that includes themselves in a campus setting chosen for its personal appeal or its influence on their choice of college, program, or degree: the hall or building reflecting their major subject, the library carrel or coffee shop used as a study space, a favorite outdoor spot or campus view, a campus monument or art work.

Writing the Pandemic may remind many writing instructors of their own experiences when the plague of 2020 descended on their communities and the world at large. Besides university and college instructors of first-year composition classes, other relevant audiences for the book are those teaching at the post-secondary level as well as teachers of English in high schools and middle schools, who also had to suddenly scramble to translate their teaching deliveries into new formats delivered through alien modalities to separated, distanced, and sometimes frightened and challenged students.

All teachers of writing will find useful practical material in this book, including the three essay assignments and opening Photo Activity with descriptions of writing processes and succinct instruction pages ready to project in a classroom or upload onto a class's online site electronically, in addition to suggestions for assessments and adaptations for different modes of instructional delivery.

College students and their families, too, may be interested in *Writing the Pandemic*. One or more of the students' stories probably parallel their own experiences. They may extract an insight out of the disruptive, often devastating, transitions demanded by remote teaching and learning or from the presumed implications for the future of higher education, particularly as these affect writing and first-year composition. Finally, any who seek a history of the uniquely tumultuous, globally calamitous opening of the third decade of the 21st century and its effects in 2020 and subsequent years on the students, teachers, classrooms, and campuses that rode out its storms might discover that the experiences related here prompt their own recalls and narratives.

Thank you for reading *Writing the Pandemic*. As challenging, and sometimes distressing as the Years—and its recurring effects during this Decade—of the Pandemic have been, may these memories help redress past shortcomings, reform current practices, and spur and shape future successes in our teaching and learning. May the trials of the 2020's and our continuing adaptations to COVID-19 lead to future gains in growth, hope, and resolve in teaching first-year writing as well as in mutual healing across educational institutions and communities in this and other countries. Teachers of first-year college writing, especially—for our classes include almost every student at the university or college, often at the beginning of their studies—are perfectly positioned to help redirect the tone of our fractious times as well as the tenor of teaching practices and classroom protocols toward wellness and wholeness, which are so needed now and in the future.

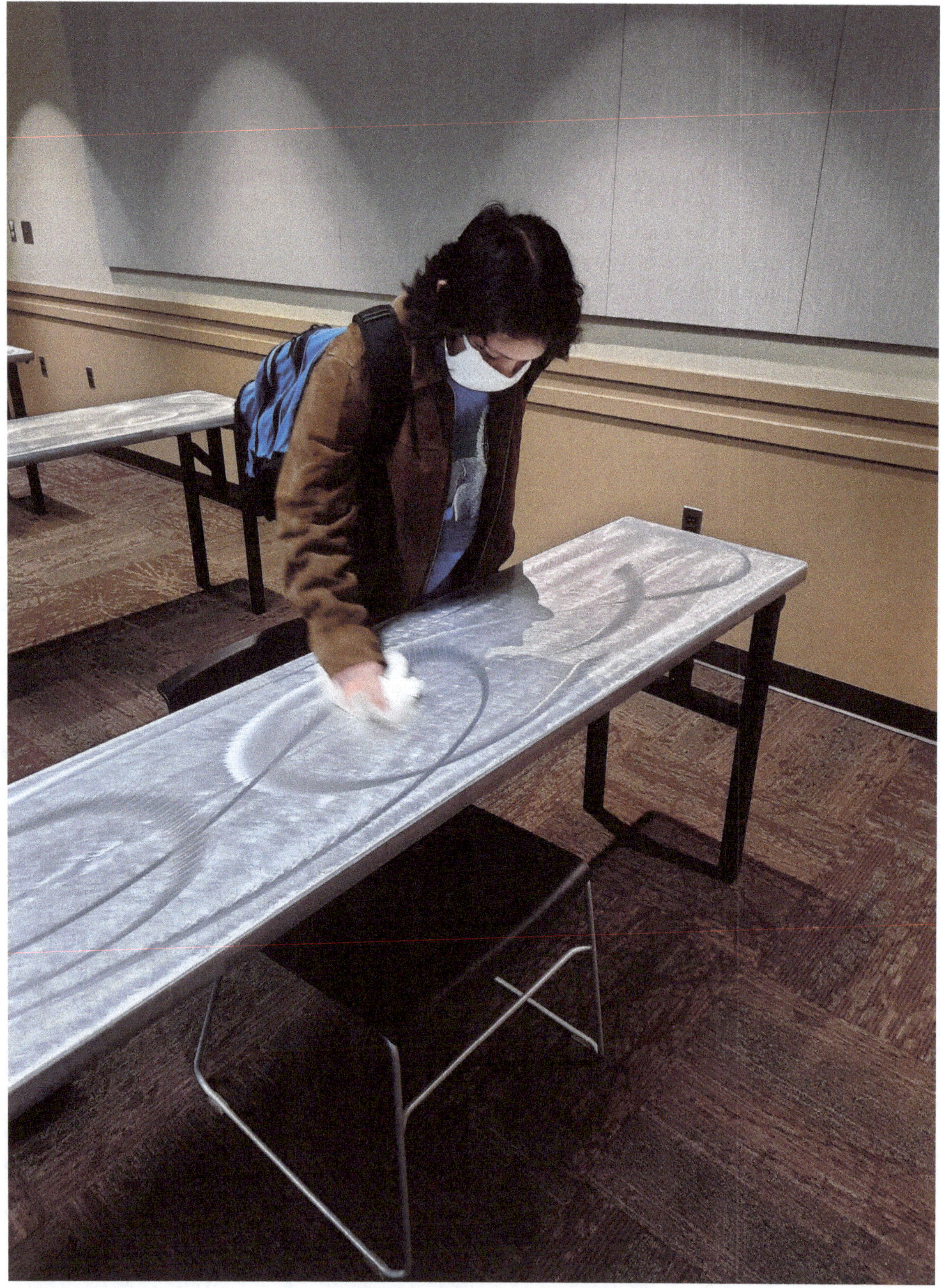

Figure 3. Could continually cleansing furnishings boost students' feelings of ownership toward the classroom? Photo by Author.

COVID Quote–2020

The United States averaged one death every minute from COVID-19 during the week of Thanksgiving.

—**PBS News Hour, November 30, 2020**

COVID-19 Notes: "Snow Flurries"

Only one day after my school announced its college-wide switch to all-online, Aaron (not his real name) dropped our composition class. All semester, he lightheartedly complained to me about taking a Saturday morning class, both for its incursion on his weekends and the morning hour. "You know, the only reason I signed up for your class was because by the time I got around to registering, it was only between yours and an online course, and it was the online course that did me in at my last college. That online course caused me to drop out of there."

Almost every Saturday, he greeted me the same, "That online class..."

Our Saturday of the semester was an inclement beginning: Slippery snows filled the city too rapidly for the weekend crews to get ahead. Side roads and parking lots were left buried. Trunk routes clogged. Freeways were fouled by vehicular slide-offs and ditchings, never mind their treacherous, untouched ramps.

Once at campus downtown, I found the building locked that contained the English Department and my opening day's handouts and syllabus. To consolidate the few weekend classes, only one hallway in one building was open. That I knew, but I had not planned for the office lockout.

Trudging to Campus Police, I asked to be let into the English Department. The weekend force's freshman officer cheerily talked me across the commons, "What a morning! The chief came only five minutes short of closing campus. She could not drive in herself, and I tell you, that never happens. They closed the freeway south: She could not even get turned around to backtrack out. I almost did not make it, neither, fishtailing all downhill to the college. Lucky, I did not end up in a snowbank myself. Would you like a key?"

No, I assured him I would be OK once inside, as neither did I want to complete the triplicate paperwork nor add another of the college's identical-looking brass keys onto my already weighty key chain.

Back at class, handouts at the ready, I met Aaron and 12 of the 15 students enrolled in the class, impressed by their braving that first Saturday morning snowstorm to attend Comp class. Attendance and registrations were to drift and melt in subsequent weeks with as many as 20 enrolled by our third Saturday but attendance rapidly shrinking back down to 15 by Week 5.

Throughout, Aaron attended faithfully, arriving promptly with his smirk, "You know, the only reason I signed up for your class ...." He never failed to elicit a chuckle, either from me or one of his knowing, nodding cohorts.

I like to pride myself on running a hands-on, collaborative, workshop-style writing class, incrementally arranging sequences of activities involving research and sentence and paragraph formation, and integrating photos, formats, and frequent excursions into the city that surrounds our campus, all skating toward the three essays we produce in English 101.

Aaron was all in—participating, revising, producing, enthusiastic—all the while grinning his sly smile.

Then the virus, COVID-19, struck Michigan the week following spring break, one Saturday past midterm.

My online roster revealed the red Ghostbuster slashed circle over Aaron's name. Aaron was my first class casualty of the early campus closure and its necessitated change to all-online remote instruction.

But was he really spooked at being buried online again, or had all his snow flurry assertions predestined the drop?

—Noted on March 22, 2020

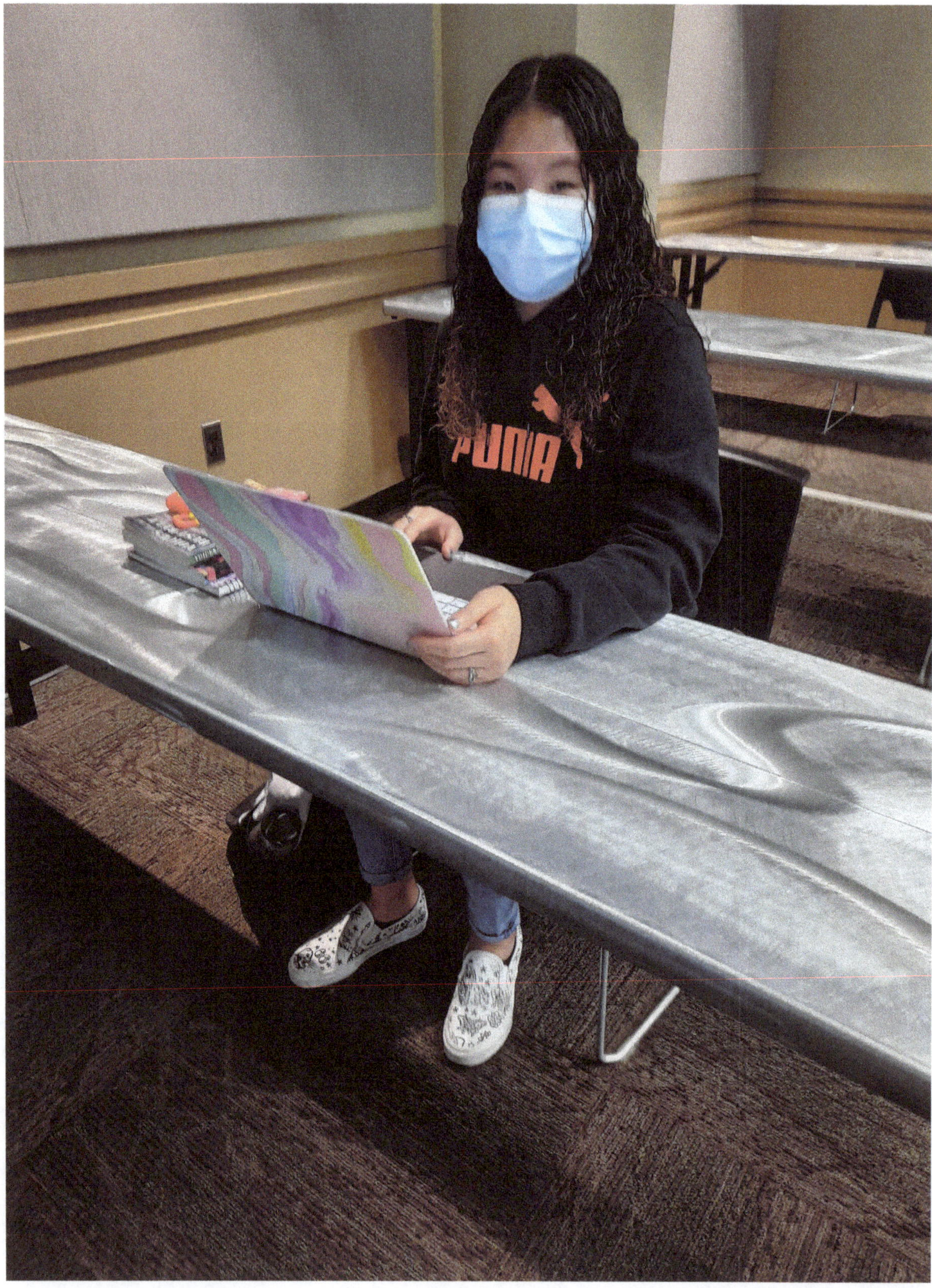

Figure 4. Cynthia Liu sitting distanced in a culinary conference room converted into a 1st year composition classroom. Photo by Author.

Chapter 1. Distanced

Place-based inquiry and writing should play a larger role in our first-year writing curriculums because it allows students to analyze their place in the world, express their experiences to audiences, and respond to challenges they see within their communities.
—Rosanne Carlo

Remote

My in-person English Composition I classes all filled in the fall term of 2020. Hungrily, many students wished for some restoration of a prepandemic, teeming college campus replete with a return of all the vibrant smorgasbords of collegiate activities, despite an ever-present viral threat. Some students simply missed the presence of live classmates and a stand-up teacher inside a physical classroom. Others were still licking wounds from rocky bouts of online learning: Too many lacked the computer hardware, wi-fi access, or technical knowledge to switch and sustain virtual classwork. One student whose family lived far afield rurally told me about her distances from internet connections, which were finally lost when their nearest town's public library and sole fast-food outlet both closed. A few told tales of grade-fatal procrastinations without the regularity of physical attendance and the mutual accountability of student cohorts together with regular reminders from their teachers. Emailed assignments were too easy to ignore, and lounging bedridden in pj's did little to spur top quality schoolwork. Two relayed horror stories of crowding one computer, every sibling competing for online time. Another added a parent's work obligations to the family's homebound computer scheduling challenges. Many simply figured that they would grasp for as much normalcy as they could, taking whatever the college offered, before the looming boom lowered: The next expected retreat to remote learning—hopefully striking later rather than sooner in the semester.

Classrooms were scattered around the campus. Instead of teaching on the top floors of the main classroom buildings, the traditional habitat of the College of Arts and Sciences where most English classes settled, mine were removed to double-length rooms in the college's fieldhouse and culinary arts center. Both rooms were twice the size of standard classes, and they had separate doors temporarily labeled Entrance and Exit to assist with distancing during class gatherings and exchanges. Both were fitted with a half-dozen rolls of paper towels, aerosol bottles of disinfectant—*bactericidal-tuberculocidal-fungicidal-virucidal*—to spray equipment and furnishings, along with hand-sanitizer dispensers for "cleaning in and cleaning out." Recirculating fans hummed overhead to diffuse any viral discharges.

"Can you speak louder?" students courteously persisted as my voice faltered in the first two weeks trying to project over the fans' constant droning. After one week, we gave up on the thumb-up signal I suggested initially to request I increase my verbal volume. Not only did I miss most of their hesitant signals from the distant back of the classroom, but they tired of the constant gesticulating and sympathized with my faded voice. I requested a headset to tap into the health science room's powerful speaker system, designed not only to overcome the ceiling fans' rumbling buzz, but also to outpace spinning cycles and workout groans. (I did not want to imagine instructing a class pedaling from a cycle seat or stretching on a yoga mat!)

"If you need 'em, you can find extra batteries for the belt pack inside a plastic tray that's on top of the projection console," I was assured over the phone.

I hoped the batteries never died in the workout room, for I could not reach, let alone see, anything atop the tall black box parked in a front corner of that room and filled with electronics stacked behind its clasped glass door. Apparently, the box was designed for taller—and probably much more fit—instructors than I. Before carefully snapping the headset over the ear straps of my facemask, I gave it a thorough spraying and wipe-down with the classroom cleanser. Before me, who knows what perspiring hands had handled and sweat-soaked heads had sported that headset, and what germs were suspired into its cushioned mic?

"Sorry, we don't handle the culinary department," the IT rep intoned, responding to my repeated request for electronic projection in the culinary arts conference room, now composition classroom. Surely speakers were available to communicate over clattering tableware and luncheon munchers. "To use their *lav*, you have to contact that department directly. They don't do headsets with mics."

Lav? What's a lav? Lavatory? I knew where that was: I studiously washed my hands there before and after every single class I taught. But that has nothing to do with microphones and speakers. Maybe it's something that attaches to a chef's toque hat or connects somehow onto one of their culinary white lab coats with the wearer's name stitched in blue?

Ever obliging, the culinary department's rep assured me that he would have a *lav* set out for me before the next morning's class when I inquired about a mic. "I'll watch for you tomorrow and show you how to operate it. Is 10 minutes before your class time OK?"

"Sure." My curiosity piqued overnight.

Lav, as revealed to me the following day, is short for *lavaliere,* simply a mic attached to a tie clip and wired down to a battery belt pack. It was fitting, all of a piece with the college's culinary arts center, now repurposed into spacious, luxe classrooms, walls paneled and papered and trimmed with rich blond oak, cushioned in deeply plush carpeting. Three separate projectors with screens that scrolled down from recessed ceiling trim, and the layered ceiling shone with recessed lighting, theater light fixtures, and ceiling backlighting. I could not access the half of all that room's (more accurately, plural *rooms'*, for there were sets of room dividers tucked between walls mid-length to divide the large space into several smaller breakouts) sight-and-sound capacities. In fact, I was relegated to an IT cart with portable projector and two whiteboards on wheels (one of which would never erase thoroughly even when slathered with dry erase spray), all placed safely distant from the decorative oak wainscoting that paneled the place.

"Cool," the culinary rep chirped, "you're wearing a tie; otherwise, you'd have to attach this alligator clip onto a pocket or collar since you don't wear a chef's jacket."

Figure 5. Kyla Scobey seated six feet apart from any classmates in the converted classroom with portable projection cart and whiteboard added. Photo by Author.

Deathly

The campus itself was rendered a ghost town that 2020 autumn. Regardless of the time I drove into the faculty parking ramp, I never failed to find a spot—often on the ground level, a plum position—without ever circling up or down levels. Entering campus, I had no double-parked obstacles; in fact, it was a rare day that the streets were lined with even singly parked cars. Buses no longer lined up to circle among the campuses downtown, and the bus stops themselves were deserted as often as not. No one recruited passersby for student clubs. No representatives stood at entryways armed with petitions and pens, dispensing Bibles or brochures, or brandishing signs seeking recruits for causes or cults or military service.

Traffic patterns indoors, too, staggered students' class entries and exits, so none overlapped. A quiet pall had settled over us. Nobody "hung out." Former campus hot spots had had furnishings removed or distanced so as to keep students all at a certain remove from each other. The cafeteria, food court, and culinary program's diner and restaurant were secured. Whole buildings of single-entry, standard-sized classrooms had been closed for the semester. In fact, cutting through a hall to cross into the English Department's offices, themselves closed and darkened, I noticed only one student, slouching on a seat left in the corner of a study lounge. We two appeared to be the only beings haunting that entire five-story building.

The numbers of first-year college students resigned to or opting for online learning was not the only reason for fewer students on campus. Madeline St. Amour, using data from the National Clearinghouse, reported a drop of 10% from the previous year in the number of high school graduates immediately enrolling in college, including a decline of greater than one fourth from high schools with a majority population of minority students, and a reduction of one fourth from high schools situated in U.S. cities (St. Amour). Salmaan Farooqui wrote in January that one-fifth of college-age students in Canada planned not to return to college in the coming year, primarily due to the limitations of online learning resulting in the loss of classroom and social interactions, and laboratories and internships (Farooqui).

Collegiality also expired. My encounters with a colleague on campus were rare, and the very few interactions were cautious and cagey, as they invariably involved someone standing in the sole office doorway that afforded escape, collegially removing the facemask that assured suspiration safety, or delicately declaring just a bare modicum of pleasantries before both parties beat a relieved retreat. Each considered where the other might previously have been, to whom that other had been virally exposed if coming from a classroom or mandated meeting, and how soon both could safely yet sociably extricate themselves from the encounter. Safety reigned. Merely selecting one of the common workspaces, logging onto one of the college-furnished PCs or making use of the department's photocopier/scanner, could trigger existential rationalizations and avoidances never considered before.

Gatherings were discouraged as they could cause microbursts of coronavirus outbreaks. No student clubs or organizations met. Meetings dwindled until they occurred only virtually or not at all. Anything essential happened via streaming. Few offices opened. Fewer buildings opened. Only a handful of classrooms ran live, in person. Hallway lights, many set to sense movement, were mostly continuously extinguished.

Only a handful of athletic programs ran in 2020—those that were both outdoors and individual or distanced: baseball, softball, and cross country. The fieldhouse's basketball courts, pool, weight room, and practice rooms all were locked shut with limited openings by appointment as county and state health department restrictions stipulated. Individuals, their faces buried beneath bulky, athletic department-issued facemasks sporting the college logo, slipped surreptitiously through partially opened doors to lift weights or meet their team training protocols.

The remains of campus life floated ghostly with the odd professor returning to use a campus technology lab, quiet office, or tech-furnished classroom to record, livestream a lecture, or zoom through the airwaves and cloudbanks, then fading away with the person's departure. Only skeleton crews of custodians, police, administrative office staff, and smatterings of instructors and students drifted about, gliding quietly to and from the several scattered cavernous classrooms, or settled briefly in some suitable alcove for study or catch-up texting before or after class.

Beyond their classes, instructors also vanished. Nobody lingered for between-classes camaraderie, coffee klatches, shared office hijinks—*nada*. Congenial emails or texts occasionally erupted, addressing any of the many changes and additives that teaching, communicating, accommodating, and planning required in online, in-person, and hybrid Comp classes. Otherwise, most email communiques hung suspended, unacknowledged, while staff scrambled to mitigate the risks of their own children's at-home or back-home learning, their elderly parents' living concerns, or their own scramble to rescue a course or a student's stability and success.

Only once did I arrange to meet up with a teaching buddy socially—at a picnic table in a chilly city park after driving thru McDonald's. We commiserated over burgers and fries, shivering under a picnic pavilion, the park to ourselves, just weeks before Lake Michigan's winter snows and arctic winds froze the state under.

Even the infrequent student tours of campus were subdued, modest. Without any student body present, a campus guide spoke softly with a shrunken audience of a single student with a sole parent or guardian, stepping slowly through an emptied commons, past locked and darkened buildings toward Admissions—hushed, underwhelmed, removed. Besides the emptied commons, all of the cafeterias and the coffee shop, Student Life office, campus bookstore, athletic fieldhouse and natatorium, and the library-media center—normally busy, buzzing, focal spots—were completely deserted, darkened, dead.

COVID Quote–2020

The spring semester of 2020 was significantly disrupted by the spread of the coronavirus as more than 1,300 colleges and universities in all 50 states canceled in-person classes or shifted to online-only instruction. By fall, many campuses merged in-person instruction (with social distancing) and online learning, with varying degrees of success. 44% of institutions developed fully or primarily online instruction, 21% used a hybrid model, and 27% offered fully or primarily in-person instruction. Freshman enrollment in fall 2020 declined by an unprecedented 13.1%. This led to an overall postsecondary enrollment dip of 2.5%. Enrollment declines varied by institution, but public 2-year institutions have generally seen the largest declines in first-time student enrollment (–21.0%) followed by public colleges and universities (–8.1%). New international student enrollment dropped by 43%.

—**Andrew Smalley**

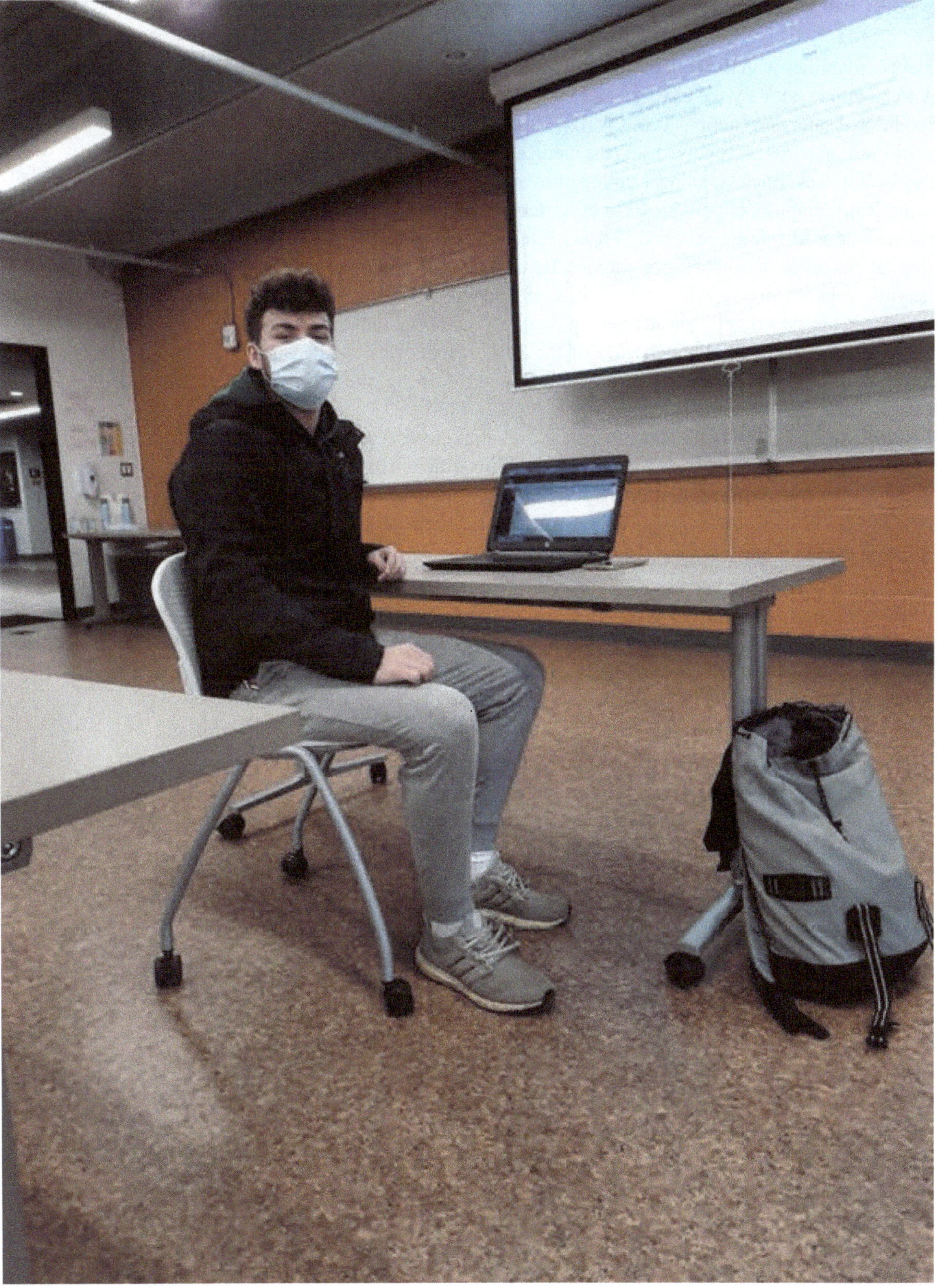

Figure 6. How will learning college composition separated from the dialogical interactions of a group setting (here in a twice-the-normal-size health sciences classroom inside the college fieldhouse) affect first-year students' language, thinking, and emotional skills? Note the cleansing supplies alongside the hand sanitizer dispenser beside the entrance door. Photo by Author.

Placed

Students unfamiliar with the college campus and its cosmopolitan setting had to learn how to negotiate not only the changes of a typical postsecondary transition but all of the additional safety precautions for COVID-19 as well as the changing adaptations to this novel coronavirus as it evolved, and the medical and scientific communities learned more about it. Nevertheless, citing a survey of over 40,000 college students conducted by American Campus Communities, Greta Anderson reported that 85% claimed they could achieve academic success, and 57% expected a "sense of community" even with the limitations of social distancing on campus. By comparison, Anderson noted a Strada Education Network survey, which found 58% of students who moved home or lived off campus reported struggling academically, and 56% said they could not find a place to study adequately. Still, although 96% of the ACC respondents claimed that they followed their colleges' distancing, gathering, and mask-wearing rules, 62% believed that their classmates did not (Anderson).

Laurie Patton, president of Middlebury College in Vermont, observed four distinct features of colleges and students that "counterintuitively" positioned them for a "renewed, more dynamic sense of place" (Patton). Applying four principles of place from Peggy Barlett and Geoffrey Chase's *Sustainability on Campus*, she claimed the coronavirus heightened the importance of place-based learning:

> COVID was everywhere and nowhere. As an airborne and aerosol disease, COVID transcended space and yet forced us to redefine space wherever we went.

> Suddenly, the paths across our campus and hallways in our buildings did not just lead from point A to point B; we had to ask, does this path accommodate enough people? Is this classroom building capacious enough for people to talk seriously to each other while at a distance far greater than usual? (Patton)

Furthermore, students, staff, and faculty had to continually adjust their distancing and gathering behaviors as the college, local and regional health departments, and the state and federal regulations and recommendations responded to the ebbs and riptides of COVID-19 illnesses on campus, among student populations, and across the college's neighborhoods and community, as well as the prospects of local hospitals filling, anticipating tidal waves of patients, and arranging mass testing centers and eventually mass vaccination settings (Patton).

As Patton relates, besides negotiating their own classrooms, hallways, and campus spaces, and adjusting to the pivots of their colleges' gradual openings and sudden shutterings, in addition to the alterations of in-person classes, hybrids, and online learning, students frequently gained an empathy toward local employers whose stores, cafeterias, restaurants, bars, and coffee shops closed or were reduced to 25% or 50% capacity. Inconvenienced themselves by the closures and redactions, they felt for peers whose local or on campus jobs disappeared, and whose lives were jarred by the reductions in hours, staff, or occupancy of college offices, student programs and athletics, and bookstores, many of which shifted to by-appointment or online consultations only, or closed altogether.

Besides gaining empathy for classmates and community members, having experienced and adjusted to so many disruptions at their colleges, students may have become more resilient and better prepared to

> bring their newly deepened sense of place out into other places in the world.… [R]emote learning has in fact created a longing for being together in a shared environment. The primary driver for students returning next semester is whether there are in-person classes on our campus. Far from being a substitute for place, remote learning has deepened our students' place-based sensibility. (Patton)

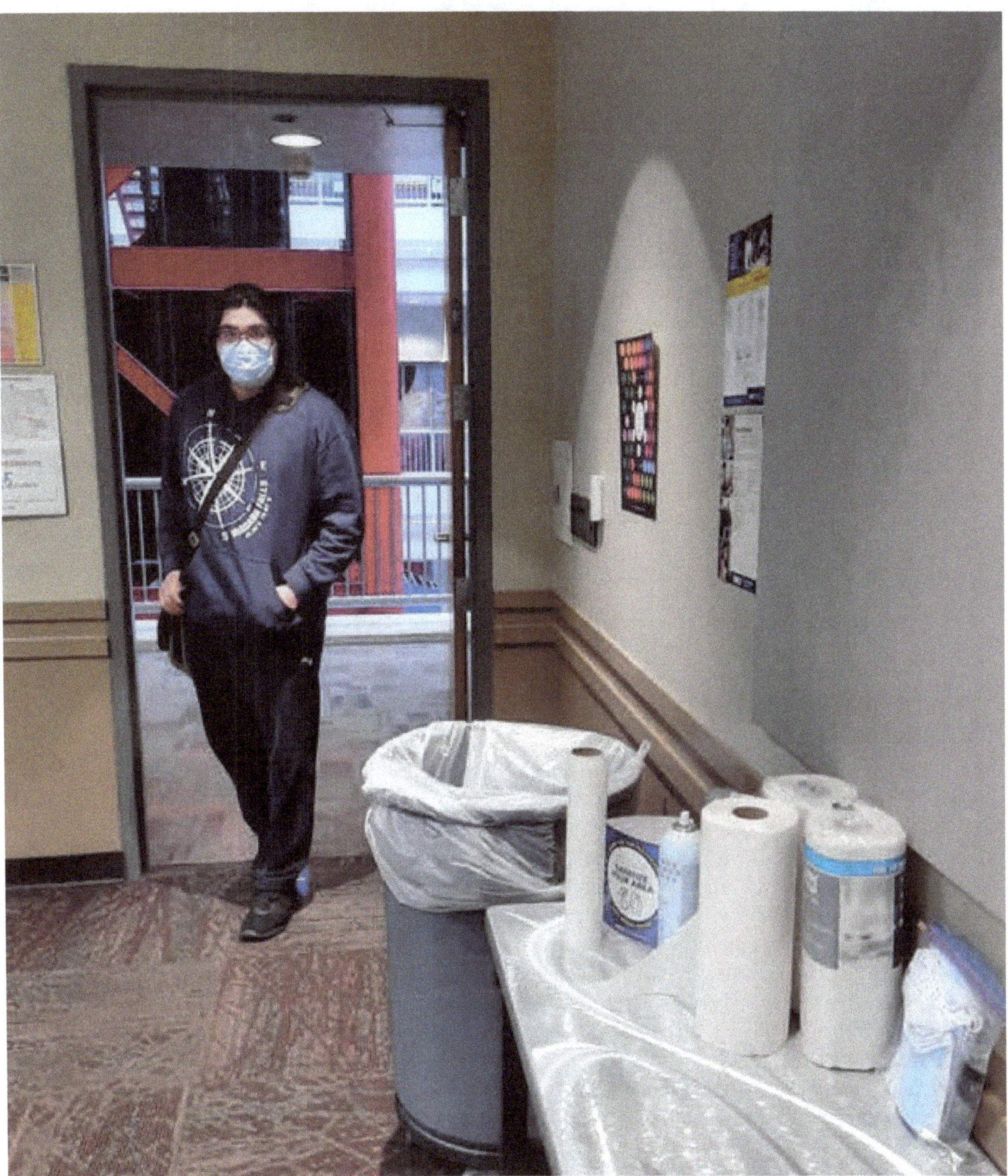

Figure 7. Could passing a stock of cleansing supplies to enter a classroom lead students to associate the class itself with a sterilized hospital room or patient ward? Photo by Author.

Construction

"Are you covering that garish orange and blue?" I asked the two maintenance department workers patching and prepping the boldly painted walls in the hallway of a classroom building I cut through to the English Department's offices. They and I together accounted for everyone populating the ground floor of that previously bustling classroom building that encompassed a student lounge, the math tutorial center, math department, other general education classrooms, and a bank of three elevators serving the additional four floors. Those other floors housed dental, nursing, and medtech programs; English, humanities, and languages; and the business and language labs and tutorial centers.

"No, they're staying the same. We're just touching them up while no one's here."

They were not the only ones "touching up." I had encountered a work crew of four aligned atop evenly spaced stepladders, with their arms and shoulders reaching into removed ceiling tiles to reroute and replace electric conduits in the technology building the week previous; and three floors of the college's original main hall were being gutted for a remodeling update.

Construction, deconstruction, reconstruction—it was a time, bereft of students and staff, well-suited to repair and improvement projects.

Bruce Feiler writes about times of uncertainty as being especially conducive to self-improvement, and how writing, in particular, can be restorative:

> I was flabbergasted by the sheer volume of people who told me that out of the blue, in the midst of their life transition, they started to write. Just as the world seemed to be its most volatile and the ground underneath their feet the most fluid, they found a table, a chair, a piece of paper, and a pencil, and started to write themselves back to life. (231)

Surprisingly, he discovered, college students who wrote of a life-changing experience, although they felt a short-term sorrow, in the long term gained more emotional introspection and expression, better health and coping skills, stronger problem-solving skills, and improved on-the-job and job-search results. "Central to the act of writing is a process of growth, of slowly gaining control of their narrative" (232). They could author their own lives—by a process of deconstructing and reconstructing their own stories through a blueprint of words. During a pandemic-induced time of remoteness and distancing, such composition could prove a restorative, reflective, and reforming activity. Writing's cathartic capabilities would help to heal students suffering the loss of campus life, friendships and roommates, in-person in-classroom interactions, and possibly the mourning of a lost senior year's culminating rituals of secondary school. Feiler adds, "We generate the meaning we need in the moment. That act of reinterpretation is fundamentally an act of agency; it gives us a sense of control and confidence at exactly the moment we feel out of control and lacking confidence" (313). College composition may have been a valuable opportunity for our students to make sense of 2020–21, that trying, calamitous year. Maybe their writing helped strengthen their own skills in coping and constructing, in addition to composing.

Works Cited

"A Timeline of COVID-19 Developments in 2020." *American Journal of Managed Care*, 3 July 2020, www.ajmc.com/view/a-timeline-of-covid19-developments-in-2020.

Anderson, Greta. "Did Students in Campus Housing Learn Better?" *Inside Higher Ed: Higher Education News*, 3 Dec. 2020, www.insidehighered.com/news/2020/12/03/survey-students-campus-housing-had-better-social-and-learning-outcomes?

Barlett, Peggy F. and Geoffrey W. Chase, editors. *Sustainability on Campus: Stories and Strategies for Change*. MIT Press, 2004.

Carlo, Rosanne. *Transforming Ethos: Place and the Material in Rhetoric and Writing*. Utah State University Press, 2020, p. 138.

Farooqui, Salmaan. "Online Classes Put Post-Secondary Students in Hard Place: Many Consider Deferring Courses as Institutions Limit in-Person Learning." *Toronto Star*, 18 Jan. 2021. *Press Reader Digital Newspaper*. Available by subscription at https://www.pressreader.com/.

Feiler, Bruce. *Life Is in the Transitions: Mastering Change at Any Age*. New York: Penguin, 2020.

Gannon, Kevin M. *Radical Hope: A Teaching Manifesto*. West Virginia University Press 2020, p. 5.

Patton, Laurie L. "A Surprising Fruit of Our Pandemic Fall Semester." *Inside Higher Ed: Higher Education News*, 7 Dec. 2020, www.insidehighered.com/views/2020/12/07/pandemic-has-revealed-academe-dynamism-place-based-learning-opinion?

St. Amour, Madeline. "Report: Fewer High School Students Went Straight to College." *Inside Higher Ed: Higher Education News*, 10 Dec. 2020, www.insidehighered.com/quicktakes/2020/12/10/report-fewer-high-school-students-went-straight-college?

Smalley, Andrew. "Higher Education Responses to Coronavirus (COVID-19)." *National Conference of State Legislatures*, 22 March 2021, www.ncsl.org/research/education/higher-education-responses-to-coronavirus-covid-19.aspx.

Q1.

When COVID-19 disrupted your community, college, and classroom, what teaching transitions were you required to make? Which of these changes have continued to the present? Which ones do you predict will persist in the future?

Figure 8. Justin Duhimbaze, author of "COVID Refugee." Photo by Author.

Student's Story—"COVID Refugee," by Justin Duhimbaze

Working full-time for a local warehouse in the city, I believed I would never get touched, that my life and that of all refugees to the US were going to be saved as we had been from deadly diseases in refugee camps from which we had come. I did not seem to hear any other stances about the global fight. I even ignored safety precautions that were in place, and I wondered why things were closing when no one in the neighbourhood disappeared. After 5 months, I realized that masking was a ticket that I needed to go into church, work, a grocery store, or school.

Articles claiming the virus to be on its way to the rest of the World from BBC, CNN, Africa News, ABC, and others filled the notification centre of my iPhone. I only saw overtime opportunities come up to my pupils. The warehouse, unaware and unprepared, did not make any official announcement until employees started requesting paid days off and voluntary leaves to take care of family members or loved ones who were said to have either come in contact with or contracted the virus itself. I was shocked by the company's slowness distributing required materials for protection. We all doubted the company's commitment to caring for its employees. An employee questioned a manager, "When are we going to get sanitizers at work?"

The transition back to school especially online has not been easy, and neither has helping my young siblings with homework, dealing with family responsibilities, and personal life. It took me a few weeks to settle down and find a rhythm for how to do things; however, I have recently felt some comfort with the online world. Everyone at home has been deemed a special or necessary employee, and we have all been in strong health and thank the creator for it. I have learned about organization with daily agendas and goal setting sheets. Furthermore, these stay-at-home orders taught me teamwork with family members, how we can support each other, and communication skills. Another lesson is innovation in technology, and my familiarity with new meeting apps such as Zoom and Google Meet has broadened.

Figure 9. When overhead air-recirculation fans buzz, portable electronics consoles hum, and students are distanced six feet apart in enlarged classrooms, what is lost from the transmission of communication? Photo by Author.

BP/DP/AP—Before, During, and After Pandemic Casualties

BP, at my two schools, all college staff members were subjected to regular active shooter drills, required to watch training videos with their varied responses of fight or flight: when to retreat, when to barricade, and when to counterattack. The post-stream, multiple-choice quizzes' definitive answers notwithstanding, on-campus contingencies entail this one always-right answer: *It depends*. In classrooms with floor-to-ceiling windows, it may not be advisable to extinguish lights and pretend you are invisible to a hallway gunman. In end-of-corridor classrooms, there may be no escape route, and top floors do not always allow for flight, even if Icarus-like we could slip on wings, since windows typically are permanently sealed for central climate control. Regardless of setting, then, classroom doors remained locked, opened briefly for 10 minutes before and after classes, and afterwards closed to avert the threat of shooting casualties.

    DP, doors are opened continually, kickstands down or wedges permanently jammed in place. One of my double-sized classrooms is furnished with red paving bricks, one or two per door, to hold open both the entrance and exit sets of double doors, so that no one besides possibly the building custodian or the first and last instructors assigned to teach in that repurposed storeroom may have to handle its levers or doors. Fewer touches help prevent the passing of pandemic virus through cross contacts of people pressing levers, pushing crash bars, entering and exiting constricted passageways. Wide-open doors also improve the flow of fresh air into and out of a classroom. We weigh the risks during a pandemic. What gunman, no matter how deranged he might be, in seeking to stage a mass casualty shoot-up would target such a separated, single classroom of distanced learners on an already mostly emptied college campus?

    AP, as the pandemic is willed into submission by vaccinated instructors returning on campus to teach vaccinated students, with additional classrooms and buildings returned to service, safety may dictate a newly balanced, hybrid approach of weighing the risk of viral infections with automatic gunfire preventions. When either threatens an outbreak, vigilant instructors, always keeping an eye on the campus and local climate, must pivot to prevent and protect students and themselves from both germs and guns. One day, this may necessitate replacing red bricks and wooden-wedge doorjambs with automated door releases like those used with firebreak doors, possibly necessitating another light switch near each teacher station to toggle them open or closed.

    In the meantime, continue to read the signs of these tumultuous times, ever ready to pivot from propping or locking doors from class to class and maybe hour to hour. Also, rapidly learning every student by name and disposition, you may want to assign alert and responsive exemplars near doorways, windows, and light switches. And be prepared at a moment's notice to call out, "Andrew, quick, pull that door shut," "Pedro, turn off the lights," and "Alyssa, close that blind."

    "Then squirt some of that hand sanitizer, too."

Bottom Line: Arrive at classes alert and remain vigilant—and learn your students' names and inclinations.

COVID-19 Notes: "Avalanche"

My mid-March 2020 weekend was piled with reprepping my writing classes from hands-on, onsite, writing workshops to remote, online all-the-time learning. My challenge was to simplify and clarify with concise, step-by-step, bulleted, once-a-week directions without clogging students' email inboxes with avalanches of explanations.

In the meantime, I tried to dig my own email boxes out from under the avalanches of updates and snowballing expectations.

Both of my colleges' professional development directors invited instructors to any of a number of hurried learning opportunities for projecting lessons, demonstrating labs, inviting participation, and evaluating virtual work. (This switched soon to small-group study of 25, then 10 or fewer, and finally to online virtual meetings, when Michigan's Department of Health and the U.S. Centers for Disease Control communiques stipulated changes as they discovered more and more about the virus and its spread.) Each email seemed followed by an aftershock pile-up of clarifying and practical messages from school deans, department heads, committee reps, the union rep, and sundry other colleagues with suggested apps, programs, techniques, and ideas for dealing with COVID concerns. Finally, several more cast their collegial offers to assist.

That was not all: Another wave of offers came from a half-dozen textbook publishers and their reps, along with menus of online options to streamline delivery of their content during that special and limited time. Finally, a spattering of pay-per-view offers rolled down from authors, speakers, and conference sponsors, most happy to cut 10%, 20%, even 50–60% off their regular rates to help out in a trying time. Throughout March, I was avalanched. However, I chose not to bite. Instead of piling on new or different apps or programs, I would try to keep on with keeping on, sticking with my original assignments and essays delivered via the same college online delivery platforms that my students were used to. Besides having to cope with working from home, possibly attaining or upgrading any technology to complete assignments, students should not have to learn additional layers of tech as well. That was my reasoning.

Since many students found their schedules upended by changing work demands, homeschooling their kids, or helping teach younger siblings—sometimes even competing with family members who were working from home or studying at home for computer access—I tried to open the weekly calendar as wide as I could. Instead of teaching everyone online at the same assigned time, I switched to asynchronous instruction: I posted and emailed all class work for the next week with explanations and examples on a Friday or Saturday, and I collected assignments online via uploads on the colleges' delivery platforms or by email with attached forms, documents, or snapshots, whichever the student felt was most convenient. At first, I accepted all late work through the month of March to grant students enough time to set up and get situated in their new surroundings; then I extended my acceptance of late work until the semester's end in April to allow anyone who needed to catch up and keep up. I accorded full credit to any assignment submitted any time.

In class, I had signified my "quality control" by initialing students' drafts and collaborative assignments when completed to my satisfaction, but online I labeled them *complete* or *incomplete* using the college's online platform. The work still had to pass my muster before it was deemed *complete*. I aimed to set up assessments to remove all summative scoring that could adversely affect students' course grades; on the contrary, I relied on their completed preliminary pieces to assure them of success.

I had to do a lot of reminding, cajoling, and reviewing during that lengthy month-and-a-half period. What I could have accomplished in class with a walk-by observation and suggestion, or a sit-down group collaboration with a quartet of students all together, usually turned into an out-in-the-cloud, one-after-another, one-on-one, seek-and-explain exercise. Oh, did my eye drops rain regularly!

Even with individual attention, many students struggled with this midstream switchover—as did I and not just a few of my colleagues, even with the avalanches of proffered assistance and advice.

—Noted April 12, 2020

Figure 10. Example Opening Photo Activity: "The College Stairs Signify My First Steps Toward My Unknown Future."
Photo Courtesy of Student.

Chapter 2. Breaking the Ice

The real question is whether we want higher education to be about life.
—Parker Palmer and Arthur Zajonc

Opening Photo Activity

Some bemoan the fact that so few students read their syllabi, and outside of the one or two instructors who may sonorously read it aloud during the first class meeting—an unwelcome introduction to any class—several seem to go to great lengths to cajole or trick students into reviewing theirs. Some bury entertaining snippets throughout in the hopes that students would plow through the rest of the text to uncover its gems. Others quiz afterwards on the contents. One college where a friend of mine teaches requires all instructors to read the syllabus on the first day of class and automatically drops any students absent on Day 1.

With more and more colleges and departments of English and Writing dictating subject matter and learning objectives on course syllabi, they read ever more like the contractual arrangements of online service providers, with their pages of minutiae and legalese in too-tiny font sizes—bringing to mind the cellphone apps for which everybody cursorily checks off their agreement to gain access to the good stuff. That is how we ought to treat syllabi, too. Sign off if you must, but use class time to skip on to the important things—one of the most important being the college itself. Especially when so many of our students felt alienated from their schools while studying remotely online or isolated apart, a good use of at least part of the first class session is for students to gain an acquaintance with the physical campus by finding the sites of most import to them.

So, after greetings and an introduction to the class, syllabus, text, and schedule—kept as brief as feasible—I finished our first in-person meeting with an Opening Photo Activity assignment, which could be completed either individually or with distanced assistance. Using the cameras on their phones or asking a classmate to take a picture, students were assigned to snap a creative selfie with a collegiate backdrop or another suitable setting, preferably outside for safety during the pandemic; in addition to the picture, an MLA-formatted caption that included the student's name, where it was taken, why that setting was chosen, and how it was arranged using a creative camera angle, point of view, lighting, or other creative element, and the photographer's name if a different person from the subject. The photo then was emailed to me with the assignment's name and course number and section in the subject line. At our second class, I clicked through my email box from last to first, asking each student for a brief introduction with name, setting chosen and why, as well as their creative element added to the photograph, and the photographer's name if taken by someone else. I managed the classroom's mouse and projector myself, so nobody besides me had to sail up front or handle any devices that I or others had touched.

This Opening Photo Activity gets students out of the classroom and around the campus, searching for a site or backdrop that is personally significant—one that will represent them representing their school, usually their new place. Furthermore, it acquaints them with email protocol when communicating with me—a helpful skill when distanced in the classroom or forced to pivot suddenly to online learning again. In addition, it introduces them to MLA formatting and captioning, which could prove helpful later with their assigned essays, should they wish to incorporate a photo or graphic in one.

Finally, it grants them an immediate success in using a handheld technology that nearly all have already mastered and applying it to a new writing skill.

If you want to try the Opening Photo Activity with your students, you can project or distribute the Instruction Sheets below in class or post them on your class's learning management system. If you assess the Opening Photo Activity, the *Assessment: 6 Points Possible* page is a time-saver. Instead of reviewing assignments yourself, you can use this straightforward assessment to have students self-assess, instead. Often, I add a Bonus Point to assessments to motivate additional creative effort, and I aim to be liberally generous with the dispersion of these negligible, one-point bonuses. Earning an early bonus point can generate some initial enthusiasm for the writing course and spark students to motivate themselves and one another to seek to achieve more than the basic requirements.

Once adherence to safety procedures or a thoroughly vaccinated populace has defeated the virus, or progeny is so weakened that it no longer threatens so many, this Opening Photo Activity can readily become an ice-breaker assignment for new groups, or a prewriting or scaffolding activity for the later Tour essay (Chapter 4). Prepandemic, I have assigned students working together to snap whole-group photos staged at their consensus choices for the most scenic spot on campus; the classroom building where most of their classes meet; the best group-gathering study space in the library; and what they and their collective study space would look like after pulling an all-nighter. When it is not safe to be in huddled gatherings of groups—and even when it is—students sent outside to explore may welcome the outside access to fresh air as much as the openness to generate a creative project through an opening photo activity.

Work Cited

Palmer, Parker, and Zajonc, Arthur. *The Heart of Higher Education: A Call to Renewal: Transforming the Academy through Collegial Conversations.* San Francisco: Jossey-Bass, 2010, p. 36.

Q2.

How have you changed your class and course introductions during the coronavirus pandemic? How could you involve outdoor or campus explorations?

Figure 11. Example Opening Photo Activity: "B & W on Campus." Credit: Que'Anna Jackson.

<u>Instruction Sheet 1.1</u>

Opening Photo Activity Assignment

Email your instructor a creative photo of yourself with an iconic, suitable school setting and MLA caption.

1. **Choose an <u>individual, creative place</u> that reflects you and your interests—some ideas:**
    - School sign, banner, logo, or promotional materials.
    - Artwork such as a statue, frieze, painting, on campus.
    - Building entrance, sign, study spot, stairwell, library—where you expect to spend your time.
    - Try <u>not to repeat</u> anyone else's.

2. **Snap a <u>creatively arranged photo</u>, such as:**
    - Angled from above, below, or one side—make sure you and your setting can be seen clearly.
    - Positioning yourself and your setting at different angles with nothing horizontal or straight.
    - Crop out any blank spaces like floors, ceilings, or sky, so that you and your setting fill the frame.

3. **Type an <u>MLA-formatted caption</u> below your photo, like this:**
    Fig. 1. Your First and Last Name at Place with a Descriptive Reason why you chose it to reflect you. Credit: Photographer's First and Last Name.

4. **Email your creative photo with MLA caption to your instructor and <u>present</u> it at your next class:**
    - Write **Opening Photo** with your **First & Last Name** and **Course Name & #** on the <u>email Subject line</u>.
    - <u>Next class:</u> Stand and introduce yourself, the place you selected and the reason why, your creative angle, and the caption.

Figure 12. Example Opening Photo Activity: "College Multiplicity." Photo Courtesy of Student.

Instruction Sheet 1.2

Opening Photo Activity Scoring

Assessment: 6 Points Possible
(3 pts = C, 4 pts = B, 5 pts = A, 6 pts = A+)

1. You are recognizable in the photo.
2. Photo incorporates a representative, identifiable, or iconic campus spot.
3. Picture is creatively composed.
4. MLA caption is accurate and complete.
5. Email, attached photo, and Subject line description are thorough.
6. Bonus Point: Spoken presentation compellingly introduces yourself.

Notes

Figure 13. Example Opening Photo: "The Lion Reflects My Roots as a British Citizen—The Lion Is on England's Coat of Arms, So It Reminds Me Where I'm from and, Consequently, Where I Am Returning." Credit: Reece Mellish.

<u>**Instruction Sheet 1.3**</u>

Opening Photo Activity Alternatives & Adaptations

1. **Different Settings**
   - Home—You in study spot with college logo or website on monitor
   - Neighborhood—Selfie with dorm, home, or apartment
   - Campus greenscape—Yourself in the garden, arboretum, greenhouse
   - Fitting building—Selfie with building entrance representing your major, such as "Social Sciences Building"
   - Artwork—Selfie beside sculpture, painting, mural, or another artwork
   - Commute—Yourself walking, scooting, biking, skating, driving

2. **Different Subjects**
   - Yourself typing with a computer, laptop, or tablet
   - Yourself pensively pondering topics
   - You reading the textbook or reader
   - You frustrated with discarded drafts and scribbled starts
   - Yourself in a group conference—Distanced "live" or remote "virtual"

Figure 14. What are the advantages of students working in their own comfortable and private workspaces? Photo Courtesy of Student.

COVID-19 Notes: "Chew Toy"

Somewhere, I heard the coronavirus molecule described as looking like a dog's chew toy. If so, it appears covered in artificial bacon bits—you know, the kind that looks flaming red like the spicy hot chips dispensed in bags from the vending machine aisle that students crunched en route to classes. You still remember those scenes, don't you?

Initially, splattered all over webpages' mastheads and news segments' topic series, I thought the COVID-19 graphic looked rather like a sock pulled over a ball and stuck with cloves poking out all around—much like a holiday ham, but instead of a healthful pink, it was gray meat covered in red sprouts, floating around the computer screen like a corrupted screen saver threatening harm. As COVID's symptoms became known, I suspected briefly that I may have caught it way back in February. For the first time in 10 years, I had to call in sick and visit the doctor. Achy, exhausted, light-headed, raw throat, fever—yes, I had succumbed to a virus, but already 10 days through its progression, I was assured that it would pass. It did, and I was good to go, again.

No, I had not lost taste, nor had I lost my appetite, and I could still smell. My breathing was no more laborious than seasonal allergies could account for. I had caught a bug, but it did not seem to be the monster currently prowling the globe.

From season to season, I figure that I have accumulated whole reservoirs of immunities. Holidays, weekends, family events, and students come and go, the latter often catching and carrying maladies to and from school. In close quarters and crowded classrooms they share, how could they not?

When flights from China were curtailed in February and from Europe in March, and Americans were advised to return to the U.S, both before and during that global rush the coronavirus hopped continents. Possibly some had hitched onto me in MI—something I am chewing on.

—Noted 29 March 2020

Figure 15. A Workstation Where Others' Zooms Don't All Talk Over Mine. Photo Courtesy of Ally VanTimmeren.

Chapter 3. Electronic

Even with shifts in technology, the purposes of literacy are still tied to building on, changing with, and addressing the needs and concerns emanating from the social contexts where students live and interact.

—Antero Garcia and Cindy O'Donnell-Allen

Virtual

Between the Spring and Fall semesters of 2020, which both began in person on campus but ended remotely for me, I taught a wholly online class, virtually, during the summer. Paradoxically, connecting online was a boon since the pandemic threat had shut down any face-to-face social interactions. There was nowhere to go locally, as Michigan's vacation wonderlands all closed to curtail the viral flare-ups that had begun around Detroit at the outset, then spread with sparks of unmasked and unheeding beach partiers, wedding and funeral congregants, and agnostic clans of science-deniers. Restaurants, bars, arenas, theaters, and other gathering spots shut down, only offering pick-ups, curbsides, drive-thru's, and deliveries. Farther afield, airline and cruise travel had shut down to prevent more worldwide spread and proliferation of the virus. Safely sheltered in place, I hunkered down at home and duly logged onto my college's online platform and its learning management system every day.

Tasks that I had performed intuitively and reflexively when teaching in person required considerable additional thought for preventative troubleshooting. Accommodations had to be made for students who were sick or attending ill roommates or housemates, as well as those who had to spend inordinate effort to obtain Maslovian basics such as adequate shelter and food for themselves and family members before accomplishing schoolwork. In addition to these considerations, access to competent technology, online capability, and the criteria of best-accessibility or user-friendliness had to be taken into account when choosing among the available options for course delivery. And all demanded time and effort put into discovery and dissemination. Finally, what allowances would be granted for glitches in technology, timing, or tenacity—both for my students and myself? In other words, how willing was I to give them a break, not to mention to grant myself some slack, given all the novel scenarios we were continually acting in—often impromptu—together and separately, during that summer semester?

Teaching online, I adopted a daily ritual that I have since continued with every class—whether it be remote, hybrid, or in-person—involving a six-click electronic sign-in: First, I clicked the PC's mouse or laptop's keypad onto the college website. Then, I clicked the *Sign-in* button—second click. After waiting for my Username and Password to self-populate, I signed in again—third click. "Close" the *Password Recovery* reminder that I constantly skipped, I selected the college's Learning Management System (LMS) by clicking on its icon—fourth and fifth clicks. Next, I chose the English 101 class—sixth click—which offers the same eight, vertically arranged menu items that I use with first-year writing classes: Academic Service Learning Option, Assignments & Activities with Weekly Folders, Discussions, Grades, Groups, Instructor, Syllabus & Schedule, and Tools.

Before a class began, I sent an announcement:

> ***Welcome*** *to Comp. I!*
> **<u>Thank you</u>** *<u>for enrolling</u> in our class. I look forward to meeting you on [first day the class meets] and working with you this semester.*
> *Please take your **phone** to class (if you carry one) along with a notebook and pen or laptop—whichever you prefer to write with.*
> *During the COVID-19 coronavirus pandemic, we will follow these [college name] **requirements**:*
> * *Wear a **face mask** that covers your nose and mouth,*
> * *Maintain **6-foot distance** from the rest of us (this includes entering and exiting the classroom),*
> * *Consider everyone's **well-being**, including your own, by taking good care.*
> * *Check out this website of [college & community] COVID reminders [link added].*
> *As you plan: normally, students average about 3 hours of writing each week during a regular semester. **Don't worry:** I consider myself <u>your personal</u> (although 6-foot distanced) **<u>writing guide</u>**, so think of me as your coach—and <u>check your [college] email</u> regularly.*
> *The good news is college semesters can go fast. Maybe that's the bad news, too ☺. I divide every major assignment into bite-size, week-by-week pieces, and I usually post the next week's assignments on Friday or Saturday so you can get a <u>preview of the coming attractions</u>. Normally, we do the <u>nuts-and-bolts business</u> assignments **in the first half of class** and the <u>essay writing</u> drafts and revisions in **the second half**.*
> *Please click around in [the college's LMS] and let me know any questions you have.*
> *See you [first class day],*
> *Tom*
> *[email address]*

Altogether, that task required seven clicks of my mouse to access before I could begin typing the Announcement.

Concluding every one of the first 14 weeks of the 15-week summer semester, I added another folder to the *Assignments & Activities with Weekly Folders* tab and populated it with each week's assignments, involving additional clicks: Four clicks required to add a new week's folder, color-coded with a bulleted list of its contents, regularly arranged like this:

<u>Inside This Week's Folder</u>
* *5 Criteria Reading Assignment Questions for This Essay: [Text, Title, Page Numbers]*
* *(Virtual) Tour Essay Plan: Participants, Stops, Theme, Dates, and MLA Sources*
* *Opening Quote #1*
* *Sentence Combining Activity #1*
* *Group Discussion Response & Replies #1*

Inside each folder, I uploaded additional folders and posts with detailed instructions, illustrative examples, explanatory suggestions, and supportive videoclips and weblinks. I tried to make every week's assignments succinct yet thorough, logical and intuitive, to assure students' ease of access. I aimed for clarity and consistency from task to task by assigning the same succession of five assignments, communicated in the same sequence week to week. Anything we instructors can do to assist students in negotiating colleges' complex LMS's and to reduce our own sometimes dense textual blocks of instructions is considerate.

My own regular forays online ate up hours. Posting a document inside a folder, for example, normally involved eight steps, each requiring a click to open another section of the course management system: Launch it (1), name it (2), add text (3), browse my files (4) and select one (5), choose when I wanted the file to become accessible (6) and how I wanted it released (7), then click the "Submit" button to confirm its posting (8). Adding a graded assignment or test required 14 clicks: all of the previous ones—launch, name, browse and select, choose when and how, and the finishing "Submit"—plus choosing what type of assignment (9), how many times students were allowed to turn it in (10), whether or not it should be scanned for plagiarism (11), how its score would be shown to students (12), and whether or not it would be averaged into the term's grade (13); in addition, several of the choices necessitated choosing from among separate categories to complete each (14). Posting a discussion required 12 clicks in total. Optimistically, I estimated that I could adroitly manage about one-fourth of the college's LMS features before IT upgraded it midyear to handle the additional demands in usage and capabilities as more and more courses and programs were shifted to remote mode.

Although there was a lot to manage, online delivery for me was bliss. Asynchronous delivery allowed me to log in anytime to post assignments, review essays, and reply to questions. Instead of what normally involved 20 to 30 minutes to commute one-way to and from either the downtown main campus or one of the college's satellites, I had only to climb the stairs to my study at home. Shower, shave, dress professionally—all were peripheral on those days I did not have to communicate using a camera, with all its attendant arranging of online invitations with links, framing myself onscreen, testing sound, engaging everyone, and desperately trying to figure out if the participants were indeed connecting and not merely electronically logged on. Still, only once a month did I have to gas up my car, which sat in my garage, mostly immobile, parked safely inside as was I while COVID stormed without.

Unfortunately, online delivery was also hellish. All communications were electronic, so they necessitated logging in myself—oftentimes having a merely tenuous "how to" knowledge of the process—then either talking others through the sequences of joining a meeting, checking video and sound, or getting talked through a parallel sequence on another program myself. Learning different delivery systems and electronic supplements to my schools' LMS's was at turns frustrating, tedious, and enervating. Never did it grant me any Eureka feeling of having mastered something new and valuable; instead, it invariably left me wondering why my communications felt always incomplete and fragmented. It seemed I never could sense a whole picture within a completed frame for any interaction. Alternately, it felt like spending, biding, and doing time—time itself having become commodified. It felt never-ending, as though I were always on display, always on call, expected but never able to tidily conclude. It felt like some sitcom episode that begged the presence of some small-screen Hollywood persona and frequent commercial breaks, not a writing prof juggling a lesson along with unflinching eye contact and perpetually on-point delivery remaining in character in only one take through sporadic disruptions and interruptions. I dearly missed my half-hour commutes, cranking up my music and decompressing to and from classes.

Like everything online—gaming, shopping, browsing, chatting—teaching electronically can rapidly spill into a great drain of time. Unlike teaching in person, with its set beginnings and endings and its personable transactions, in distance mode, online inquiries, posts, and chats pop up any time, all the time, and are usually terse and disjointed—which is probably to be expected when students are stacked onscreen in miniscule boxes like a brick wall of word bubbles. With censors and strictures seemingly tossed aside online, some students have little compunction about asking to chat at odd hours, requesting alternate modes of communications to the college's learning management system, sometimes bypassing the LMC altogether with cryptic emailed assignments sent from phones. Initially game to try any new approach to streamlining communications—*anything had to be better than the clunky college platform I had to contend with*, I thought—and going extra miles toward helping my students succeed, I quickly found that I had to limit all interactions to an established schedule using only college media and modalities, in order to protect my sanity and my time while also standardizing a system through which I could communicate clearly to all students. There are simply too many unsynchronized options out there, each with its own individual quirks, strengths, and demands.

It seems unimaginable to picture a shift to remote learning before the late flurry of technologically enabled connections and applications designed for, and adapted for (e.g., Zoom), educational purposes became available. Had the pandemic occurred twenty years ago, we would have resignedly declared a COVID-induced extended period of "snow days," acts of God requiring a full shut-down of instructional delivery until a healthful "thaw" allowed all to gather again to face a fallout of makeup days to complete credits. Paradoxically, today's useful technologies may have condemned learners and instructors to a perdition of perpetual online presence, schooling ever on call, and never another serendipitous surprise of a bad weather day canceling classes and freezing assignments—unless perchance the electricity fails.

Figure 16. Why might a student choose to work in a basement corner space? Photo Courtesy of Student.

Polysynchronous

During a time of pandemic, I tried to alleviate some strains on students by accommodating their requests and schedules as well as teaching both straightforwardly and simply. One way I attempted to attend to students' shifting schedules was by adapting instructional delivery. I regularly posted the next week's assignments and materials on the school's learning management system every Friday. Students then had the weekend beforehand to familiarize themselves with the next week's expectations, and those who worked during the workweek could get a head start if they so chose. In addition, I usually made assignments due either at the end of a day or before a class's scheduled beginning to allow them time at night to finish if they needed, and so flourish.

Yes, I accept late work, normally "docking" it 10%, but I readily agreed to all students' requests for additional time to complete classwork, granting them full credit for any late submission. Instead of threatening a reduction in grade—or no grade at all—I simply asked when they could submit it. Most who did request an extension only did so once or twice, but a few came to rely on a grace period every week. All appreciated my flexibility. Nearly all turned in their assignments eventually. With the myriad demands and stresses that many of my students underwent during the year, "I'm sorry, but I slept through my alarm" was a newly viable excuse, as was "My employer extended my work hours today and required, 'mandated,' me to stay" and "I agreed to cover a fellow employee's shift whose kids were doing schoolwork from home." All now sounded genuinely legitimate, often laudable.

Many students in my classes were employed, as it so happened, in the medical profession; furthermore, quite a few worked irregular and lengthy shifts, frequently exacerbated by the several waves of COVID-19 washing across the state. With their accentuated stresses during these viral surges, many were "mandated" to work additional days or extended shifts. In these instances, when their career demands potentially disrupted class attendance, participation, and timely completion of course work, any allowance on my part seemed justified. Additionally, many worked for employers who promised them long-term employment, advancement, and often other benefits, and some offered college scholarships to assist their employees—*my* students—to attain valuable credentials, skills, and promotions at their hospitals, medical offices, and clinics. Attached to many of these perks were often required attendance and grade-point average stipulations—paradoxically the first casualties of these students' added work mandates—potentially posing a cruel Catch-22 for these typically conscientious students. Surely these mandates, and students' successes, futures, and contributions to a beleaguered medical profession, as well as to a community's health and welfare—especially during the COVID-19 pandemic when medical interventions were particularly vital—were as important as any of my classroom assignments.

Besides medical students, other frontline workers among my students had work schedules upended during the pandemic. Stockers, delivery workers, cashiers, transit suppliers, some manufacturers, in addition to drive-through, curbside, and take-out staffers, experienced amplified hours and shifts as their supermarkets, retailers, restaurants, and door deliveries operated under increasing demands—many times with reduced personnel when colleagues fell ill, required quarantining or isolating, or had to give up work due to family responsibilities. At the other extreme, a large number suffered unemployment and cutbacks as many hospitality and service industries, along with other businesses, were closed or limited by state and local health departments, as well as by a heightened safety consciousness among consumers, who sought to limit the potential for viral exposures by reducing all kinds of outings. Even if unemployed, many college students invested hours completing and submitting the necessary paperwork to apply for benefits and to update resumes and sharpen job-searching skills. More than one of my students told me it was at least as hard to go look for work as to go to work, especially when pandemic cutbacks and closures were causing many employers to release their employees and many owners to close their shops.

Along with work stresses, some students had to homeschool or care for their own children or younger siblings whose schools were closed, many learning remotely. Besides studying for their own classes, some were drafted into a teacher's role, too. One of my students took a full course load at college, homeschooled her three children, and worked as the primary wage-earner for her household. Her spouse worked nights, cooked meals, and walked the dogs. Several found themselves as caregivers to family members who had contracted COVID-19 or were contending with other conditions that required special care, interventions, quarantines, and shifting household schedules or duties. The multifarious demands on students all seemed cruelly intensified by the vicissitudes of a raging COVID-19 pandemic.

My routinely posting assignments early to allow students to log in to the course site and to turn in their work over an extended stretch of time helped many students complete assignments, and many appreciated this act of understanding. As a practical matter, I normally collected (electronically) assignments twice each week to synchronize with the college's standard weekly class schedules: either Mondays and Wednesdays, or Tuesdays and Thursdays. Assignments were due at the end of the two days unless class met in person, in which case, they came due before class to have the results readied for discussion, further applications, or a next step in the writing process. Twice weekly due dates appeared to keep students engaged, whether in person or remote, participating in classwork and logging in regularly and frequently. As noted before, exceptions were accepted.

Besides accommodating students' schedules, I found that maintaining a consistent routine within class sessions from weekly meeting to meeting was comforting and assuring to them. When so much else around them may have been unpredictable and felt tumultuous, having access to an early preview of each coming week's attractions during the previous weekend and knowing what to expect for each class meeting's sequence of activities helped students thrive, so I scheduled a routine sequence of class activities. Normally, the first meeting each week was for "practice" workshops using sentences, paragraphs, and samples from students' own constructions and other sources. The second meeting was devoted to writing process and workshop activities targeting different writing stages or parts of an essay. If meeting in class, I bulleted the class session's components in sequence on the whiteboard, or if remote, they were noted in a weekly announcement posted on the college's LMS. This gave students an overview of expectations in class and assignments to be completed before classes in addition to a checklist of expectations and accomplishments. Students usually find a simple and clearly ordered sequence of online assignments that are uploaded onto the school LMS helpful (Loepp). Programs that cannot be uploaded and delivered simply and seamlessly via an LMS should probably be avoided for both your students' and your own sake. Time and effort, both your students' and yours, is far too valuable, especially when threatened by the recurring possibilities of pandemic pivots requiring you and them to wade through upswells of textual instruction or technical terminology before jumping into the writing processes.

Reading about one's own writing and self-analyses of students' writing processes is no substitute for actually engaging in the writing process and tackling its various tasks—choosing and then narrowing a theme, developing a unique viewpoint on a topic, and exploring a personally interesting and meaningful research process that results in an original, well-organized, and well-written composition. Diving directly into a student's composition as you guide students through plans, drafts, revisions, and edits toward their personal best writing is as meaningful for instructors as it is for students, who may have become too used to writing about topics chosen for them, assigned to them, and all-too-often disembodied from them, their interests, and their experiences.

Figure 17. When most or all school work is home work, how does a university's purview shrink—
or expand? Photo Courtesy of Student.

Electric

"They're the best. I love teaching hybrid classes," one of my colleagues exulted mid-semester. "The face-to-face in-class sessions let me get to know my students and catch some of what makes them tick, and the online lets my nerdy side geek out with all the cool new programs and improvements. It's really the best of both worlds right now."

"I hate these damned hybrid classes," another colleague despaired. "All the extra setup and staging is like having to prep two extra-demanding classes simultaneously, and I can't help but feel like I'm always barraging students with extraneous technology and badgering them with constant reminders of where to be when. If I have trouble remembering when to set up an online meeting and when to show up in class, I can only imagine what they're experiencing."

What do we lose when opting for technical expediency to assure physical safety while in a rampant pandemic? Technology both helps and hinders. On the one hand, it allows us to post assignments making them accessible in class as well as remotely to students who are stricken by illness, family obligations, essential work demands, and other pressures. Zooms, Skypes, Teams, and Meets allow instructors to take the course content to students and provide some opportunities for interaction as well. College centers for teaching and technology can offer smorgasbords of technology, applications, and accoutrements—a full course and then some of electronic instructional options—seemingly something to appeal to everyone's tastes (Marsicano; Peterson-Ahmad and Keeley). Cathy Davidson, writing in *The New Education*, paints an optimistic picture of the potentials of social media for students:

> … [S]tudents' constant interactive lives online, rather than making them dumber or lonely, make them more connected and engaged with one another, with the large culture, and even with printed, old-fashioned books…. This generation wants to know what is important and wants to communicate what they know. Writing well is important to them …. (94)

There is plenty to geek out on. And there is also plenty to become buried beneath.

No panacea, technology always comes at a cost. Along with the money, it costs time and effort, and bandwidth and bytes, too. Teaching center directors and staff, technology trainers, department heads, and faculty must learn a new technology well enough to decide whether it is worth adopting and applying. Too often at a point of panacea-induced pivotal panic, instructors, students, trainers, and programmers all immediately need the shiny new program up and running, crystalline-clearly user-friendly, with amply accessible and personable support. Afterwards, we are left with the question: How useful will it prove when we all—or most of us—pivot relievedly back into classrooms? Would it still be beneficial after another immediate pandemic-spike panic is past? Will today's Zoomed solution be around for next semester's or next year's panicked pivot? Will there in fact be a *back to before* classroom? I suspect not.

Class Zooms, Skypes, Teams, and Meets can also accentuate, often uncomfortably close up, students' breakdowns and breakups. On a computer screen, everyone appears incarcerated into a diminutive isolation cell, usually a streamed headshot, with those mugshots stacked like class photo rosters of students stacked vertically sans legs and torsos, or with a student's picture blanked out, leaving a disembodied voice behind a plain gray screen. In their online presence, students can be found logged in, logging in, muted, unmuted, glitching in and out, freezing and thawing, distracted or self-conscious, many scanning the microslides probably seeking themselves. Any intended or unintended movement commandeers everyone's eyes and attention. An attempt at discussion may fragment and halt when every sound suddenly mutes others' mics and triggers scattered gaps mid-conversation. Some profs resignedly resorted to lecturing, displacing classroom conversations and interaction altogether. Furthermore, clearing throats, slammed energy drinks, roving dogs, traffic, and other background noises, even a budged mouse—any one of these and many many more accidental interrupters can disrupt a purposeful online video interaction. Worse, the fatigue that many experience from always having to appear alert and stay engaged, while examining themselves and one another close up, perpetually, can drain and disquiet many already emotionally vulnerable electronic participants (Denworth; Lee; Schroeder).

Electronic teaching, although freeing and enabling in so many ways that make learning and teaching more accessible, and sometimes even feasible, in a time of novel coronavirus, can alternately constrict and cripple with its never resting, relentless and evolving, ever in-our-faces, extra-demanding omnipresence. While a useful accessory and now necessary means to personal interactions, electronically mediated interaction is at its best a simulacrum, beneficial to the degree that it leads to an in-person transaction or interaction and stimulates more live, face-to-face communications, even if distanced and masked.

Works Cited

Davidson, Cathy N. *The New Education: How to Revolutionize the University to Prepare Students for a World in Flux*, Basic Books, 2017.

Denworth, Lydia. "Why Zoom Fatigue is Real and What You Can Do About It." *Psychology Today*, 31 July 2020, www.psychologytoday.com/us/blog/brain-waves/202007/why-zoom-fatigue-is-real-and-what-you-can-do-about-it.

Garcia, Antero and Cindy O'Donnell-Allen. *Pose Wobble Flow: A Culturally Proactive Approach to Literacy Instruction*, Teachers College Press and National Writing Project, 2015, p. 63.

Lee, Jena. "A Neuropsychological Exploration of Zoom Fatigue." *Psychiatric Times*, 17 Nov. 2020, www.psychiatrictimes.com/view/psychological-exploration-zoom-fatigue.

Loepp, Eric. "What Students Want: A Simple, Navigable LMS Course Design." *Faculty Focus: Higher Ed Teaching Strategies from Magna Publications*, 1 Feb. 2021, www.facultyfocus.com/articles/online-education/online-course-design-and-preparation/what-students-want-a-simple-navigable-lms-course-design/.

Marsicano, Christopher R. "Embracing Break-and-Bake Cookies." *Inside Higher Ed: Career Advice, Teaching Today*, 10 Apr. 2020, www.insidehighered.com/advice/2020/04/10/professor-inexperienced-zoom-teaching-shares-lessons-learned-his-first-weeks-it.

Peterson-Ahmad, Maria B., and Randa G. Keeley. "Five Ways to Engage Students in an Online Learning Environment." *Faculty Focus: Higher Ed Teaching Strategies from Magna Publications* 27 Jan. 2021, www.faculty-focus.com/articles/online-education/online-course-delivery-and-instruction/five-ways-to-engage-students-in-an-online-learning-environment/.

Schroeder, Ray. "Zoom Fatigue: What We Have Learned." *Inside Higher Ed: Higher Education News*, 20 Jan. 2021, www.insidehighered.com/digital-learning/blogs/online-trending-now/zoom-fatigue-what-we-have-learned.

Q3.

What technologies have you used with your writing instruction during the pandemic? Which was most beneficial to your teaching and your students' learning? Which was least helpful?

Figure 18. Ashtyn Stewart, author of "Resilient." Photo Courtesy of Student.

Student's Story—"Resilient," by Ashtyn Stewart

Although I am optimistic, it would be ignorant to ignore the fact that this virus has taken the lives of many and created financial chaos; in addition, it has taken away the sense of normalcy that we once knew. It has taken away my own "bubble," a bubble that I felt trapped in and only discovered the way out of when COVID came to town. Every day that I wake up I am grateful. I am truly, deeply, sincerely grateful.

I almost feel a sense of guilt because other than mentally, I have not been affected by COVID-19. The guilt comes from knowing that people have it worse off than me and for once I am not being knocked down; in fact, my life is better now than it ever has been. However, I will admit during the summer I experienced some of the worst anxiety and panic attacks that I have ever had in my life. They came out of nowhere, which I attribute to the psychological effects living in a pandemic has combined with the personal experiences taking place at the same time. The emergency room saw me four times because the panic attacks made me feel like I could not breathe. After seeing multiple doctors, I have now realized that anxiety can be debilitating; but if anyone is going to get through it, that will be me.

Since I live by myself, COVID-19 has caused a feeling of isolation; moreover, I have spent more time alone this year than any other. Despite it being scary sometimes, I have never in my life been so able to focus on myself, nor have I been able to heal at this rate. During the summer I started to see a therapist and that propelled me further into a deeper healing state.

This virus has shown me how tough and resilient I can be. I graduated from high school in 2017. I was not a good student academically as I was constantly living in survival mode, but I have always loved to learn. I thought about going to college for 2 years, but I was not confident that I would succeed. During the summer, when I was not at the pharmacy I work for, I spent hours reading and journaling. I dedicated time and put work into myself that allowed me to realize that I was capable of going to college. In June, I decided that I was going to college and a global pandemic was not going to get in my way. I would adjust and get through it.

Living through this has not been easy for me all of the time and I don't want to make it seem that way. I have struggled and continue to have days when I am anxious, depressed, and feel a sense of deep guilt. There are people truly struggling right now with circumstances out of their control. I cannot fathom what it must be like to lose a loved one to this virus. I have not been sick with it to my knowledge, but I still worry every day about catching it.

I want to end on a positive note. I genuinely believe that we will get through this. We as a collective, as a society and as resilient people will make it out of this. I believe that it is ultra-important that we do our part and control what we can while also remembering to be mentally tough. I know for myself, I cannot let myself spiral down the hole of What If. COVID-19 has made me realize that all I and anyone else has is today; in other words, we need to appreciate and take advantage of today, pandemic or no pandemic.

Figure 19. How does taking—or teaching—first-year writing online affect the balance of school and home life? Photo Courtesy of Student.

BP/DP/AP—Before, During, and After Pandemic Crossings

BP, I clustered students together in small groups and roamed freely around the classroom, joining groups at their tables, asking about their writing plans and progress, reading their drafts and assignments, and contributing to their discussions and group activities. I taught standing at a podium at the front of the room, pacing past whiteboards at the back of the room, seated on a wheeled stool and scooting among groups, table to table. Instead of the 2020 and 2021 incessant droning of circulation fans recycling air, classrooms normally had a collaborative, conversational hum. All were unmasked, often clustered closely, leaning in, with laptops and the classroom electronic console used primarily in support roles, projecting instructions, class activities, or sample writings.

DP, I stand in place, parked at the projector's console, and remind individuals to distance, and curtail moving around in the classroom. "Keep distanced, but call out some ideas to the person sitting across from you to work out an agreement together," lacks intimacy and harms some of a class's camaraderie. Masked and distanced, some struggle to make out what their partners say. Sidling close to a partner or baring a mouth to help a classmate decode a pronunciation draws my reprimand and sometimes a fearful retreat of a student from peers: "Hey, distance up, dude!" Collaboration is limited, mostly forced, and often electronically mediated, even inside an in-person classroom. The gives and takes of healthy discussions and lively collaborations—essential to the English classroom, especially in an age of social, cultural, racial, and political fragmentation—are hard to develop, as much is lost to electronically isolating, individualized learning. "Don't clump up your group at a laptop. Share a doc together, or send something electronically, instead. Work together by yourselves."

AP, although we are bound to experience setbacks and blowbacks, and we can expect the continued exhaustion of having to back up classes with online and individualized alternatives as receding waves of COVID-19 and its variants continue to break across states, regions, and campuses, too, as they ebb and flow seasonally, we can hope for a gradual return toward the Comp 1 collaborative workshops we created and facilitated before March 2020. Still, for some who thrive online and others who have learned to prefer remote learning or its hybrid arrangements, continued student and faculty demand as well as administrative appreciation for the reduction in overhead now that the technical infrastructure is largely established—and those jarring glitches of our first few pivots have been patched up—should ensure that the demand for these options continues for future semesters.

Bottom Line: Expect to continue crossing additional, ever-evolving electronic programs and applications with ever-wider arrays of hybrids with in-person, onsite instruction.

COVID Quote–2020

January 10–12, 2020, the World Health Organization reported a novel coronavirus outbreak in Wuhan, Hubei province, People's Republic of China and publishes a comprehensive a comprehensive package of guidance documents for countries, covering topics related to the management of an outbreak of a new disease.

On January 16, The Pan American Health Organization/WHO Regional office for the Americas (PAHO/AMRO) issued an alert on the novel coronavirus. The alert included recommendations covering international travelers, infection prevention and control measures and laboratory testing, and after the first case in the Americas is detected in Washington state, the United States on January 21, the PAHO urged countries in the Americas to be prepared to detect early, isolate and care for patients infected with the new coronavirus, in case of receiving travelers from countries where there was ongoing transmission of novel coronavirus cases on January 24.

—"Listings of WHO's Response to COVID-19"

Figure 20. Even when students enjoy taking classes from home, what are some disadvantages? Photo Courtesy of Student.

COVID-19 Notes: "Wuhan–Milan–Michigan"

Daily, I take a walk through our neighborhood, a routine that my wife and I often double each day, now that we both work from home and springtime beckons us outdoors. We are not the only ones. Often, we meet couples strolling an infant, families bicycling, and individuals walking dogs—many whom we had not met before. And it may be my imagination, but folks seem friendlier, waving a hand and calling greetings when before you were lucky to exchange a terse head-nod.

On a walk recently, a neighbor, safely socially distanced 6 feet apart, told us about her child, a traveling nurse, moving to Detroit for 6–8 weeks to work in a hospital's COVID-19 Intensive Care Unit. We wondered whether to congratulate or comfort her.

Four blocks farther on that same day, another neighbor shared that she had moved her elderly parents—her father, a dementia patient—from a local nursing facility, where several residents and employees tested positive for the novel coronavirus, and one died. She pulled her parents to quarantine 14 days in her house. A complicating factor: Her husband is compromised with diabetes, so he is quarantining upstairs for the same two weeks.

In Cedar Springs, Michigan, a nursing home reported 31 cases of COVID-19 and 6 deaths (Tunison). However, Michigan does not require its nursing homes to report illnesses and deaths, so we likely do not know the extent of coronavirus infections (Roelofs).

On our daily walks, we heard of two more local nursing homes with unreported coronavirus cases and fatalities, but it is difficult to assess their accuracy.

Grand Rapids seems sheltered in the heel of Michigan's pleasant peninsular palm, settled far from the explosive epicenter of the viral COVID-19 pandemic enveloping Detroit, beneath the thumb. As the coronavirus threatens 10x the virulence and 10x the contagion of a run-of-the-mill annual flu, it appears that the Detroit area, with its automakers' travel lines to Italy, Europe, China, and other parts of Asia, may be struck with 10x the number of illnesses and fatalities as the rest of the state. The Grand Rapids Press reports that Michigan was the last Great Lakes state to confirm that a patient had COVID-19. The Press also reports that Michigan's Governor Whitmer was rapidly proactive in issuing shelter-in-place and other safety precautions, and Michigan residents and businesses were very amenable to the state's stay-at-home orders (Mack).

COVID Quote–2020

The Great Lakes State was the last in the Upper Midwest with a confirmed case of COVID-19.

—**Julie Mack,** *The Grand Rapids Press*

Holy Week and the week preceding hit Michigan hard. Some 100 deaths a day were reported across the state, with the vast majority in Wayne, Oakland, and Macomb Counties encircling Detroit City. Detroit was whacked with a "perfect storm of circumstances," including extreme poverty, many industrial ties to hotspots overseas, an international airport allowed to continue travel to those hotspots, and an especially popular democratic presidential primary election (Mack).

Apparently past its peak—at least its first peak—Motown is declining in COVID-19 cases, and so is Michigan overall. Grand Rapids, West Michigan, and Michigan's rural regions, however, continue to climb (Wilkinson). Grand Rapids and its suburbs expect to continue accelerating cases into May. The mid-sized city's distance from larger Midwest metropolises like Detroit and Chicago helped delay its rise and allowed time for hospitals to repurpose hospital rooms for COVID, stock supplies for essential services, and promote adherence to social distancing and sheltering in place—all policies that appear to mitigate the spread of the virus.

We pray the expected spike here will not metastasize, but we worry for our most vulnerable populations, especially residents of nursing homes and multigeneration and multifamily households, as more reports and rumors spread of infestations. Our hunkering down at home may be as much keeping others safe as it is ourselves.

—Noted May 19, 2020

Works Cited

"Listings of WHO's Response to COVID-19." *WHO: World Health Organization*, 29 June 2020, www.who.int/news/item/29-06-2020-covidtimeline.

Mack, Julie. "Why Did It Get So Bad Here?" *The Grand Rapids Press.* 19 Apr. 2020. pp. A.1, 6.

Roelofs, Ted. "Michigan Nursing Homes, Where Information on Coronavirus Goes to Die." *Michigan Healthwatch, Bridge Magazine*, 21 Apr. 2020, www.bridgemi.com/michigan-health-watch/ michigan-nursing-homes-where-information-coronavirus-goes-die.

Tunison, John. "West Michigan Nursing Home Now Reporting 6 Coronavirus Deaths of Residents." MLive. 10 Apr. 10, 2020, https://www.mlive.com/news/ grand-rapids/2020/04/west-michigan-nursing-home-now-reporting-6-resident-coronavirus-deaths.html.

Wilkinson, Mike. "Michigan May Be Past Coronavirus Peak, but Cases Grow Outstate." *Bridge Magazine*, 19 Apr. 2020, www.bridgemi.com/michigan-health-watch/ michigan-may-be-past-coronavirus-peak-cases-grow-outstate.

Figure 21. How might a student's enjoyment of a solitary moment outdoors inspire their writing? Photo Courtesy of Student.

Chapter 4. Exploring the Local Scene

Place- and community-based education—an approach to teaching and learning that connects learning to the local—has become ... an antidote to one of the most serious ... dilemmas in American education: the alienation ... from the real world right outside their homes and classrooms.

—Gregory A. Smith and David Sobel

Essay #1: Place-Based Writing—The Virtual Tour

"Who is your reader?" I like to get my students considering and visualizing actual audiences and purposes for writing at the outset.

"Maybe the people we ask to go on our tours?"

"That could work, although you are introducing them and connecting them to your chosen tour stops in the essay, too, so it may sound rather awkward."

"You."

"Yes, definitely, I will read your essay, probably more than once."

"Do we have to read each other's?"

"You will, both to give some ideas and possibly to get some, too. Could some of your classmates be interested in taking the tour?"

"What about other friends or maybe family members?"

"Yes, could you suggest some others besides your chosen tour group who might be interested in taking it, as well? What adjustments would you make or suggestions could you give for other tour groups?"

When I taught in a "far west" suburb of Chicago, I simply told people that I was from Chicago, or if we were meeting somewhere in the U.S. Midwest, I might specify "Chicagoland," generally taken to include most of northeast Illinois as well as the section of northwest Indiana adhering to the Central Time Zone. Now that I teach in West Michigan, I readily reply, "Grand Rapids," although I commute to campuses in the towns of Allendale or Holland, too, and I live north of a smaller town, Hudsonville, that is nearly a suburb. With the ubiquity of malls, chains, brands—maybe colleges and universities, too—places in many ways seem to resemble one another, and we can take comfort in the conveniences of McDonald's, Starbucks, and all those Amazon Prime delivery vehicles prowling about. However, it is their differences that define places. As Laura DeLind and Terry Link characterize it,

> ... place is a concept of many dimensions—a shape shifter of sorts. It can be tangible, sensual. It can exist under our feet; it can literally ground us, anchor us, give us roots. But place can also be social and spiritual. It can be as intangible as history, as creative as culture, as mystical as creation myths. Instead of something absolute, place can be a matter of shifting identities, shared understandings, and relationships not only among ourselves but among all living creatures. (124)

Exploring a college's campus and neighborhood, ferreting out the study nooks and crannies, discovering a bohemian coffee shop and tattered used bookshop, then mapping the dreadful weather shortcuts and meandering pathways between or among them help us stake territory, make a place ours, and identify as a resident—if only for a few years. A sense of place can augment identity and enhance communal pride; in fact, it can also develop democratic dispositions (Pretty and Barlett 312–313) and foster the practice and learning of a Deweyan democratic community beyond the classroom (Jenlink 277–280). In addition, "[c]olleges and universities are inextricably woven into the communities in which they exist, and their programs, commitments, and connections provide opportunities to make significant differences off campus as well as on campus" (Barlett and Chase 5).

Normally, when I teach on Main Campus, downtown, I assign students to plan and write a tour of the city of Grand Rapids for friends or family; however, now in the throes of a viral pandemic, I ask them instead to research and compose a virtual tour. Whereas before, I sent them out into the city to visit museums, restaurants, coffee shops, art installations; participate in festivals, celebrations, or parades; and walk parkways, river paths, the skywalk, even a cemetery—now I ask them to boot up a Google map and click on the different sites to get ideas for their websites before visiting the college's library as well as their local city or county public library to research in-depth. Of course, as venues and businesses reopen, I encourage them to get out, visit, and patronage them—as they feel safe and comfortable doing so. As important as the simple act of going outside and walking was to alleviate student stresses and anxieties before the COVID-19 pandemic of 2020, its importance was magnified during the times of shelter-in-place and open-again, shut-again campus protocols (Massey).

A commuter campus, my college is settled at the confluence of several thriving downtown districts, including a tourism hub with a convention center, arena, three concert venues, high-rise hotels, and a multitude of restaurants and breweries; a "medical mile" of two medical teaching colleges, two hospitals, and many medical specialty buildings; a government corridor with federal, state, and local centers along with courts, law firms, and law enforcement; and three other, separate colleges' downtown campuses. Parks and the city plaza usually schedule outdoor concerts, art shows, festivals, parades, and ethnic heritage celebrations; and street corners may feature buskers, too, weather and city permitting. Many students, unfortunately, have neither the time nor the inclination to explore or experience what their city offers: they typically park or disembark a bus to a classroom, possibly stopping in the campus cafeteria or sitting in their cars to eat lunch, then finish their classes and commute off to home or work.

Besides eliminating stress and anxiety, walking proffers all manner of benefits to students (and instructors alike), as Shane O'Mara notes in *In Praise of Walking: A New Scientific Exploration*. In O'Mara's view, walking helps "clear the clamour of the day …. Gives … the freedom to think things through … [and] have a quiet dialogue with myself" (145)—all advantageous to planning and processing an essay assignment. Along with its promotion of mental and physical health as well as social interactions and creative thinking, walking is a superb approach to explore a downtown, community, or college campus (99).

More and more, I attempt to weave the city into my curriculum, with the Tour Essay a prominent strand. Given the many Michiganders who have grown up without ever or hardly ever visiting a Great Lake, and others from the city or a suburb who have never experienced downtown Grand Rapids even if attending classes there, I aim to instill in them a sense of place by requiring them to plan sites to visit in Grand Rapids. For starters, the college's Student Center offers enrollees a card granting free admission to four downtown museums, an avant-garde film theater, and the city's zoo. Most are unaware of this student perk until I require that they acquire one of those cards. Also, fewer than half in a typical first-year composition class have a library card for their local public library, so they miss out on community events and news, as well as all of the local history, books, periodicals, media, and electronic materials and access available there. Besides the college's free pass, I require them to obtain a library card, too. While many of the school's resources are no longer available to them after they graduate or transfer to another school, their library and their city, with all of the cultural, educational, entertainment, and community opportunities they offer, remain for lifelong access—when the pall of pandemic passes, that is.

Assisting students—many having grown up hereabouts and all now achieving an education at its namesake college—to see themselves as being an integral, contributing part of this place may be reassuring, especially when under the threat of a ruthless virus that has isolated, threatened, harmed, and killed so many. "I grew up here, but I never knew about all the places and things we learned. Now I'm going to tell my parents because I don't think they ever learned it either," several have commented.

The Virtual Tour essay is an opportunity to share students' newfound knowledge and appreciation of their city with family or friends. Importantly, the tour is theirs: They choose who takes it as well as where and when they go, how they get there and get around, and how much time and money participants would spend. Also, I ask them to snap a selfie—either solo or of their whole group if they are safely able to do a group shot—to upload into their essay and to add an MLA caption beneath it. Picturing themselves as guides of the city also may help them identify this place as their own and themselves as belonging to the place. In addition, students' positive response to this essay assignment is a reminder that even reluctant writers can become deeply engaged in a writing task involving personal interest and choice.

Students start by considering their audience, identifying 3–6 individuals to lead on a tour of the city of Grand Rapids. Some select their friends, others family; and many choose people who live out of town but plan to travel here to visit. They are required to select actual individuals and to consider their ages and interests, so that the tour stops can be aligned with characteristics of their tour group or audience for the virtual tour. Even if students decide to include the college, their place of employment, where they live, and some of their own favorite spots, they still must find a way to gear the tour to their selected tour group audience. For example, if their tour group includes a secondary school student, the writer might include the college's counseling and placement building in addition to the cafeteria, science building, and library where the guide spends each school day. Tours including young children, elderly, or less mobile participants may limit distances and avoid stairways and hills.

With their tour group members chosen, writers next select 3–6 stops to include on their tours. They are welcome to impose a theme, such as outdoor artwork, farm-to-table restaurants, child-friendly parks, challenging disc-golf parks, brewpubs, favorite taco stands, places of worship, or historical sites—to name several essay themes of former students. Many piece together a "Best of the City" hodge-podge of museums, businesses, parks, walkways, restaurants, coffee shops, breweries, art works, or scenic river views to fit their own as well as their tour group members' varied interests.

For every stop, they research a source or two, including its website if it has one, for descriptions and details such as recommended menu entrees and prices for a restaurant or permanent and featured exhibits in a museum that match their audience's affinities. Between stops, they furnish directions and distances as well as modes of transportation:

walking, free shuttle bus, public transportation, scooter, bicycle, longboard (skateboard), private vehicle, kayak, boat—all examples from students' essays.

Besides transportation, they must schedule the times of the tour activities. First, determining when the participants are visiting and whether they are from out of town or local; whether they are available only mornings or afternoons, evenings, or weekends; and whether there is a need to accommodate a work or school schedule. If choosing to include a concert, when is the performer or ensemble touring? If it includes a baseball or soccer game, the tour may need to be arranged for the summertime; if hockey or basketball, it will be in the winter. If venues' schedules are not established due to closures and restrictions caused by the coronavirus and state and local safety strictures, I let students check the calendars of previous years and apply the dates to coming seasons. In addition, they may need to limit their tours to the reduced numbers of places open during the pandemic and the smaller percentage of patrons allowed inside; or, for those hardy enough to brave the open air, they might consider those establishments that serve outdoors, as many have opened their summertime patios for fall, winter, and spring times, too, or augmented patios with tents, "bubbles," and other shelters.

Finally, they should calculate prices—costs for admissions, meals, and transportation— and tally them individually or by group for their selected participants.

I allow students to plan the tour individually or together with one or a few classmates as long as they work at a distance or remotely during the pandemic; but I caution them about the possible complications: planning a common audience, agreeing about tour stops, arranging suitable transportation, writing multiple drafts together, and all accepting the same grade for the assignment. Scheduling to do all of the work together, even electronically, can be a nightmare, and regularly reporting everyone's equal input adds another demanding layer of accountability. While most prefer designing their own tours, a few do enjoy the efforts of collaborating with one or more classmates.

For the writing process, I posted five steps with what I intended to be simple and clear requirements. In fact, these are the same five steps that I assign for all essays, so that if my class members have to scatter remotely mid-semester, as we did twice in 2020, students leave with a basic understanding of what to expect for each, regardless of how far along in the writing process they may be.

Although students are not tied to them, I propose specific research sources and provide links for them, so they know where to search as well as what I expect. Besides sparing them the frustrations of fruitless Google goose-chases, it steers them to specific, place-based, local sites and sources, so that even when they do meander along rabbit trails within them, they should encounter locally useful information for potential future area explorations—thus not a useless diversion. Besides, with all the tangles of online algorithms and advertisers, along with the drifting clutter of irrelevant or out-of-date sites, it seems fairplay to introduce students to those sites of most current value and utility for their essay that may also be of potential value for future personal excursions.

Works Cited

Barlett, Peggy F. and Geoffrey W. Chase. "Introduction," pp. 1–26. *Sustainability on Campus: Stories and Strategies for Change*, edited by Peggy F. Barlett and Geoffrey W. Chase, MIT Press, 2004.

DeLind, Laura B. and Terry Link. "Place as the Nexus of a Sustainable Future: A Course for All of Us," pp. 121–137. *Sustainability on Campus: Stories and Strategies for Change*, edited by Peggy F. Barlett and Geoffrey W. Chase, MIT Press, 2004.

Jenlink, Patrick M. "Transforming the School into a Democratically Practiced Place: Dewey's Democracy as Spatial Practice," pp. 274–296. *Dewey's Democracy and Education Revisited: Contemporary Discourses for Democratic Education and Leadership*, edited by Patrick M. Jenlink, Rowman & Littlefield Education, 2009.

Massey, Mike. "Encountering Nature: Outdoor Walks to Reduce Stress and Increase Focus in Students." *Faculty Focus: Higher Ed Teaching Strategies from Magna Publications*, 23 Sept. 2020, www.facultyfocus.com/articles/teaching-and-learning/encountering-nature-outdoor-walks-to-reduce-stress-and-increase-focus-in-students/.

O'Mara, Shane. *In Praise of Walking: A New Scientific Exploration*, W.W. Norton, 2020.

Pretty, Jules and Peggy F. Barlett. "Concluding Remarks: Nature and Health in the Urban Environment," pp. 298–319. *Urban Place: Reconnecting with the Natural World*, edited by Peggy F. Barlett, MIT Press, 2005.

Smith, Gregory A. and David Sobel. *Place- and Community-based Education in Schools*, Routledge, 2010, p. viii.

Figure 22. Might writing in or about a favored place outdoors bolster a student's emotional affinity toward an assignment and its rhetorical purposes? Photo Courtesy of Student.

<u>Instruction Sheet 2.1</u>

Virtual Tour Essay Assignment— Grand Rapids

3–6 pp. MLA Instructions

<u>Overview</u>

Choose a group for whom you could serve as tour guide to Grand Rapids such as friends from out of town or visiting grandparents, then choose appropriate tour stops for their ages and interests, or think of a good theme (like African American owned shops and restaurants, with the African American Museum and "People of This Place" in the Grand Rapids Public Museum, and famous statues and artworks), and plan your tour. Calculate dates, costs, directions, distances, and transportation, and anticipate any concerns or special considerations for your visitors. Consider other groups who could take your tour and any considerations relevant to those audiences.

<u>Audience</u>

1. Begin with some <u>questions</u>:
    a. Whom do you plan to take on your tour?
    b. What are their ages?
    c. What are their interests?
    d. What theme could you consider?
    e. When will you take them on your tour?
    f. What accommodations might you make for them?

<u>Tour</u>

2. Include <u>3–6 tour stops</u> with <u>3–6 research</u> <u>sources</u> in your background research:
    a. **Required Websites**
        1) <u>Experience Grand Rapids:</u> www.experiencegr.com
        2) <u>Library's Grand Rapids Subject Guide:</u> [hyperlink removed]
        3) <u>A Grand Rapids business, restaurant, coffee shop, or organization's webpage</u>
    b. <u>Map</u> with directions
    c. <u>Interview</u> of business owner, artist, city employee
    d. <u>Another</u> webpage or source

<u>Photos</u>

3. Include <u>1–2 photos</u> with MLA captions beneath and squared text around them:
    a. Self-portrait (or tour group) at a tour stop with identifiable sign:
    b. Historical or site picture credited correctly with a caption:
4. a. MLA rough draft, revised draft, and peer reviews   Due: ___/___/___
    b. MLA final edited copy & Reflection/Analysis form   Due: ___/___/___

<u>Instruction Sheet 2.2</u>

Virtual Tour Essay Plan

Email your instructor or upload on the class's LMS your answers to these questions:

1. **Whom would you lead on your tour?**
    - List the names, ages, and interests of 3–5 individuals taking your tour.

2. **When would you take your tour?**
    - List the season, month, day(s) of the week, and time(s) of day.
    - Note which places or events affect your tour's season, day, or time.

3. **Where would you take them?**
    - List 3–5 tour stops, and relate them to group members' interests and ages.

4. **What supporting details require researching?**
    - Prices, hours, schedules, menus, tickets, reservations?
    - Parking, transportation, directions?
    - Descriptions, reviews, personal visit, interview?

5. **List 3–5 websites and other sources you plan to research.**
    - Websites: museum, restaurant, business, park …
    - Interview: owner, employee, docent …
    - Library book, database, historical journal or photo …
    - Brochure, menu, newspaper, magazine …
    - Personal visit (if safety precautions taken)

Instruction Sheet 2.3

Virtual Tour Essay Plan Score

Assessment: 6 Points Possible
(3 pts = C, 4 pts = B, 5 pts = A, 6 pts = A+)

3 pts. 3 Tour group members listed with ages and interests
3 Tour stops listed with detailed descriptions
3 MLA Works Cited sources

4 pts. 4 Tour group members listed with ages and interests
4 Tour stops listed with detailed descriptions
4 MLA Works Cited sources

5 pts. 5 Tour group members listed with ages and interests
5 Tour stops listed with detailed descriptions
5 MLA Works Cited sources and in-text citations

6 pts. 5 Tour group members listed with ages and interests
5 Tour stops listed with detailed descriptions
5 MLA Works Cited sources and in-text citations
1 Photo, map, or graphic with MLA caption

Notes

Figure 23. How could visiting a favorite event and researching a favored team, club, or activity instill enthusiasm for a writing task and composition itself? Photo Courtesy of Student.

Instruction Sheet 2.4

Virtual Tour Essay Rough Draft

Email your instructor or upload on the class's LMS a rough draft of your essay that includes these items:

1. **An MLA-style template** (saved as… from an earlier essay or uploaded new).
   - Running head with your last name and page numbers in top right corners.
   - Name block with your name, instructor's name, course name, and date.
   - Title centered in plain text.
   - Works Cited page with an MLA in-text citation matching every source.

2. **Introduction**
   - Personal backstory of your own experience influencing your choices.
   - Introductions to tour group members, ages, and interests.
   - Brief overview of tour stops and timeline.
   - Effects of COVID-19 safety protocols on your tour plan.

3. **Body Paragraphs**
   - Detailed descriptions of 4–6 tour stops related to tour group members.
   - Clear directions and transportation modes between every tour stop.
   - Variety of facts, stories, histories related to tour stops.
   - Recommended experiences, sights, entrees at eating establishments.
   - Maybe a map, photo, or chart.
   - MLA in-text citations in parentheses within every paragraph.

4. **Conclusion**
   - Summary review with highlights for readers.
   - Totals: Distances, costs, time.
   - Suggested alternatives for prospective tour groups with different ages or interests.
   - Optional personal reflection.

<u>Instruction Sheet 2.5</u>

Virtual Tour Essay Rough Draft Score

<u>Assessment: 6 Points Possible</u>
(3 pts = C, 4 pts = B, 5 pts = A, 6 pts = A+)

3 pts. 3 tour group members with ages and interests in Introduction
3 tour stops with detailed descriptions in body paragraphs
3 MLA Works Cited sources and in-text citations
3 highlights summarized in Conclusion

4 pts. 4 tour group members with ages and interests in Introduction
4 tour stops with detailed descriptions in body paragraphs
4 MLA Works Cited sources and in-text citations
4 highlights summarized in Conclusion

5 pts. 5 tour group members with ages and interests in Introduction
5 tour stops with detailed descriptions in body paragraphs
5 MLA Works Cited sources and in-text citations
5 highlights summarized in Conclusion

6 pts. 6 tour group members with ages and interests in Introduction
6 tour stops with detailed descriptions in body paragraphs
6 MLA Works Cited sources and in-text citations
6 highlights summarized in Conclusion
1 photo, map, or graphic in "squared" text with MLA caption

<u>Notes</u>

Instruction Sheet 2.6

Virtual Tour Essay Revised Draft

Email your instructor or upload on the class's LMS a revised draft of your essay that includes these items:

1. **An MLA-style template**
   - Running head matches font and size of essay text.
   - Name block is typed in plain text, doubled-spaced, with no additional spaces.
   - Title has two parts connected with a colon, and is centered in plain text.
   - No additional spaces between paragraphs.
   - MLA in-text citations appropriately match Works Cited sources.

2. **Introduction**
   - Personal backstory includes specific and sensory details.
   - Introductions to tour group members are varied and individualized.
   - Transitional words and phrases unify paragraph's components compellingly.

3. **Body Paragraphs**
   - Every tour group member is specifically related to at least one tour stop.
   - Directions, details, and descriptions are thorough and varied for all stops.
   - Every tour stop includes a specific recommendation.
   - A map, photo, or chart is uploaded with squared text and MLA caption.
   - An MLA in-text citation follows every direct quotation.

4. **Conclusion**
   - Final paragraph is unified with transitions.
   - Closing ideas add possible stops for a future tour or different group.
   - Optional personal reflection.

Instruction Sheet 2.7

Virtual Tour Revised Draft Score

Assessment: 6 Points Possible
(3 pts = C, 4 pts = B, 5 pts = A, 6 pts = Bonus A+)

3 pts. 3 substantive changes made to essay

4 pts. 4 substantive changes made to essay

5 pts. 5 substantive changes made to essay

6 pts. 6 substantive changes made to essay

Email your instructor or upload on the class's LMS a list of the 3–6 substantive changes you made to your essay for the revised draft.

A *substantive change* may involve rewriting the Introduction, rewriting the Conclusion, adding a body paragraph, rearranging the body paragraphs, adding an introductory transitional word or phrase to every paragraph, or combining and rephrasing the sentences inside a paragraph.

Notes

Instruction Sheet 2.8

Virtual Tour Essay Peer Review

Email your revised draft of the Virtual Tour Essay to your group members or upload it on the class's LMS for your group to access.

Send or share your replies to the questions to the writer, then email your instructor the names of those whose essays you peer reviewed as well as those who peer reviewed your essay.

Normally, you receive one point for each essay you peer review (limit 3) + the number of group members who reviewed your essay (limit 3) to match the number of sentences inside your resulting changes paragraph = Peer Review Score (maximum 6).

- Write **Virtual Tour** with your **First & Last Name** and **Course Name & #** on the email Subject line.

- List the names of students who peer reviewed your essay as well as the names of those whose essays you peer reviewed.

- After reading the peer reviews of your essay, write a 3–6 sentence paragraph explaining what changes you plan to make in your essay.

1. **Is the two-part title both accurate and appealing?**

2. **What could be changed in the Introduction and the Conclusion?**

3. **What is one additional thing you want to learn about a tour stop?**

4. **What was described with the most specific details, sensory portrayal, narrative illustration, or historical background?**

5. **What is something the author did that you might like to try writing yourself?**

Instruction Sheet 2.9

Virtual Tour Essay Peer Review Score

Assessment: 6 Points Possible
(3 pts = C, 4 pts = B, 5 pts = A, 6 pts = Bonus A+)

Email your instructor a list of the names of your classmates whose essays you peer reviewed as well as those who peer reviewed your essay, as well as a 3–6 sentence paragraph detailing what changes you plan to write as a result.

Normally, you receive one point for <u>each essay you peer review</u> (limit 3) + the number of group members <u>who reviewed your essay</u> (limit 3) <u>to match</u> the number of sentences inside your <u>resulting changes paragraph</u> (3–6) = Peer Review Score (maximum 6).

- Write **Virtual Tour** with your **First & Last Name** and **Course Name & #** on the <u>email Subject line</u>.
- List the names of students who peer reviewed your essay as well as the names of those whose essays you peer reviewed.
- After reading the peer reviews of your essay, write a <u>3–6 sentence paragraph</u> explaining what changes you plan to make in your essay.

Notes

Instruction Sheet 2.10

Virtual Tour Essay Final Draft with Editing and Formatting

Follow these five final steps before turning in your essay:

1. **Check your <u>MLA formatting</u>**
   - **Running head** with your last name and page numbers in top right corners on all pages,
   - **Name block** with your name, instructor's name, course name, and date written out formally with no punctuation (e.g., 28 October 2023), on separate lines aligned at left margin on first page only.
   - **Two-Part Title** with a colon (:) and centered, plain text, double-spaced with no additional spaces between the name block and Introduction.
   - **MLA in-text citations** with last name of author and page number or webpage's or article's title within parentheses in every body paragraph.
   - **Works Cited** page with complete MLA citations in same font style and font size as essay, double-spaced with no additional spaces, set up in hanging indentation, in alphabetical order.
   - **No bold or underlined** text, **all double-spaced** with no additional spaces between paragraphs or sources.
   - **Any Photos** have an **MLA caption** beneath and text wrapped "square" around the picture, so there are no blank gaps on the page.

2. **Run a <u>spell check</u> and double-check words for usage and variety.**

3. **Run a <u>grammar check</u> to ensure clarity and lucidity.**

4. **Check every page for varied <u>sentence styles</u> and <u>paragraph organization</u>.**

5. **Use the LMS program to <u>scan</u> for plagiarism and <u>turn in</u> your essay. Congratulations!**

<u>**Instruction Sheet 2.11**</u>

Virtual Tour Essay Editing and Formatting Score

<u>**Assessment: 6 Points Possible**</u>
(3 pts = C, 4 pts = B, 5 pts = A, 6 pts = Bonus A+)

Email your instructor a total from your tally of the Editing and Formatting score, giving yourself 1 point for each of these 6 items:

- Write **Editing & Formatting Score** with your **First & Last Name** and **Course Name & #** on the <u>email Subject line</u>.

1. **Checked <u>MLA formatting</u>**
   - **Running head**
   - **Name block**
   - **Two-Part Title**
   - **MLA in-text citations**
   - **Works Cited**
   - **No bold or underlined text, all double-spaced**

2. **Ran a <u>spell check</u> and double-checked words for usage and variety.**

3. **Ran a <u>grammar check</u> to ensure clarity and lucidity.**

4. **Checked every page for varied <u>sentence styles</u> and <u>paragraph organization</u>.**

5. **<u>Scanned</u> to remove plagiarism and <u>turn in</u> your essay.**

6. **Photo, graphic, or chart included with MLA caption and "squared" text.**

<u>**Notes**</u>

<u>Instruction Sheet 2.12</u>

Virtual Tour Essay Reflection/Analysis Score

<u>Assessment: 6 Points Possible</u>
(3 pts = C, 4 pts = B, 5 pts = A, 6 pts = Bonus A+)

Email your <u>instructor</u> a 3–6 sentence paragraph answering the questions below, including the number of sentences you wrote for each paragraph (3 pts for each paragraph = C, 4 pts/each ¶ = B, 5 pts each ¶ = A, 6 pts/ each ¶ = A+):

- Write **Essay Reflection/Analysis Score** with your **First & Last Name** and **Course Name & #** on the <u>email Subject line</u>.

1. **What 3–6 things that are new to you did you attempt in this essay?**

2. **What 3–6 things do you like most about your writing?**

<u>**Instruction Sheet 2.13**</u>

Virtual Tour Essay Final Score

<u>**Assessment: 6 Points Possible**</u>
(3 pts = C, 4 pts = B, 5 pts = A, 6 pts = Bonus A+)

Email your instructor a total of your scores for every step of the Virtual Tour Essay.

- Write **Essay Reflection/Analysis Score** with your **First & Last Name** and **Course Name & #** on the <u>email Subject line</u>.

1. **Essay Plan Score: ___**

2. **Rough Draft Score: ___**

3. **Revised Draft Score: ___**

4. **Peer Review Score: ___**

5. **Editing and Formatting Score: ___**

6. **Essay Reflection/Analysis Score: ___**

= Total Score (1+2+3+4+5+6): ___ divided by 6 = Average Score: ___

Figure 24. Sebastian Benavides, author of "Eating Vegan in the City: A Tour of Grand Rapids." Photo Courtesy of Student.

Virtual Tour Sample Student Essay

Sebastian Benavides
Professor Tom Mulder
English 101-5877
18 February 2021

Eating Vegan in the City: A Tour of Grand Rapids

2015 is the year I moved to Grand Rapids and started living a vegan lifestyle. Over the years, I have had my fair share of experience eating at the different restaurants we are fortunate enough to have in town. While conducting additional research for this essay, I was able to find even more vegan options in the city that I did not know about beforehand. One of my favorite activities when I visit somewhere new, no matter the place, is to pull out my phone, do a little research on Google or Instagram, and plan out where I can find something tasty to eat. This exact activity was the inspiration behind my tour. On this tour, guests will experience a full day of vegan eating throughout Grand Rapids. For some, it may be hard to find something that can accommodate their diet. For others, they may be interested in learning more about the vegan lifestyle and the options that so many restaurants have to offer (Allen and Dunn, Hubbard, *Vegan Grand Rapids*). On the tour, guests will make six stops and get to see several areas of the city. From a dive bar in the heart of downtown to a tiny coffee shop on the West Side, guests will take a trip around the city of Grand Rapids, eating along the way.

The one thing that all six guests of this tour have in common is their desire to learn more about the vegan food options that Grand Rapids has to offer. For this tour, I am bringing along a small group of my closest friends. E------ and M------ are both from Grand Rapids and eat 100% plant based. M----- and M----- are from Hudsonville and are both vegetarian. Additionally, my friends B----- and M----- are coming up from Chicago to take my tour. B----- considers herself a vegetarian and M----- actually eats meat, so I will be introducing both of them to some things they have never had before. They are all in their late 20s, so they should get along very well, with similar interests outside of their eating habits. While some of the tour stops may be in close proximity to each other, it is recommended that the guests have a vehicle available to get around and experience this tour completely. My car can fit 4 people, in the event that anyone does not want to drive. Since this tour will be taking place in the Summer of 2022, the COVID-19 Pandemic will have passed. Therefore, we will be able to utilize the Grand Rapids Dash to help navigate around the city, if needed. One perk of doing this is we will not have to deal with parking. What we order at each stop is completely up to the guests, though I would encourage them to plan on spending roughly $10–15 at each stop and allowing some wiggle room for proper gratuity. This is all completely dependent on what they want to eat. We will be starting with breakfast and ending with dessert, so I would recommend planning on spending roughly $75–100.

Our tour will begin on the West Side, not far from the John Ball Park Zoo, at Rise Authentic Baking Co. This vegan, gluten free, and soy free bakery is located 1220 Fulton Street West and began selling their baked goods at local coffee shops back in 2016. They opened a storefront, partnering with Squibb Coffee, in 2019 ("Our Mission—Rise Authentic Baking Co"). This is one of the first vegan bakeries I ever had the opportunity to try, and I have been a loyal customer ever since. They are even doing the dessert for my wedding, where we will be offering 3 different donut flavors for guests to choose from. Given that the bakery has so many delicious options, it was a little difficult for us to narrow it down to just three. Ultimately, we ended up choosing Blueberry Lemon Lavender, Classic Glazed, and Cookies & Cream. Their bakery menu changes daily, offering different flavors of donuts, muffins, yum tarts, and cookies, among other things. Because their flavors also change, their menu can be found on their Instagram story every morning. Additionally, they have a rotating seasonal menu offering different sandwiches, soups, smoothie bowls, and shakes. My personal recommendation to the group would be to find someone else on the tour and each get a few different flavors of donuts and maybe an apple fritter. That way, they will get to try a little bit of everything. With so many different flavors of donuts, it would be impossible to narrow it down to just one. These donuts could easily be paired with an Oat Milk Matcha Latte or Iced Coffee and my guests will be ready to tackle the rest of our tour with plenty of energy.

Once we have had our caffeine and sugar fix to start the day, we will take the 5-minute drive over to the Roosevelt Park area and stop at 570 Grandville Avenue Southwest, which is home to the restaurant MudPenny. Although it is only a short distance, it would not be feasible for us to walk. MudPenny has an additional location in Ada, with a different menu, but we are staying in close proximity of downtown for the purpose of the tour. This location opened in December 2018, with two dining spaces and a full coffee bar. Whether the guests are in the mood for homemade vegan biscuits & gravy or a quinoa salad, MudPenny does not disappoint with a wide variety of options for vegans and vegetarians ("Roosevelt Park Menu—MudPenny"). It is worth checking out their specials as well since they have had some vegan options in the past. One of the best things about MudPenny, is that they have committed to giving back to their community. Quarterly, they donate 1% of their sales to neighborhood efforts and organizations ("About | Grand Rapids, MI—MudPenny"). By stopping at this restaurant, we will be helping give back to the community of Grand Rapids as it continues to grow.

Our next stop is not too far away from our stop for breakfast, and is located in the heart of Downtown. Guests can choose to drive 4 minutes or take a 17-minute walk to 53 Commerce Avenue Southwest, though I would personally recommend driving, depending on how hot it is that day. Once we have arrived and finished taking photos along the mural of skulls outside, we will find Stella's Lounge. While this restaurant was named the Best Burger in America by GQ in 2012, they surprisingly have a full vegan menu with plenty of options for anyone who is interested in eating something plant based, instead ("Stella's Lounge—Stella's"). Stella's Lounge brings a whole new meaning to vegan bar food, from their beer battered avocado nuggets to their breaded potato wedges, tossed in your favorite sauce. Guests can also snag a sweet potato burrito, featuring their house made vegan ranch, or try the ever-popular Impossible Burger. ("Stella's Menu—Stella's"). Stella's Lounge has a very inclusive atmosphere, and they are accepting of people that come from different communities and backgrounds. This is evident just from walking in the front door and seeing their very diverse staff. There are arcade game machines and old shows on the televisions above the bar. There is an additional entrance on Ionia Street, which is one of the most popular streets in Downtown Grand Rapids. This offers several opportunities to browse around the downtown area, while also working up their appetite again.

After spending a little bit of time in the main Downtown Area, we will take the 2-minute drive (or 7-minute walk up the hill) to Bangkok Taste, located at 15 Jefferson Avenue Southeast, a Thai restaurant located between Downtown and Heritage Hill. We could not go on a vegan food tour without making a stop for Thai food at least once. This particular Thai restaurant is down the street from my old apartment, so I have become quite familiar with the menu. With several options that are already plant based, Bangkok Taste notes on their menu that most of their dishes can be made with tofu and without fish sauce. The servers are so friendly and have never had an objection to modifying something to accommodate a plant-based diet. Some of the best things on the menu are their curry dishes, served with a side of freshly steamed white rice, but we will not be stopping here for a full meal as part of the tour. My personal recommendation would be the Fresh Rolls, filled with veggies, rice noodles, and served with a peanut dipping sauce. If we were to pair this appetizer with the crispy fried tofu, served with cucumber sauce, I know that the guests of my tour will be very satisfied ("Bangkok Taste Cuisine"). It is the perfect amount of food for a light snack after walking around downtown and before heading to our next stop in Eastown.

As we move east of downtown, we will take a quick 5-minute drive, and will end up at 1017 Wealthy Street Southeast, the home of Brick Road Pizza Co. From just hearing the name, someone might think that a pizza place would not have many vegan options, but they would be very surprised. Nearly everything on the menu at Brick Road Pizza Co. is either already vegan or has a vegan option available. They even offer a fully vegan brunch buffet on Sundays with a changing menu every week, which I have most certainly missed over the past year. While we are at Brick Road Pizza Co., guests will find that the menu has much more to offer than just pizza, although their pizza is delicious—especially the buffalo tofu, with creamy vegan ranch, tomato, and green onion ("Menu–Brick Road Pizza"). They have a wide variety of sandwiches, ranging from their vegan take on a classic club to their Philly steak sandwich. This is one of my favorite restaurants in town and my go-to when I do not know what else to get. Additionally, it is one of the best places to take someone who is somewhat unfamiliar with vegan food, since they have so many different options to choose from. One of my friends ordered the BBQ Jackfruit sandwich a few years ago and could not believe it was not real pork. In fact, this is the restaurant that I go to every year for my birthday. Since I am a creature of habit, the servers have even predicted my order a few times, which was only a little bit embarrassing, since it showed how often I go there. However, I suppose there are worse things to be embarrassed about.

Someone reading about this tour might be wondering how we can possibly fit more food into our day, but I promise that our last stop of the tour is the perfect way to end our night. Located at 958 Cherry St Southeast, Furniture City Creamery is a 1-minute drive from our stop for dinner. This area of town is considered uptown, just east of downtown, but not quite to Eastown. While there are several different options for restaurants and bars in this area, Furniture City Creamery offers some of the best vegan ice cream in town. Their ice cream is made in house, using coconut milk, to create delicious vegan options for those who are plant based. Their menu changes frequently, so it is best to follow them on Instagram to stay up to date. They offer fresh scooped ice cream or a variety of options in their cooler right inside of the store, including vegan chocolate tacos and Oreo sandwiches (*Hand Crafted Ice Cream*). The guests might end up leaving this place with more ice cream than they need, especially after our morning donuts, but what is so bad about that?

So, what is the biggest takeaway for the guests of this tour? The guests of my tour will get to see several areas of town, all with something a little different to offer. Additionally, there are so many delicious plant-based food options throughout the city of Grand

Rapids. Some may be at locations people would never expect, such as a pizza shop or dive bar known for its stuffed burgers. Sometimes it just takes a little research to find out what different restaurants have to offer, but thankfully there are so many resources these days to help narrow down the search for good vegan food. Most of the time, I have discovered places by hearing from other people, but there are websites such as Experience GR, Vegan GR, or simply looking around on Google Maps. The greatest thing about a tour like this is that we could do it again going to six different restaurants. We could try the Vegan Chicken & Waffles at Field & Fire Care or the Tempeh and Cactus Tacos at Tacos El Cuñado in the Downtown Market. Moreover, it would be very easy to bring different guests on this tour and still have a wonderful time, including those who are not interested in vegan food, but just want to come along for the trip. In the end, I would ask my friends to take a look at some resources online and suggest where they would go next time. That way, when I hold this tour again, I can plan a brand-new itinerary, with exciting new establishments.

Works Cited

"About | Grand Rapids, MI—MudPenny." *MudPenny*, www.mudpenny.com/about. Accessed 13 Feb. 2021.

Allen, Kolene and Jon Dunn. "Epic Grand Rapids Brunches According to Vegan GR." *Grand Rapids Hotels, Events, Restaurants, Things to Do & Vacations*, 1 Aug. 2019, www.experiencegr.com/blog/post/vegangr-brunch/. Accessed 13 Feb. 2021.

"Bangkok Taste Cuisine." *SinglePlatform*, places.singleplatform.com/bangkok-taste-cuisine/. Accessed 13 Feb. 2021.

Hand Crafted Ice Cream, my-site-106441-108280.square.site. Accessed 13 Feb. 2021.

Hubbard, Ashley. "A Vegan & Sustainable Weekend Itinerary for Grand Rapids." *Grand Rapids Hotels, Events, Restaurants, Things to Do & Vacations*, 17 Jan. 2020, www.experiencegr.com/blog/post/vegan-weekend-itinerary. Accessed 13 Feb. 2021.

"Menu—Brick Road Pizza Co." *Brick Road Pizza Co.—Specializing in Gourmet, Traditional and Vegan Pizzas!*, brickroadpizza.com/menu/. Accessed 13 Feb. 2021.

"Our Mission—Rise Authentic Baking Co." *Rise Authentic Baking Co*, www.riseauthenticbaking.com/our-mission-1. Accessed 13 Feb. 2021.

"Roosevelt Park Menu—MudPenny." *MudPenny*, www.mudpenny.com/new-page. Accessed 13 Feb. 2021.

"Stella's Lounge—Stella's." *Stella's*, stellaslounge.com/stellasgr. Accessed 13 Feb. 2021.

"Stella's Menu—Stella's." *Stella's*, stellaslounge.com/stellas-food. Accessed 13 Feb. 2021. "Take-Out Menu."

Vegan Grand Rapids, 13 Oct. 2018, vegangr.com. Accessed 13 Feb. 2021.

Figure 25. What is risked when a college composition takes its shape from experiences that begin in places significant to the students? When does the risk negate any potential value? Photo Courtesy of Students.

Virtual Tour Essay—Students' Reflections

For many, the Virtual Tour with its place-based research and opportunities to explore in person as the pandemic ebbed and flowed was their highlight of the class, as attested in these semesters' end recollections:

- I felt it was a fairly tall order to find not only a limited audience but also a limited area to explore to provide this theoretical tour. I soon found that these limitations were an absolute necessity, however, as they would put into focus the small rabbit holes that contained the required information to construct a cohesive plan. Being able to identify my audience and describe them within the context of an objective and how it would serve them was a clever exercise that allowed me to clearly identify the who, what, and where of this assignment.

- I found my writing of the Grand Rapids Tour to be most enjoyable as it helped me learn more about the city I live in. There were so many things in Grand Rapids I thought I had known, but I would end up being wrong 90% of the time. It was one of the few essays I enjoyed writing due to the fact it is about my own city and knowing I didn't know much of the city.

- A favorite essay of mine was MLA Grand Rapids Virtual tour paper. Our assignment was to cater to our audience of friends and family members by choosing hand-picked stops in Grand Rapids and combining them into a well-planned tour with directions. I enjoyed writing this essay because it gave me the chance to explore Grand Rapids and go to places that I normally would not; in fact, I learned that there are a lot of different things downtown. An example of that would be that both the GRAM and GRCM have reduced-priced family nights. This essay was fun to write as I was able to focus completely on my audience and what they would like.

- The first assignment that I would say drastically improved my writing process was the Grand Rapids Virtual Tour. This was the first paper that I had written that was more than three pages long and that scared me. Not only was I to write in a new format (MLA) that I had never used before, but this assignment required me to organize my writing for my audience. I had to make a tour for a group of people that had never had a full taste of downtown Grand Rapids and needed to make sure it could flow well.

- I learned the importance of planning, drafting, and revising for the Grand Rapids Virtual Tour. Planning was advantageous because in the process of planning for this essay I had to choose my audience and the theme for the tour. I also had to write down times and dates for the tour. When it came to writing the rough draft, a well-developed plan is fundamental. After the rough draft, I found that re-reading my essay was useful, for I caught many mistakes when it came to making sure that my essay made sense. In the essays I've written before this semester, I never made a plan; in addition, I would write my essay and never revise which resulted in essays that were not well written.

- Writing about a tour trip downtown Grand Rapids with several individuals that I chose immediately sparked my interest for several reasons. First, I was expecting a bland assignment filled with must-haves and page requirements. However, I was excited that the theme of my essay and the audience were completely my choice and could be tailored to my interests. Never before did I write an essay about a topic that interested me. It was a completely different experience writing about real life experiences and plans as opposed to one area of required research. Also, having the ability to choose the audience of my essay was a great change. Knowing the particulars of my audience gave me additional motivation and enthusiasm to write about something my audience and I had in common. All in all, the writing process of this essay looked vastly different from those I had completed before and introduced me to a dynamic of writing I had not known.

- When we started the class on the first week we got the first essay assignment, the Grand Rapids (virtual) tour. I was terrified because it was my first time writing an essay this long. The thing that helped me finish was doing a plan before I write. The plan seemed irrelevant, but when I got to the writing, I saw how important it was.

- In the Grand Rapids virtual tour, I wrote about one of my favorite pastimes, disc golf. Having the ability to write a topic that I was passionate about helped me with the writing process. I believe this is why it was one of the reasons I did well on this assignment. Writing about a topic I knew about, I was able to better my writing by giving first hand experiences.

- It helped me during the transition of moving to Grand Rapids. An essay to learn about Grand Rapids and explore its inner riches helped me be more confident in my new home, and it showed me some really great locations. This paper was the most fun for me to write because it allowed me to use real world experience in an academic setting and vice versa.

- This semester, I learned quite a bit about the city of GR, for example, the log jam of 1883 that took out the predecessor of the Blue Bridge. Another thing that I learned about is that in GR Rosa Parks Circle was designed by famous artist Maya Lin. It is a place that I have visited on multiple occasions without knowing a lot about the history.

- Something about this course that I particularly enjoyed and found interesting was the focus on Grand Rapids. Although I have grown up only 20 minutes away from downtown Grand Rapids, I really did not know too much about it before taking this course. But now, I have learned so much, I feel like I could talk about Grand Rapids for hours!

COVID Quote–2020

Higher-education leaders should seize this period of upheaval as an opportunity to focus on learning, shift to student-centered instruction, and look for new opportunities the online setup affords. The move to virtual classrooms is a chance for institutions at every level to make learning more effective—off campus or on. It is an opportunity to refocus on student outcomes, on the development of universal skills that will enable graduates to respond to the next crisis, to create resilience and adapt to unfamiliar territory, and to help lead society forward.

To remain relevant in the post-COVID world, universities must be able to demonstrate real progress toward better teaching methods with clear outcomes, driven by the science of learning. Many educators have implemented methods such as flipped classes and project-based learning. It's time for the wholesale adoption of such innovations across institutions.

—Mazur and Kerrey

COVID-19 Notes: "Earth Day #50"

Normally, I filled up my Civic once every other week, commuting from campus to campus. Now, with both of us working from home, my wife and I alternate cars on the few trips we take, and it has been over a month since I last stopped to fuel. At $1.48 when I passed my neighborhood Speedway, pump prices were so low for a lack of demand that I almost wished I needed to refuel to take advantage.

Economically, I feel fortunate to continue drawing a paycheck. Luckily, instead of closing shop and laying off its contingent workforce, my colleges made all instruction remote and directed us to translate our onsite to online learning platforms. Challenging, yes, but devastating, it was not.

Ecologically, what has been daunting to so many economies, employees, and employers, may prove a boon to the environment. Watching *Good Morning America* today, I was impressed by the clarity of otherwise smoggy and polluted famous places including the Himalayas, the Taj Mahal, and the LA freeways, as well as the otherwise churned, contaminated canals of Venice. Where people usually trafficked, penguins toddled over curbs and through crosswalks, mountain goats conferred on boulevards, and bighorn sheep jogged city streets. A park ranger in Yosemite exclaimed about four frolicking bears romping around, climbing trees along the emptied village's normally traffic-jammed thoroughfare, "They're having a party!" (Zee).

What is a hazard to human health and commercial growth may spark a natural and wildlife rebound. Why must it require a global pandemic for humankind to lift its polluting footprint?

—Noted April 23, 2020

Works Cited

Mazur, Eric and Bob Kerrey. "Higher Ed's Coronavirus Opportunity." *Wall Street Journal*, 11 May 2020. ProQuest, http://grcc.idm.oclc.org/login?url=https://www.proquest.com/newspapers/higher-eds-coronavirus-opportunity/docview/2400255906/se-2?accountid=11183.

Zee, Ginger. "Earth Day Boasts Beautiful Before and After Photos in Nature." *Good Morning America*, 22 April 2020, www.goodmorningamerica.com/news/video/earth-day-boasts-beautiful-photos-nature-70283163.

Q4.

How has your college and community coped with the COVID-19 crises? What characteristics of your place affected its responses? How have they influenced how (and what) you teach?

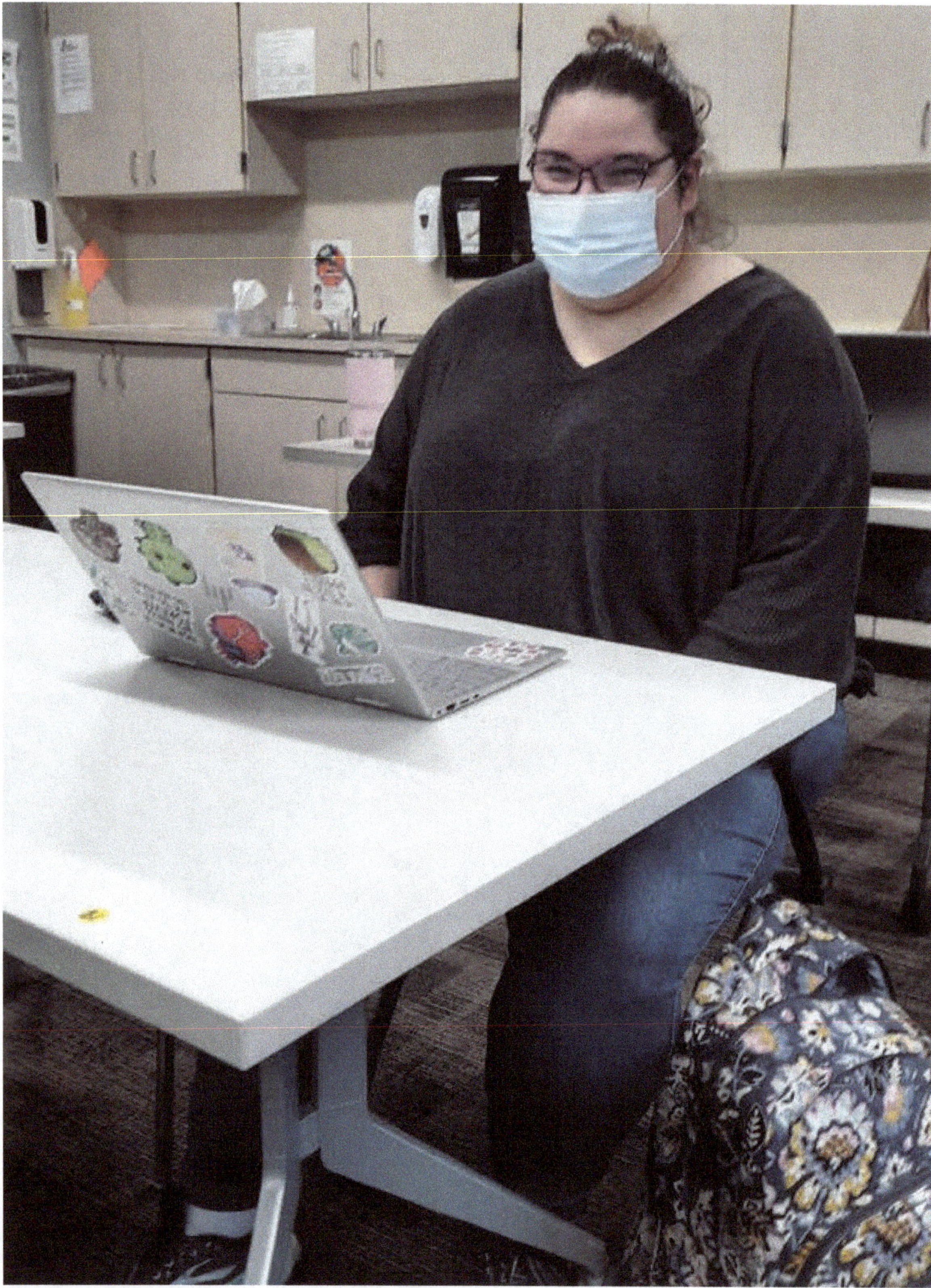

Figure 26. Megan Bolema waits for Middle College English 101 Composition I class to start in a designated high school classroom with faucet, sink, and soap dispenser in addition to a hand sanitizer dispenser and a spray bottle for disinfecting classroom furnishings. Photo by Author.

Chapter 5. Detailed

The experimental attitude ... is not merely one facet of democracy; its cultivation ... is the culmination of democratic social life itself.

—Nathan Crick

Protocolic

(or, The Annoyingly All-Consuming Demands of Keeping Caught-up with
Ever Evolving Classroom, College, and Community Protocols)

Standing outside the front entrance of a local high school, where I taught a "middle college" writing class (essentially, college first-year writing for advanced high school students), I waited for the front office secretary to return to her desk, where she had a sightline through an outdoor window to see anyone at the entry. Already that morning, I had scanned into the school's Daily Staff Health site and indicated that no, I was not spiking a fever, coughing persistently, or losing my senses of taste or smell; no vomiting, diarrhea, headache, muscle ache, sore throat, or shortness of breath. I had not recently taken a cruise. Neither had I been diagnosed with COVID-19, tested for COVID-19, nor had an immediate family member or member of my household contracted COVID-19. All *no's* resulted in my receiving a clearance *du jour* to enter the building that Fall of 2020.

Spotting her opening the office door, I knocked on the window to catch the secretary's attention. No buzzer for electronic access, I waited for her to angle around the countertop, out the office door to the vestibule and to the school's double front doors to let me in.

"Hey, Tom, been waiting long? Your classroom is opened, the lights are turned on, and the heat is notched up for you."

With only one door for access and egress, the classroom had a faucet and sink as well as a hand sanitizer dispenser. I dutifully soaped my hands, and vigorously rubbed them the obligatory 20 seconds before crossing the classroom and firing up a laptop, projector, and sound system. Tables were spaced four feet apart, with chairs arranged near either end of them to stretch another foot between students.

I taught from the front, seated behind a teacher's desk opposite the classroom door, only on occasions sitting atop a corner of the desk when I could maintain distance from the nearest student. Perched apart, I tried curtailing my own and students' movements while maintaining as much distance between students, under the assumption that stasis may slow spread of airborne droplets, the coughed, sneezed, or exhaled carriers of the COVID-19 novel coronavirus.

Students were supplied Chromebooks, textbooks, and access codes to the publisher's online components. Unfortunately, the transition from my college's LMS to the high school's separate service was proving a trial: The Word documents that I had uploaded were blocked or opened blank by their computers. I tried converting them into pdf files. "Any luck?"

What did this DOCM Macro-enabled document setting do? I tried it. "How about now?"

Half connected.

"Maybe refresh or reboot?"

While I was playing with my program up front, a quartet had clustered around one student's machine, animatedly instructing one another, demonstrating on their collective keyboards how to revive the program.

"Whoa! Hold on, distance, distance, distance, OK?" I scattered them apart.

Not one week earlier, their high school had experienced a viral breakout, resulting in some hundred students getting tested, isolated, or quarantined. I had not been immune to its fallout, receiving a flurry of phoned and emailed messages from both the college and high school: *Call [principal] ASAP.* One of my students tested positive. Had I been within six feet proximity for a sustained 90 minutes? (No, I had not.) Was I manifesting any symptoms of COVID? (No, I was not.) Which students sat before, behind, and at either side of the one going into isolation? (I looked them up on my seating chart—required this year.)

In days to come, I received mandated forms emailed from the college, the high school, and the county health department, all direly informing me that I had attended a class (one size fit all: instructor and students) with someone who had tested positive to the virus and should be vigilantly alert to a host of possible symptoms which might result, and then opaquely suggesting that I consider testing if perchance there were a testing site available. (There was not, and unfortunately testing was not possible without a doctor's directive.)

The Centers for Disease Control and Prevention indicated that there were two tests available: a Nucleic Acid Amplification Test (NAAT), which checks genetics in a laboratory, and an Antigen Test that scans proteins, and can report faster, although it is not as accurate as the NAAT ("Coronavirus Disease"). Locally, coronavirus tests could be scheduled immediately or within 7–10 days, and results could be procured in as little as 24–72 hours, or as much as 7–10 days and longer, depending on the demands and availability of kits or materials (Kransz).

During my semesters on campus, I was to receive several more of the notices, unfortunately, oftentimes after the student in question had already completed the mandated 10- or 14-days' quarantine (to remain at home if exposed) or isolation (kept apart from family members at home when tested positive). Meanwhile, the unidentified student invariably had already contacted me directly to alert me of the mandated absence as well as the experienced symptoms, and the number of other students who had contracted it, and where and how—altogether TMI. The happy medium, I imagine, lay somewhere between the student's detailed forthrightness (HIPPA regulations notwithstanding) and the slow opacity of information and action by the schools, the health departments, and their medical testing—regardless of the pandemic's wildfire spread.

Mine were the first scheduled morning classes, so I reckoned the furnishings needed no additional precleaning. Nevertheless, conscientiously refraining from touching my face should my hands pick up germs from a projector screen's pull cord, projector remote, sound system switch, or whiteboard eraser, I carried my own supply of whiteboard markers. Outside of pushing my glasses uphill, hiking my mask up-face, or tightening the ear loops or head strap to prevent mask sag, I kept hands and head safely separated. After classes, I liberally squirted desktop and chair arms with the provided hand sprayer's yellow liquid or coated furnishings with the aerosol cleanser spray and wiped it all around with paper towels, then applied those dampened towels to the remote, mouse, keyboard, projector screen's finger-ring pull, and whiteboard's eraser. Next, I wiped down door handles and adjacent surfaces, along with the light switches while simultaneously clicking them off, and disposed of the sodden towels. Finally, I gave my own hands a thorough washing at the sink or cupped and spread a couple squirts of hand sanitizer before kicking the door closed and exiting classroom and building, using hip or elbow to push the doors' exit bars in order to keep my hands sterilized.

Cleanliness *is* next to godliness—and it can be as demanding.

COVID Quote–2020

August 17—COVID-19 Now the Third-Leading Cause of Death in the US
In just 4 days, there's been a 3.2% uptick in COVID-19—related deaths, to 170,434, giving the disease a No. 3 ranking behind heart disease in the top spot and cancer at No. 2. Deaths now exceed 1000 per day and nationwide cases exceed 5.4 million. Testing has dropped off by an average 68,000 per day, despite death being 8 times more likely in the United States vs in Europe.

—"A Timeline of COVID-19 Developments in 2020"

Figure 27. How can we ensure students are welcomed, engaged, and participants in the classroom community, instead of isolated and apart, especially when distanced inside a classroom? Photo by Author.

Masking, Cleansing, Distancing

There are masks, and there are masks. Beginning Fall semester on the last day of August 2020, students arrived duly masked, cautiously allowing ample berth to one another, waiting patiently to enter the class one by one, maintaining space by stepping slowly from measured arrow to arrow, and carefully picking the separate seats not to crowd any peers. Once secure at a desk, each eyeballed the room and then silently unsheathed a phone.

Before introducing them to one another and to me, I acquainted them with the classroom COVID-19 protocols, pointing out the rolls of paper towels, spray cans of disinfectant, dispensers of hand sanitizer, and containers of spare face masks should they forget theirs. "Thank you for keeping six feet apart, washing your hands before coming to class, and keeping your nose and mouth covered with a mask." I applauded their carefully distanced classroom entry and pointed out the exit door, encouraging them to dismiss themselves row by row, beginning with the one nearest the exit. If our class was not the first of the day, I suggested they disinfect their chair and tabletop before sitting, and if we were not the last, asked them to clean again before leaving. "I'll do my best to dismiss 5–10 minutes early, so you have time to clean afterwards while keeping your distance."

Half of the students religiously cleaned their workplaces, many doing so both before and after classes. Several visited lavatories to cleanse hands before and afterward, after I quoted a doctor whom I had heard admonish Michiganders, "Never walk past a sink without washing your hands, eh."

Then there were the masks. Some were Darth Vader-like extrusions with popped-up plastic knobs that opened or closed as the wearer chose to allow in fresh air. They soon fell out of favor as we learned that their airway openings defeated the purpose of filtering all inhalations and exhalations. Some masks came spangled with glittery sequins, showy and gauzy things looking like an accessory from a glitzy-glam Halloween costume. They, too, filtered few germs. Homemade masks proliferated. "My grandmother sewed this," responded one student when asked about his sleekly fitted, custom-colored mask's cloth and edging. Several sported University of Michigan or Michigan State University colors and logos, and a couple referenced their favorite professional sports teams. The school's athletes sometimes came to class wearing a sweat-streaked practice mask adorned with the college's mascot. Others came from jobs sporting corporate logos. Light blue, pleated, meant-to-be disposable, medical masks grew more and more abundant as production outpaced demands for initially scarce personal protective equipment. Although I suspected many were reused, day to day, I could not help wondering what effect all that blue refuse—masks and other personal protective equipment from essential workers as well as students and shoppers—was wreaking on sanitation landfills. As time wore on, some masks appeared as facial accessories with flowers or patterns to match an outfit; but for every masking action, there came a nearly equal and opposite reaction. Many began dampening, sagging, and discoloring, like facial diapers dripping from a mouth's moist emanations, drooping down jaws and chins, exposing noses, and bending ears forward. I shared another doctor's dictum, "Face masks should be laundered as often as underwear."

Although normally I mentioned in a first-class meeting where the nearest bathrooms were located, I added to that, "... where you can find sinks and soap to wash your hands before coming to class and after leaving, so you don't have to rely on squirts of hand sanitizer."

Who knew that Comp class would incorporate the necessary lessons of healthy hygiene amidst a viral pandemic? Maybe some of this cleansing course content ought to remain behind when the virus departs.

Works Cited

"A Timeline of COVID-19 Developments in 2020." *American Journal of Managed Care*, 3 July 2020, www.ajmc.com/view/a-timeline-of-covid19-developments-in-2020.

"Coronavirus Disease 2019 (COVID-19) Test for Current Infection—Viral Test." *Centers for Disease Control and Prevention*, 2 Sept. 2020, www.cdc.gov/coronavirus/2019-ncov/testing/diagnostic-testing.html.

Crick, Nathan. "Rhetoric and Dewey's Experimental Pedagogy." In *Trained Capacities: John Dewey, Rhetoric, and Democratic Practice*, Edited by Brian Jackson and Gregory Clark, University of South Carolina Press, 2014, p. 186.

Kransz, Michael. "Kent County Sees 'Sharp Decline' in People Seeking COVID-19 Tests." *Mlive*, 21 Sept. 2020, www.mlive.com/news/grand-rapids/2020/09/kent-county-sees-sharp-decline-in-people-seeking-covid-19-tests.html.

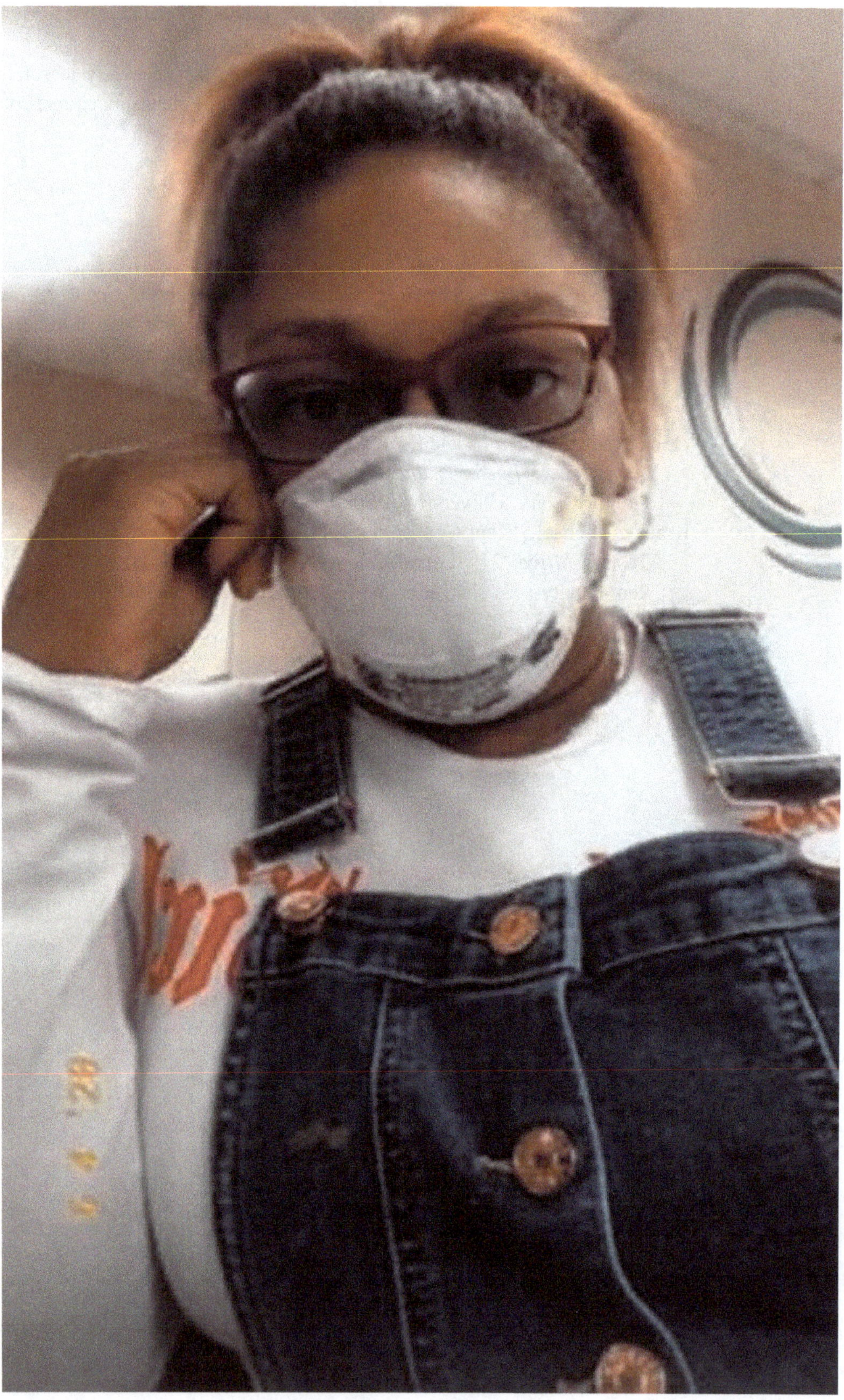

Figure 28. Denise Jones, author of "Proper Personal Protection." Photo Courtesy of Student.

Student's Story—"Proper Personal Protection," by Denise Jones

Although I am proud to be an essential worker, during this time the constant changes, stress, and limited equipment and protective gear has made it difficult to enjoy the work I do. I am currently a registered medical assistant who is also a mother of three and a student trying to complete my nursing degree. I work with the older population in a nursing home that includes assisted living and skilled nursing.

Everyone is saying wear a mask even if it is not the appropriate N 95 mask. Most are wearing surgical masks or cloth masks that were made by volunteers in the community. At first it was said that only older people 65 and above would be affected. Then it was said children are the carriers. There was even a rumor African Americans could not get COVID; however, now the numbers are showing we African Americans have a higher death rate for the virus. There has been a lot of miscommunication and misunderstandings with this virus to the point where nobody knows what to do except wear a mask, constantly wash your hands, and practice social distancing by staying 6 feet away from people. However, the job that I have does not allow me to be 6 feet away from people, and the fact that there is a shortage of the proper personal protection equipment is not only frustrating but mind boggling.

As a healthcare worker, I want to protect myself and patients; as a mother, I definitely don't want to bring anything home and need to protect my children as well. We have been on this lockdown since March, and the lockdown orders keep extending since the death rates and positive cases keep rising. I myself have been battling, trying to keep everything in order—from completing my assignments on time for school, to homeschooling my three children since all schools are closed the rest of the year, and staying professional and mindful of what I do and touch in the workplace. My place of employment currently has a positive COVID-19 patient and because of that people have quit or reduced their hours, and they are just plain afraid to come to our side of the building. However, because of the shortage in equipment there are only a few that have the proper personal protective equipment to wear to deal with that patient, which makes it hard because if one of those individuals is not present on the shift, someone else has to take care of that patient without proper equipment.

I do not know how long this will last, but we are working hard to keep some of the world going. Instead of criticizing us because we don't have the right equipment or because all of our rooms are filled or for just plain old being tired because of the long hours with the growth in cases and decrease in employees, just know we're doing our best. We are trying to make it work with the little bit we were given, and we are hoping for the best.

BP/DP/AP—Before, During, and After Pandemic
Grant Grace

BP, requiring essays and assignments on time and enforcing due dates, while making allowances for unanticipated, uncontrollable obstructions or disruptions, seemed fair.

DP, with unanticipated, uncontrollable obstructions and disruptions the norm, additional allowances should be, too. Excuses such as technology failures, technology-sharing arrangements with siblings, parents, and other household members, and intermittent wi-fi failures are commonplace and excusable. Illnesses, quarantines, and isolations; COVID tests causing schedule conflicts, trips to doctors, ER's, or out-of-town homeplaces; caregiving for family members or day-caring younger siblings or neighbors; providing transportation for household members or awaiting transport from others; and receiving work mandates as essential workers—all are acceptable excuses. Actually, they are laudable. Grant full credit, accept late work, make allowances for any unforeseen occurrences, and give grace—yes, always, even when students' excuses could be questioned.

Similarly, allow students a redo for every essay assigned. After marking and scoring a paper, encourage another revision after the writer has had an opportunity to read the comments. More process does often lead to a yet-better product. In fact, I offer students up to a 10% grade-gain for making substantive changes that attempt to implement my suggestions, and I grant them one more opportunity to re-revise before the end of a semester, as well. This allows those who have additional time at various points within a term to commit to reworking an essay—or at least to rescue it—should they for whatever reason have not had sufficient time to produce a paper of college-level quality on the first try. For those who elect to revise their essay, the opportunity allows them to apply additional writing skills gained since its first submission and also grants them the freedom to attempt another approach and take their paper in a new and different, potentially better, direction.

Finally, grant some grace to yourself. Encouraging multiple revisions can demand an inordinate amount of time and effort if I let it. One way I attempt to curtail a pile-up of papers is to ask students to list for me the substantive changes they made since the last draft, and then I simply add points based on their tally. Another is merely to ask them to identify their one latest and greatest revision's resultant paragraph, and score the revision based on that representative sample. Simply put, trust them. That in itself demonstrates grace. Students are always grateful, often more gracious towards one another (as well as to you), and sometimes return to their classwork working all the harder. This granting of grace to the students also frees you from policing and gotcha games; in other words, it rescues you from the role of perpetual enforcer of punitive writing standards.

AP, carry on with the grace-granting. Students can use some more, and so can you.

BP/DP/AP (2)—Before, During, and After Pandemic Peppermints

For a chuckle, separately, **BP**, I used to chug some 8–10 cups of coffee daily in, out, and between classes, but now, **DP**, I pop a peppermint before class. It keeps my mouth moistened, and the face stays masked. Peppermint helps me remain alert although I question whether it delivers an equivalent to the comforting jolt of a steaming hot mug of java, especially during the dark days of a Michigan winter. Just don't tell my dentist about the peppermint candy changeover, please.

AP, I intend to return, full circle, to coffee consumption. Although I anticipate waiting until receiving a health department's "all clear," I do miss visiting the local coffee shops—on campus and off.

Of course, if, as William Garvelink, former director of the U. S. Agency for International Development (AID)'s humanitarian assistance and Office of Foreign Disaster Assistance (OFDA) direct relief operations, maintained, we should expect more frequent pandemic outbreaks and plan for their recurrence ("The Future with Pandemics"). Even after the COVID-19 coronavirus is masked and vaccinated into remission, as we hope and pray happens, we can expect to turn more sudden instructional pivots in the years ahead to contend with fresh novel viral breakouts. It appears I can plan to purchase many more packages of peppermints.

Bottom Line: Grant grace generously—to your students as well as yourself, and consider sucking on a mint as a sweet alternative to the jolt of java while the coffee shops are closed.

COVID Quote–2020

October 19—Global Cases Top 40 Million
Data from Johns Hopkins University indicate that COVID-19 cases have topped 40 million worldwide as the United States and other countries see their highest rates of new cases in months. More than 1.1 million people have been killed by the virus worldwide so far, and nearly 220,000 of those deaths were in the United States, which remains the hardest-hit country in the world.

—"A Timeline of COVID-19 Developments in 2020"

COVID-19 Notes: "Imbalanced"

How do we find a right balance between lives and livelihoods?

Having sacrificed so much effort and expense already to flatten the tidal curve that threatens our poorly equipped yet resilient medical community, why would we consider the risk of another wave that's worse?

On the other hand, what do we answer to those who have placed themselves and their employees in harm's way, in a restaurant, a hair salon, or a garden center?

Time magazine reported that 26% of whites and 28% of Asian Americans working in the United States in 2020 were able to work from home, but only 13% of Latinx and 18% of African Americans could. By comparison, 47% of Americans with a 4-year college education worked at home at times during 2017–18 ("Remote Work by the Numbers").

The ramifications of one diagnosed or undiagnosed COVID-19 carrier could drown residents and staff in a nursing home, neighbors in an apartment building, co-workers in a meat packing plant or staff and customers at a restaurant, a hair salon, or a garden center. And the undertow from one local closure can suck under a restaurant's employees, its supply line, local farmers who grow its ingredients, and the gathering community that relies on its presence and support.

Losses of loved ones, compromised innocents, essential workers, and medical warriors are unconscionable. Expired jobs, paychecks, savings, insurance plans, retirements, children's futures, families' aspirations may be irredeemable.

Let us tread cautiously and thoughtfully, with care and conscience, fearful fortitude, placing every step gingerly forward, for our lives—and our livelihoods—hang in this balance.

—Noted April 24, 2020

Works Cited

"A Timeline of COVID-19 Developments in 2020." *American Journal of Managed Care*, 3 July 2020, www.ajmc.com/view/a-timeline-of-covid19-developments-in-2020.

Garvelink, William. "The Future with Pandemics." Presentation, January Series, 8 Jan. 2021, Calvin University, Grand Rapids, Michigan.

"Remote Work by the Numbers." *Time*, Vol. 195, Nos. 12–13, 6–13 April 2020, p. 47.

Q5.

During the blizzards of often opaque and occasionally contradictory instructions that blew through the changing seasons of COVID-19, what institutional interventions, departmental directives, media crackpot conspiracies, or social media maladroit misinformation have you encountered? Which did you clarify (or attempt to clarify), correct, modify, or possibly ignore in order to shield students? What literacy practices do you find best suited to assist your students in seeking and proving truth?

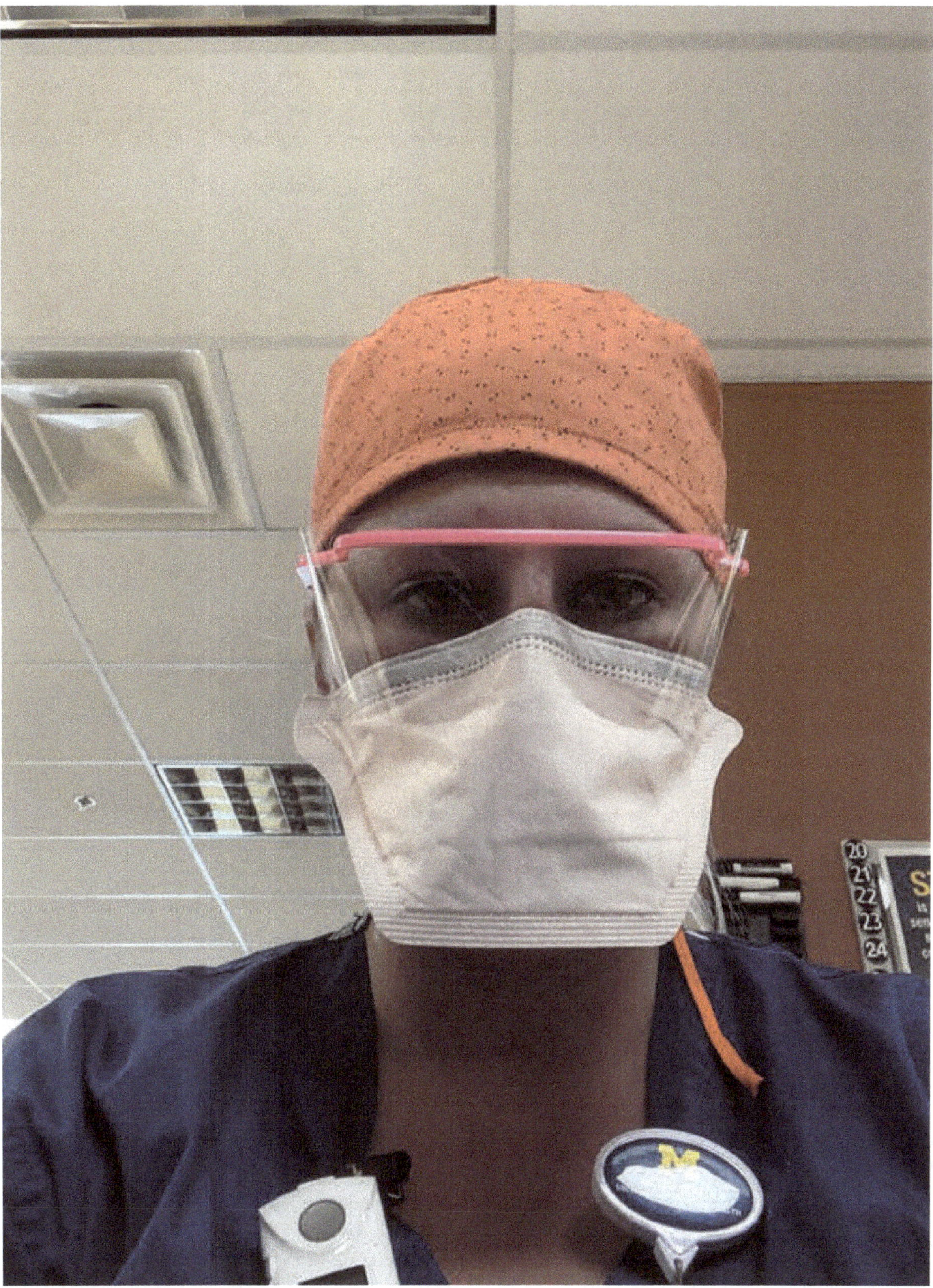

Figure 29. What are the implications of having students write about their distressing personal experiences (such as, in this case, working the ER during the COVID-19 pandemic)? Photo Courtesy of Student.

Chapter 6. Exploring Careers

*It is **our job** [emphasis added] to help these students **want** [original emphasis] to be in English classes …. We need to **work** [emphasis added] to help students **discover, experience,** and **feel** [original emphasis] the joys of reading and the magic of written communication.*

—Patrick M. Sullivan

Essay #2: Career Exploration

"Who is your reader?"

"You and our groups again?"

"Yes, primarily, so you should write the essay up to above-average college students' reading level and an English prof's expectations, eh? Who is researching about writing teachers? Nobody? That's too bad: there's no better job out there, you know. Since I'm not very interested in learning about mechanical engineering, radiation technology, or most other jobs, it's important for me that you relate your own interest in the occupation, or better yet, share your own story or maybe a conversation with someone that illustrates how you became interested in it, yourself. Who else is your reading audience?"

"Our parents?"

"Maybe, if you want them to be, or they want to be. If they pay your tuition, or if you live at home, they probably should be invited to read, eh?"

"What about business owners or hiring departments?"

"Good question, but maybe not because they might not be as interested in your reasons for going into that occupation, and probably they already know the field very well. Information that you researched about the job is likely not news to them, so they might not appreciate your asking them to read it.

Instead, how about yourself, maybe to convince yourself about a career and its preparation, or possibly for yourself after you graduate or after you're on the job a few years, to read what your former self was thinking when you decided to study for that career?"

Besides overcoming concerns about the physical safety or fiscal advisability of pursuing a college education while a viral pandemic rages, researching and writing about a professional career could help students train their gazes on an academic prize, the degree that may gain them access to the job, opportunity, wages, and self they initially projected when enrolling. With the exponentially and perennially rising costs of college—tuition, room and board, fees, incidentals—the question arises: Is it worth it? Before the COVID-19 coronavirus pandemic, the answer was usually a resounding *yes* for many.

Nevertheless, there were exceptions, as Sarah Goldrick-Rab reported in *Paying the Price*:

> The new economics of college is undermining the fundamental connection between education and democracy that has helped our nation thrive …. With inequality on the rise, and low-income and middle-class Americans under pressure, this generation must meet the challenge of making one of the best ways out of poverty and into the middle class—a college education—affordable for all. (260)

With wages stagnating and dropping for all but the most wealthy, college costs have grown by 33–50% as a percentage of a family's income over the two decades preceding the 2020 pandemic (Goldrick-Rab, 2–4). Reporting his Pew Research findings, Rakesh Koshhar noted that the United States experienced as much as 16% unemployment in the month of May, when accounting for all who filed unemployment claims as well as those unemployed who did not report. Hispanic women were unemployed at a nearly 20% rate, and black women exceeded 17% unemployment during this time (Koshhar).

Besides the high costs of college tuition and fees, students questioned the value of a college education without the interpersonal connections to professors and classmates, speakers and programs, and internships or apprenticeships. Could a remote education really duplicate the holistic college experience of learning on campus? Did an online education justify paying the full tuition of a university's semester? And could such a "virtual" education hinder a candidate's employment opportunities upon graduation?

In the next decade, the U.S. Bureau of Labor Statistics predicts slow growth in employment, with six million jobs added to the labor market by 2029, most coming in the healthcare fields ("Employment Projections") and requiring some college certificate or degree. It seems that college may yet be the ticket to middle class entry or continuity for most.

With many students enrolling for college classes but wondering about its payoff, especially when taking on student-loan debts, retooling skillsets or mindsets toward a new career, or returning for schooling after serving in the military or being away from the classroom for years, the Career Exploration Essay can help them correct some misperceptions and dispel some apprehensions. They select a career and research its job descriptions and demands, typical education and training, wages and locations, openings and employers, and future projections and past trajectories by consulting the U.S. Bureau of Labor Statistics' Occupational Outlook Handbook website and their college's student placement office's website and resources in addition to several more sources. These may include an interview with someone knowledgeable about the selected career and/or searches of *.org* and *.edu* domain websites of a professional not-for-profit organization, a college departmental website, a job-search website, or a company or organization website that offer information on the selected career. The Career Exploration Essay combines research reports with personal reflections and possibly some aptitude assessment, too, for those who desire it.

The Career Exploration Essay can acquaint students with their own prospects or pursue another career track that seems appealing. In addition, because the first-year writing class is more than merely another feeder course for "career prep"—the training of earners and consumers—a career exploration ought to involve students in researching various types of information to include in their essays: an introduction to the job, its attendant preparation and procurement, the resources available at college, and their own purposes for selecting that job to explore.

Using APA format for this second essay gives students the flavor of another format besides MLA, which most English teachers favor, and allows them the benefit of comparing the two. Since many of their general education classes assign them essays in APA style, and most of them seek degrees in programs that traditionally choose APA format, preparing them for APA style in their first-year writing class is valuable. In fact, students often inform me that they had already been assigned an APA paper in another class, and most of my students had never written or been shown how to format in APA style previously, especially when taking classes online.

Works Cited

"Employment Projections: 2019–2029 Summary." *U.S. Bureau of Labor Statistics*, 1 Sept. 2020, www.bls.gov/news.release/ecopro.nr0.htm.

Goldrick-Rab, Sara. *Paying the Price: College Costs, Financial Aid, and the Betrayal of the American Dream*, University of Chicago Press, 2017.

Koshhar, Rakesh. "Unemployment Rose Higher in Three Months of COVID-19 Than It Did in Two Years of the Great Recession." *Pew Research Center*, 26 Aug. 2020, www.pewresearch.org/fact-tank/2020/06/11/unemployment-rose-higher-in-three-months-of-covid-19-than-it-did-in-two-years-of-the-great-recession/.

Sullivan, Patrick M. "'A Lifelong Aversion to Writing': What if Writing Courses Emphasized Motivation?" *Teaching Composition at the Two-Year College: Background Readings*, edited by Patrick M. Sullivan and Christie Toth, Bedford/St. Martin's, 2017, p. 169.

Figure 30. Since all workers are essential, as the pandemic's heightened dependence on supply chain, medical, and emergency personnel has shown, should instructors allow students to research any occupation—and not only those requiring a college degree? Photo Courtesy of Student.

Instruction Sheet 3.1

Career Exploration Essay Assignment

3–6 pp. APA 1st & 3rd Person Report

Overview

Choose a career that you are interested in researching, whether or not you want to pursue it yourself, and share why you want to research this job. Learn its job descriptions, required education and training, salary range, expectations now and for the future, and the companies and locations where openings are posted. Make comparisons of what you learn to your own interests, aptitudes, and aspirations.

Personal Interest

1. Begin with some <u>questions</u>:
   a. What career are <u>you interested</u> in exploring? Why?
   b. What do you <u>want to know</u> about this career?
   c. Do you <u>know anyone</u> already working the job?
   d. What <u>degree</u> is needed?
   e. Which <u>colleges</u> offer it?
   f. What are this career's job prospects now? When I graduate?
   g. What qualifications, interests, experiences do I have?
   h. Additional question or idea:

Career Research

2. Include 3–6 <u>sources</u> in your background research.
   a. Websites—**# 1–3 are required** sites.
      1) **College Career Coach:** **Career Coach** [Hyperlink removed]
      2) **Library Careers Subject Guide:** **Careers Subject Guide** [Hyperlink removed]
      3) **US Dept of Labor Bureau of Labor Statistics:** **Occupational Outlook Handbook**
      4) Organization (.org) domain search: Google Advanced Search
      5) Career search site (like www.indeed.com):
   b. Telephone, email, or live <u>interview</u>
   c. <u>Business</u> webpage, visit, or tour
   d. <u>Four-Year College</u> webpage

Write-Up

3. a. APA rough draft, revised draft, and peer reviews   Due: ___/___/___
   b. APA final edited copy & Reflection/Analysis form   Due: ___/___/___

<u>**Instruction Sheet 3.2**</u>

Career Exploration Essay Plan

Email your instructor or upload on the class's LMS your responses to these requirements:

1. **3–6 Topic Headings from the *Occupational Outlook Handbook* website**
   - Choose from the tabs on the <u>summary webpage</u> for your career.
   - Examples: Job Description, Responsibilities, Training & Education, Salary, Locations.

2. **3–6 Subheadings for each of the Topic Headings**
   - Beneath each topic heading, list researched examples to write about.
   - Include example stories, descriptions, facts, statistics, comparison—and links.
   - Also include personal applications relating them to yourself.

3. **Two-part Working Title**
   - Write a title beginning with the career title.
   - Add a colon (:) and then a second, catchy phrase to describe it.

4. **Working Thesis Statement**
   - Draft a hefty, robust Thesis statement of 1–2 sentences about the career itself.
   - Try to include most of the topic headings in separate clauses or phrases.

5. **3–6 Websites and Other Research Sources**
   - *Occupational Outlook Handbook*—required source.
   - College's Placement Office or Career Placement webpage—required source.
   - Article from library's job-search database, weblinks, or holdings.
   - *.org*-domain website representing career and *.edu*-domain from college.
   - Interview, business, organization, or job-search site.

<u>Instruction Sheet 3.3</u>

Career Exploration Essay Plan Score

<u>Assessment: 6 Points Possible</u>
(3 pts = C, 4 pts = B, 5 pts = A, 6 pts = A+)

3 pts. 3 Topic headings listed
3 Subheadings per topic heading
Two-part working title
Working Thesis statement with 3 topics
3 research sources

4 pts. 4 Topic headings
4 Subheadings per topic heading
Two-part working title
Working Thesis statement with 4 topics
4 Research sources

5 pts. 5 Topic headings
5 Subheadings per topic heading
Two-part working title
Working Thesis statement with 5 topics
5 Research sources

6 pts. 6 Topic headings
6 Subheadings per topic heading
Two-part working title
Working Thesis statement with 6 topics
6 Research sources

<u>Notes</u>

Instruction Sheet 3.4

Career Exploration Essay Rough Draft

Email your instructor or upload on the class's LMS a rough draft of your essay that includes these items:

1. **An APA student-style template** (saved as… from an earlier essay or uploaded new).
   - Running head with only page numbers in top right corners.
   - Title page with title in bold text, your name, department, college, course section and name, instructor's name, and date.
   - Title centered at top of page 2, and topic headings centered in bold text.
   - References page with an APA in-text citation matching every source.

2. **Introduction**
   - Personal backstory of why/how you chose this career or chose to explore it.
   - Working Thesis statement (1–2 sentences) including career topics.

3. **Body Paragraphs**
   - 3rd person (Example: *Engineers must …*), then 1st person (*I plan …*).
   - Variety of facts, stories, descriptions, education, job markets, and placement.
   - 1–3 paragraphs for each topic heading.
   - Maybe a photo, graphic, or chart.
   - APA in-text citations in parentheses within every paragraph.

4. **Conclusion**
   - Reworked Thesis and summary review with highlights for readers.
   - Closing personal application.

5. **References Page**
   - 3–6 APA References sources including the Occupational Outlook Handbook and college's Career Placement site.

<u>Instruction Sheet 3.5</u>

Career Exploration Essay Rough Draft Score

<u>Assessment: 6 Points Possible</u>
(3 pts = C, 4 pts = B, 5 pts = A, 6 pts = A+)

3 pts. 3 pages in mostly 3rd person perspective
3 topic headings with paragraphs
3 APA References sources and in-text citations
3 1st person sentences including Introduction and Conclusion

4 pts. 4 pages in mostly 3rd person perspective
4 topic headings with paragraphs
4 APA References sources and in-text citations
4 1st person sentences including Introduction and Conclusion

5 pts. 5 pages in mostly 3rd person perspective
5 topic headings with paragraphs
5 APA References sources and in-text citations
5 1st person sentences including Introduction and Conclusion

6 pts. 6 pages in mostly 3rd person perspective
6 topic headings with paragraphs
6 APA References sources and in-text citations
6 1st person sentences including Introduction and Conclusion
1 photo, graphic, or chart in "squared" text with APA caption

<u>Notes</u>

Instruction Sheet 3.6

Career Exploration Essay Revised Draft

Email your instructor or upload on the class's LMS a revised draft of your essay that includes these items:

1. **An APA-style template**
   - Title page includes 2-part title in bold, five lines in plain text, page number 1.
   - Complete title repeated and centered at the top of page 2.
   - Topic headings and **References** typed in bold text and centered.
   - No additional spaces between paragraphs or topic headings.
   - APA in-text citations appropriately match References sources.

2. **Introduction**
   - Personal backstory includes specific and sensory details, maybe dialogue.
   - Robust-style Thesis statement completes Introduction and previews topics.
   - Effective transition connects 1st person backstory with 3rd person Thesis.

3. **Body Paragraphs**
   - All body paragraphs connected to topic headings and transition logically.
   - 3rd person paragraphs about career and examples related to author in 1st person.
   - A photo, graphic, or chart is uploaded with squared text and APA caption.
   - APA in-text citations included in all and following every direct quotation.

4. **Conclusion**
   - Final paragraph begins 3rd person and ends with 1st person, or vice-versa.
   - Recalls or reiterates (but does not repeat) Thesis.

<u>Instruction Sheet 3.7</u>

Career Exploration Essay Revised Draft Score

<u>Assessment: 6 Points Possible</u>
(3 pts = C, 4 pts = B, 5 pts = A, 6 pts = Bonus A+)

3 pts. 3 substantive changes made to essay

4 pts. 4 substantive changes made to essay

5 pts. 5 substantive changes made to essay

6 pts. 6 substantive changes made to essay

Email your instructor or upload on the class's LMS a list of the 3–6 substantive changes you made to your essay for the revised draft.

A *substantive change* may involve rewriting the Introduction, completing the Conclusion, adding a body paragraph, rearranging the body paragraphs, adding introductory transitional words or phrases to every paragraph, or combining and rephrasing the sentences inside a paragraph.

<u>Notes</u>

Instruction Sheet 3.8

Career Exploration Essay Peer Review

Email your revised draft of the Career Exploration Essay to your group members or upload it on the class's LMS for your group to access.

Send or share your replies to the questions to the <u>writer</u>, then email your <u>instructor</u> the names of those whose essays you peer reviewed as well as those who peer reviewed your essay.

Normally, you receive one point for <u>each essay you peer review</u> (limit 3) + the number of group members <u>who reviewed your essay</u> (limit 3) <u>to match</u> the number of sentences inside your <u>resulting changes paragraph</u> = **Peer Review Score (maximum 6)**.

- Write **Career Exploration** with your **First & Last Name** and **Course name & #** on the <u>email Subject line</u>.
- List the names of students who peer reviewed your essay as well as the names of those whose essays you peer reviewed.
- After reading the peer reviews of your essay, write a <u>3–6 sentence paragraph</u> explaining what changes you plan to make in your essay.

1. **Is the <u>two-part title</u> both accurate and appealing?**

2. **What could be changed in the Introduction and the Conclusion?**

3. **What is one additional thing you may want to learn about this career?**

4. **What is one topic that you would like to be related more to the author using 1st person?**

5. **What is something the author did that you might like to try in your own writing?**

<u>**Instruction Sheet 3.9**</u>

Career Exploration Essay Peer Review Score

<u>**Assessment: 6 Points Possible**</u>
(3 pts = C, 4 pts = B, 5 pts = A, 6 pts = Bonus A+)

Email your instructor a list of the names of your classmates whose essays you peer reviewed as well as those who peer reviewed your essay, as well as a 3–6 sentence paragraph detailing what changes you plan to write as a result.

Normally, you receive one point for <u>each essay you peer review</u> (limit 3) + the number of group members <u>who reviewed your essay</u> (limit 3) <u>to match</u> the number of sentences inside your <u>resulting changes paragraph</u> (3–6) = **Peer Review Score (maximum 6)**.

- Write **Career Exploration** with your **First & Last Name** and **Course Name & #** on the <u>email Subject line</u>.

- List the names of students who peer reviewed your essay as well as the names of those whose essays you peer reviewed.

- After reading the peer reviews of your essay, write a <u>3–6 sentence paragraph</u> explaining what changes you plan to make in your essay.

<u>**Notes**</u>

Instruction Sheet 3.10

Career Exploration Essay Final Draft with Editing and Formatting

Follow these five final steps before turning in your essay:

1. **Check your <u>APA Student formatting</u>**
   - **Running head** with only page numbers in top right corners on all pages,
   - **Title page** with two-part title including a colon (:) in bold text, writer's name, department and college with comma, course name and section, instructor's name, and date written out (e.g., November 20, 2023) on separate lines, centered in plain text.
   - **Two-Part Title** with a colon (:) and centered, bold text, at the top of page 2.
   - **APA in-text citations** with last name of author, year published, page number—or webpage's or article's title within parentheses—in every body paragraph.
   - **References** page with complete APA citations in same font style and font size as essay, double-spaced with no additional spaces, set up in hanging indentation, in alphabetical order.
   - **No underlined** text or quotation marks used with titles, **all double-spaced** with no additional spaces between headings, paragraphs, or sources.
   - **Any photo, chart, or graphic** has an **APA caption** above and beneath, and text wrapped "square" around the picture, so no blank gaps.

2. **Run a <u>spell check</u> and double-check words for usage and variety.**

3. **Run a <u>grammar check</u> to ensure clarity and lucidity.**

4. **Check every page for varied <u>sentence styles</u> and <u>paragraph organization</u>.**

5. **<u>Scan</u> to remove plagiarism and <u>turn in</u> your essay. Congratulations!**

Instruction Sheet 3.11

Career Exploration Essay Editing and Formatting Score

Assessment: 6 Points Possible
(3 pts = C, 4 pts = B, 5 pts = A, 6 pts = Bonus A+)

Email your instructor a total from your tally of the Editing and Formatting score, giving yourself 1 point for each of the 6 items you completed.

- Write **Editing & Formatting Score** with your **First & Last Name** and **Course Name & #** on the email Subject line.

1. Checked APA Student formatting
   - **Running head** with only page numbers
   - **Completed title page**
   - **Matched two-part title** atop p. 2
   - **APA in-text citations**
   - **Correctly completed References**
   - **No bold or underlined** text, and **no quotation marks, all double-spaced**

2. **Ran a spell check and double-checked words for usage and variety.**

3. **Ran a grammar check to ensure clarity and lucidity.**

4. **Checked every page for varied sentence styles and paragraph organization.**

5. **Scanned to remove plagiarism and turned in your essay.**

6. **Photo, graphic, or chart included with APA caption and "squared" text.**

Notes

<u>**Instruction Sheet 3.12**</u>

Career Exploration Reflection/Analysis Score

<u>**Assessment: 6 Points Possible**</u>
(3 pts = C, 4 pts = B, 5 pts = A, 6 pts = Bonus A+)

Email your instructor a 3–6 sentence paragraph answering the questions below, including the number of sentences you wrote for each paragraph: (3 pts for each paragraph = C, 4 pts/each ¶ = B, 5 pts each ¶ = A, 6 pts/ each ¶ = A+)

- Write **Career Exploration Reflection/Analysis Score** with your **First & Last Name** and **Course Name & #** on the <u>email Subject line</u>.

1. **What 3–6 things that are new to you did you attempt in this essay?**

2. **What 3–6 things do you like most about your writing?**

<u>Instruction Sheet 3.13</u>

Career Exploration Essay Final Score

<u>Assessment: 6 Points Possible</u>
(3 pts = C, 4 pts = B, 5 pts = A, 6 pts = Bonus A+)

Email your instructor a total of your scores for every step of the Career Exploration Essay:

- Write **Career Exploration Reflection/Analysis Score** with your **First & Last Name** and **Course Name & #** on the <u>email Subject line</u>.

1. **Essay Plan Score: ___**

2. **Rough Draft Score: ___**

3. **Revised Draft Score: ___**

4. **Peer Review Score: ___**

5. **Editing and APA Formatting Score: ___**

6. **Career Exploration Reflection/Analysis Score: ___**

= Total Score (1+2+3+4+5+6): ___ divided by 6 = Average Score: ___

Figure 31. David Austin, author of "Computer Programming: Decoding the Job." Photo Courtesy of Student.

Career Exploration Sample Student Essay

Computer Programming: Decoding the Job

David Austin
English Department, G--- R--- C---
EN 101: Composition I
Professor Tom Mulder
November 20, 2020

Computer Programming: Decoding the Job

Computers have always been a keen interest of mine, whether it be for playing video games or taking them apart to see how they work. As a source of infinite puzzles to be solved, there have always been a number of things that I could do with or to my computer. I will hardly go a day without reconfiguring some hardware setup or optimizing my software for the best possible performance. Just recently, I decided to work on my mom's old laptop to see how much better I could get it to run. After two days of trouble shooting, reinstalling the operating system a few times, and installing all of the correct drivers (which took a long time to track down), I was able to make it run like new. This most recent of examples illustrates what I love most about working with computers: the problem solving. I have come to the realization that my interest in computers will not be going anywhere anytime soon. As such, I've decided that a career in computer programming would be a perfect fit as I have always been interested in how software is made and in the languages behind it all. From my research thus far, I have gathered that an optimal computer programmer is a computer versed individual who is granted a fair amount of headroom for growth in salary; moreover, they are flexible: being able to tackle many different facets of work within the information technology industry.

Defining Computer Programming

At its most basic interpretation, a computer programmer is someone who writes and tests computer code. This means that they are tasked with a varying number of responsibilities. Computer programmers may find themselves tasked with taking a design from developers and turning it into a set of instructions that can be read and interpreted by a computer. After these instructions are made, and that job's complete, a programmer will be needed to test or troubleshoot that code. Once the developed program is finalized and distributed, additional programmer support will be needed to update and maintain that program for the duration of its lifecycle (U. S. Bureau of Labor Statistics, 2020). As I have often suspected, there will always be something for a programmer to do. This implied job security is one of the biggest reasons I am getting into the field of computer and information technology. With our ever-growing dependence on the systems humanity has put into place for itself, we will always need someone who is able to translate the underlying code into something humans can understand and vice versa. I cannot think of a better way to contribute to a work force than to have one of the single most important skillsets you could possibly have for our computer driven world.

A Typical Work Environment

Programmers appear to have quite a bit of flexibility when it comes to being able to work from home. According to a website entitled *Make me a programmer*, there are many models that a company may adopt in order to regulate their policies on the matter. One such way is being able to work fully remotely (Vuollett, 2019). As a computer programmer, you have a unique ability to do all of the necessary tasks right on your own computer; so, as long as a programmer has that computer with them, they can accomplish whatever work is needed from them. Other companies may try an in-between approach where employees are allowed to come into work for a fraction of the week; for example, allotting Monday and Friday as work from home days. The rarest work environment, according to Vuollett (2019), is accomplishing all work in a shared workspace 100 percent of the time.

Although it would be a benefit to have the flexibility of being able to work remotely, if given the option, I don't have a preference as to whether the work would need to be accomplished in the workplace or at home. Coming from a background of crazy, inconsistent scheduling, my only concern would be having a stable work week where the days spent working rarely change. Perhaps, if I do end up with a job that allows me to work fully remotely, I'd be able to set this up for myself; however, there are aspects of in-person working at an established company owned building with access to my coworkers' experience that I have come to appreciate. It'd be nice to have direct access to senior management, or to be able to bounce ideas off the heads of my colleagues.

Job Outlook for Computer Programmers

The future for the specific career of Computer Programmer doesn't look so pretty, for it is said to decline by 9 percent nationally from 2019 to 2029 according to the U. S. Bureau of Labor Statistics (2020). Additionally, many companies may opt to outsource their work to countries where the labor is much cheaper than here in the US; lately, in contrast to this trend, companies are actually finding themselves bringing those very jobs back, since the cost of operating internationally can offset any mitigated wage expenses (U. S. Bureau of Labor Statistics, 2020). Another piece of data that can be looked at to get an idea for the future of this career, for residents of Kent County in Michigan in particular, is from GRCC's (Grand Rapids Community College) Career Coach website. Since 2017, there has been a stark drop in the number of computer programmers employed, going from 446 all the way down to 395 by 2019 (Grand Rapids Community College, 2020). Thankfully, the skills attained from working with computers can be migrated into other fields within the industry. For example, someone designated as a computer programmer may be able to find work as a junior software developer, program analyst, application programmer, and the list goes on (Raise Me, 2019).

It is this job security and malleability that I often consider when I think about the reasons I would like to seek a career as a computer programmer. Even if I find it difficult to get a job specifically as a computer programmer, I predict that the skills gained from my experience will prove useful to employers in other facets of the information technology industry. Once I have a solid foundational knowledge of what all goes into making and/or maintaining a computer program, I believe that companies will be willing to make some compromises in order to get more employees in the door (due to the apparent lack of skilled employees available).

Requirements to Become a Programmer

There are a number of ways to become educated enough to find a job as a computer programmer. A website called "Get Educated" (2019) gives some ideas on how one might approach seeking a career in the field. One way the site provides is going to a technical institute. This method has some benefits as the student's studies will be focused on the skillset of their particular career, which may result in less time spent on other skills that they might not find themselves using in the real-world work environment. The most common method is to take the traditional route of going to college, which may cost more; nevertheless, graduates from college institutions are known to receive higher salaries than the other methods (Get Educated, 2019).

Another suggested method is to find and participate in an internship. With the internship, students get real world experience in the industry. Since it is hard as a student to get one's foot in the door to a company without this experience, an internship appears to be the simplest way to attain some. The last method the "Get Educated" website contributes is building job experience. As mentioned before, it may be hard to get a job based only on work experience if the considered employee had never had a job with which to gain said experience, so this method is likely reserved to those with pre-established connections to others within the field. Computer programmers seeking a job with a particular company may also be required to have specific certifications that prove their proficiency with systems and languages being used by their target employer.

Getting the work experience is the hardest puzzle to crack for me personally. Since I am starting from the ground floor, aspiring to be the first in my family to graduate from college, I do not have much in the way of connections that would make me a shoo-in for any company. The internship seems like the optimal path to take—even if its unpaid. From my perspective, the experience gleamed would be payment in its own right. Especially if it means the difference between getting a job or not.

How Much Money a Computer Programmer Makes

When compared to its counterparts in the computer information technology industry, computer programming is not much better or worse in terms of salary. According to the U. S. Bureau of Labor Statistics (2000), nationally, computer programmers make on average of $86,000 a year, whereas the average of all other computer occupations sits at around $88,240; additionally, the lowest ten percent of computer programmers earn less than $50,150. The pay ceiling is much higher than the national average with the highest paid 10 percent of workers receiving a salary of $140,250 (U. S. Bureau of Labor Statistics, 2020). Also, according to indeed.com (2020), an average base salary for a Michigander is around $69,233 a year in the city of Auburn. When compared to the rest of Michigan, this is on the higher end since the average pay in the state as a whole is a paltry $36,836. Comparing this to some nearby states with a higher average salary, one finds that Wisconsin and Illinois both pay out more, at 23 percent and 28 percent higher than Michigan's average, respectively (indeed.com, 2020).

From the beginning, I have decided that moving cannot be completely out of the question for a career like this; in fact, it is no surprise that I may consider heading to Illinois or Wisconsin since they both have considerably higher average wages. Thankfully, the cost of living likely will not be too much higher than it is in Michigan, especially when compared to the next highest states (Washington and California).

Those seeking to be computer programmers have a rocky road ahead if they are not willing to look into other fields within the computer information technology industry. While the pay ceiling seems high, and there's a good amount of apparent flexibility, an aspiring computer programmer will have to be willing to make compromises for the company they are aiming to work for—whether that compromise comes in the form of working for free in an internship, paying out of pocket for a certification, or time spent commuting or moving to a more distant establishment where the pay is objectively better. All in all, so long as one sticks with the industry, there are a great many opportunities that will not limit a computer programmer to the sole act of computer programming.

References

Get Educated. (2019, September 6). How to become a computer programmer. Get Educated: Review, Rate, Rank & Compare Online Colleges & Degrees. https://www.geteducated.com/careers/how-to-become-a-computer-programmer/

Grand Rapids Community College. (2020). Computer Programmer. Career Coach. https://grcc.emsicc.com/careers/computer-programmer?region=Kent%20County,%20MI&radius=indeed.com. (2020). Computer programmer salary in Michigan. https://www.indeed.com/career/computer-programmer/salaries/MI

Raise Me. (2019). Computer programmers: Salary, career path, job outlook, education and more. https://www.raise.me/careers/computer-and-information-technology/computer-programmers

U. S. Bureau of Labor Statistics. (2020, September 1). Computer programmers: Occupational Outlook Handbook. https://www.bls.gov/ooh/computer and-information-technology/computer-programmers.htm

Vuollett, P. (2019, January 20). Do programmers work from home? Make Me a Programmer. https://makemeaprogrammer.com/do-programmers-work-from-home/

Figure 32. Could a composition help to sustain the gratitude shown caregivers in frontline positions during the pandemic? Photo Courtesy of Student.

Career Exploration Essay—Students' Reflections

Several appreciated the Career Exploration Essay's opportunities to study a prospective job and its attendant education, training, and application, as noted in these semesters' end recollections:

- I gained the confidence I needed and was able to bust out some good essays. I was really proud of my final draft of my career exploration essay. I used many tools and websites to help me find valuable information on my topic which I applied to my paper. One challenging aspect in this essay was the fact that it was in APA format. Considering I had been using MLA format throughout my entire high school career, I had no idea how to write an APA essay. I listened carefully and it turned out that the APA essay was my best essay all semester.

- Taking this class proved to be helpful because I was able to apply skills when writing papers for my psychology class. Two APA style papers were required for that class and had I not had exposure like I did, I don't think I would have done as well. Research turned out to be a huge component in that style of paper and by having to write a paper for EN 101, it made writing the papers for PY 201 much smoother. An important skill I picked up was how to be an effective, explorative researcher; in addition, we were given great resources and examples to use to be successful in the research process. Furthermore, even in my government class, I became more aware in writing short answer responses.

- The essay I liked writing the most was my career exploration essay. In past English classes I would either have to write about a book or a memoir which I never really felt happy with. Writing essays in this class has been like a breath of fresh air because they are topics I actually find interesting. Researching about a career that interests me was fun because it is something I am looking forward to pursuing, now something that I know much more about. I found it helpful to have already become interested in studying that career early. I liked researching colleges with programs that correlate to the career we chose. This gave me an idea of the kinds of majors that different colleges offer, too. The career exploration essay was also the first time I wrote in APA style. Whenever I will have to write APA research papers in the future, I will feel more prepared after already having experienced this style of writing.

- Learning to write in these various styles prepared me for writing in other classes. I plan to continue in the medical field so learning more about APA formatting was beneficial.

- The most memorable and beneficial assignment to me was the career exploration essay. This assignment at first was very overwhelming. Not only did I have to write a paper, I also had to do research in a new site, use a new style of writing, APA format, and through all of this, learn how to make my work "college level." Though, as soon as I began my research, I realized that this paper could educate me in multiple ways. While writing this paper and learning how to write in APA format, I also learned a lot about my future career. I researched marketing/promotional managers; however, it did not feel like research. It felt more like an exploration where I could see the potential for my future and what I would need to do to get there, while also writing about it to communicate my findings to an audience. I will take with me much of the information that I have learned from writing that essay throughout the rest of my college career as well as when I begin searching for my lifetime job.

COVID-19 Notes: "Forward"

Sandwiched between two remarkable days, one of peaceful protest marches and open solidarity with the Black Lives Matter movement ("About Black Lives Matter") and another of selfless service to the city by cleaning up and repairing overnight vandalism to small businesses and downtown institutions—including the public art museum, the county court, and even the city police department—a night of shameful, wanton destruction and looting following the Black Lives Matter solidarity march on May 30. After the orderly marchers left at dusk, protesters of a violent stripe replaced them. 100 buildings in downtown Grand Rapids were vandalized that Saturday night: it was one of 150 cities nationwide where protests turned destructive. Windows were broken, merchandise was stolen, and businesses were looted by youth rampaging to protest a Minneapolis policeman's tortuous and dehumanizing killing of George Floyd, an unarmed black man. Maybe the many protests were compounded by the unjust police murders of other innocent African Americans, recently including former Grand Rapids resident Breonna Taylor, who was mistakenly and indiscriminately shot in Louisville, or Ahmaud Arbery, killed jogging in Georgia, along with far too many others who were murdered by racists or uncontrolled cops and other individuals infected by America's systemic and endemic sense of white privilege and power fueled by an angry, outspoken cohort of defiant, deluded, or deranged pundits and politicos.

Maybe my city's rioters were youth made stir-crazy by two months of sheltering in place, banned from schools' academic and social interactions to remote homeschooling, hanging out inside with little relief from the stress of the wave of pandemic engulfing West Michigan. Possibly, they suffered the indignity of being deemed nonessential workers and losing work, income, or purpose. Any attendant depression, isolation, despair, illness, and uncertainties could have backed them into a corner and spurred a breakout lash-out.

Compounding the injustice of police brutalities, blacks suffer disproportionately— more than twice the rate of COVID-19 illness relative to their populations (June 1, 2020, PBS). Probably, they had suffered indignities themselves at the hands of police: racial profiling resulting in their being pulled over or falsely accused of a crime or simply demeaned with comments and implications. In a conversation about *The Hate U Give*, the movie based on Angie Thomas's young adult novel, I remember every African American student in one class agreeing that either they or an immediate family member had experienced racial profiling by local law enforcement. When asked if they had been given "The Talk" about what to do when confronted by a police officer, all indicated that they had. Afterwards, exasperatedly, resignedly, yet patiently, they explained their realities to their white classmates, few of whom had heard of "The Talk."

Militant police, armed with military weaponry and trained in military tactics, who treat civilians of other cultural communities disdainfully as "those others" or even "the enemy," might ignite the reactive violence they aim to repress. "When you have a grenade launcher, even peaceful protesters look like enemy combatants. It's no surprise that as police departments have stocked up on military-grade equipment, they have acted more aggressively" (Editorial Board). Tear gas canisters and flash grenades fired and launched at peaceful civilians make city streets look unnervingly like conflict zones, something entirely foreign to the traditional police purpose, *to serve and protect*.

Some respondents interviewed on the local news stations suggested that rioters were not protesters at all; in fact, they were counter demonstrators not from the city but stirred up by inflammatory social media or the president's "violence glorifying" tweet repeating the racist slogan that implicitly threatened looting with shooting. In a time of escalated political trickery and combative chicanery, their claims seemed less outlandish, even feasible.

While that Saturday's smashing backlash to police brutality or white supremacy may be understandable, it is not justifiable. Another wrong, even if a lesser one than the atrocities of killer cops who disingenuously pledge to serve and protect or the emboldened white supremacists in this nation professing "liberty and justice for all," regardless, is still wrong.

Fortunately, preceding Saturday night was Saturday afternoon—a peaceful, positive protest—and afterward Sunday morning followed by restorative clean-up and repair. Saturday afternoon, downtown Grand Rapids was crowded with young people, families, groups of faith, and individuals of many races marching, chanting, listening, praying, and demonstrating—joining millions of others in hundreds of cities across the U. S. to protest a profane murder at the hands of a haughty cop. As President Obama wrote afterwards, there is hope for us: "[W]atching the heightened activism of young people in recent weeks, of every race and every station, makes me hopeful. If, going forward, we can channel our justifiable anger into peaceful, sustained, and effective action, then this moment can be a real turning point" (Obama). When I see and hear students of all backgrounds discussing, listening to one another, and working together, I agree with our former president. Thanks to our youth, our city's and our country's future can still be one of peaceful unity, active understanding, and mutual empathy—a future that accepts and applauds racial differences. We can all hope that the constructive voices in society will outlast and overcome the destructive deniers and dividers and continue to speak truth to the powers that be.

Thank God for Sunday. After it was seriously rattled, my city rallied. Families, groups, neighbors, young people, and coworkers all descended on downtown with brooms and shovels, cleansers and scrub brushes, drills, and 2 × 4s and press board to clean and secure shattered city storefronts. Restaurants fed the cleanup and repair crews at sidewalk smorgasbords. Coffee shops distributed steaming cups of java and cocoa. Officials and owners exuded thanks to everyone, and bleary-eyed TV crews asked kids and adults alike, "Why are you here doing this?"

Without exception, people regardless of race, workers and owners, children and their parents replied, "This is our city." We have to keep working to make it better, especially for Black Lives. We stand in solidarity with Black Lives Matter.

Works Cited

"About Black Lives Matter." *Black Lives Matter Global Network Foundation*, https:// blacklivesmatter.com/about/.

Editorial Board. "Opinion—America's Protests Won't Stop Until Police Brutality Does." *New York Times*, 1 June 2020, https://www.nytimes.com/2020/06/01/opinion/george-floyd-protest-police.html.

"June 1, 2020—PBS NewsHour Full Episode." https://www.pbs.org/newshour/show/june-1-2020-pbs-newshour-full-episode.

Obama, Barack. "How to Make This Moment the Turning Point for Real Change." *Medium*, 1 June 2020, https://barackobama.medium.com/how-to-make-this-moment-the-turning-point-for-real-change-9fa209806067.

—Noted June 2, 2020

Q6.

How could you acquaint students with career options and their attendant programs of study in your writing class? Conversely, to what degree should the first-year writing class familiarize students with the humanities and the fine arts as an alternative to a college environment that sometimes seems obsessed by career building and "grade grubbing"?

Figure 33. How might college writing instructors help to rectify racial disparities of colleges and communities and ensure that Black lives indeed do matter here? Photo by Author.

Chapter 7. Equitable

Diversity asks who is sitting at the table, whereas equity asks who is trying to get a seat at the table but cannot. Meanwhile, inclusion asks whether everyone sitting at the table has had a chance to be heard. Finally, justice asks whose ideas will be taken ... seriously because of who is represented at the table.

—Dafina-Lazarus Stewart

Just

Random seating arrangements, I used to think, were the best approach to breaking up cliques in classrooms. Allowing partners to choose seats together at a table for four on the first day of class, I noticed friends led their pairs to fill the two open seats across from each other, so they kept that comfort for the first few weeks of a term. So I gave them assigned seats on the first day and then scrambled the their seats again twice, assigning them new places among different classmates to assure different groups for class discussions, group collaborations, and peer reviews—all arranged in classroom quartets. As I like to justify, by rearranging seats periodically, I try to guarantee an opportunity to meet, converse, and write with as many classmates as possible, so they can gain a variety of audiences and a diversity of perspectives.

Weighed against these benefits, with which no one could disagree, was the not-so-inviting prospect of facing a classroom of faces that overwhelmingly looked unalike the majority of students since, semester to semester, a class typically had only a handful of African American, Asian American, Native American, and Latinx students enrolled. Sitting beside someone who shares your own heritage and background, and who would likely have similar life experiences and perspectives, might ease somewhat the daunting task of positioning yourself within a classroom populated predominately with whites. Especially, when first-year college is the initial experience of making your way into a school or classroom where you are not a part of the majority or at least of a significant plurality of the students, having an opportunity to select a seat among a group or near a person of the same ethnicity can be an academic lifeline when you are in the minority.

Still, given their seating propensities, almost invariably students cluster with knowns and familiars, which typically requires the disruption of assigning seats to evoke cross-cultural verbal and written interaction as I noted in my *English Composition Teacher's Guidebook* (Mulder). Fortunately, electronics can help with this. Discussion boards normally do not include individuals' photos or memes; hence, students generally do not self-sort or select based on race, at least until they have gained a familiarity in class, via a photo roster, or through an email photograph. With such electronically distributed conversations, randomly assigned conversation groups assist with diversity and variety among speakers and points of view. Moreover, for better or sometimes worse, communicating electronically, even when conversing through a college's LMS, seems to remove some students' inhibitions about a forthright disclosing of their opinions and experiences.

The challenge, as Stewart observed in the quotation opening this chapter, is how to elicit, enable, and ennoble every student's participation. While many have learned to silently fly beneath the white radar by avoiding in-depth conversation about any race-weighty subject, some simply remain quiet, self-censuring to keep their viewpoints safely locked inside. English classes by their very being can impose white bias as they disseminate the traditional, standard grammar and parlance of their privileged, educated, predominantly white practitioner-professors. Likely, not only are the majority of classmates in their college English class white, so is the professor, and they all likely share the same spoken and written language and rules for formal and informal assessments. Any other idiom or approach may be considered too inaccessible, unfamiliar, or different to be accepted by an oftentimes unwittingly biased white majority.

At first, teaching antiracism as a white man might appear to perpetuate white male privilege, traditional stereotypes, or racial insensitivity; but a conscientiously forthright and caringly assertive raising and revisiting of the fundamental human right to freedom from race prejudice is especially necessary for white teachers, and in particular white male teachers, to address. Not speaking of race could be interpreted as quiet complicity with an unjust status quo, and this was especially so in that turbulent summer of 2020. An obviously privileged white male myself, I could address matters of race personally to my students. To show solidarity with quarterback Colin Kaepernick and Black Lives Matter, I settled onto a knee myself in class while raising the most recent example of police brutality perpetrated upon an African American. Careful and explicit discussion around "taking a knee" seemed advisable after that white Minneapolis policeman choked the breath from George Floyd with his own knee pressed onto Floyd's neck for an unconscionable nearly nine minutes lying in the street. Since that egregious event, humble acknowledgement of, and apology for, my own past uninformed, color-blind assumptions seems to me an appropriate first step. Certainly, a humble and contrite admission, as well as being the right thing to do, is more amenable to opening forthright dialogue than an offensive, defensive bombast about eschewing all responsibility for any "sins of our fathers."

When a black or brown student complains about having been pulled over by a police officer—an astonishingly frequent and regular event—I cringe, and after listening to the student's story, I share the time another of my black students arrived at class shaken and "in the sweats" after he was trailed by a cop across a nearby wealthy suburb before being pulled over one block outside the city for a dim brake light. This elicited a flurry of African American students' similar experiences of police patrol "escorts," evidently seeking some infraction to justify a traffic stop. "They always find something," one of my students muttered shaking his head. "I've been stopped three times driving through that town. I always drive around that town now even though it adds 5–10 minutes getting to class. I suppose that's what they want—for me to stay out of their town." While black students nodded their heads in sympathy, many of the white students' eyes widened and heads shook side to side, and I think I detected several masked jaws drop.

"…[S]tudents need to learn how to live in a society where difference is the norm, not the exception. This skill—to be able to live and work across multiple lines of difference, to make it a blessing and not a curse, to find ways that it strengthens democracies, not undercuts them—is one that will serve students for the rest of their life" (Palfrey 126–127). Many of our African American—as well as Latinx, Asian American, and Native American—students have already mastered this skill, having had to negotiate a too-often indifferent and unobservant white-led society. Simply listening to, acknowledging, and sharing their stories while admitting our complicit silences, confessing our denials, and learning to overcome our ignorances is a needed beginning.

This is one way we can help to heal the hurts that have been caused by and exposed by this pandemic. Beyond our personal modeling of nonracist attitudes and behavior, and our spoken antiracist opinions and responses to current events—whether local, national, or international—an important addition to a first-year composition class is to incorporate assignments that encourage students to share their own experiences and observations about the racial disparities and inequities uncovered in a raw social and political climate and exacerbated by the COVID-19 pandemic, and to give students a voice for their own concerns and cares about racial justice.

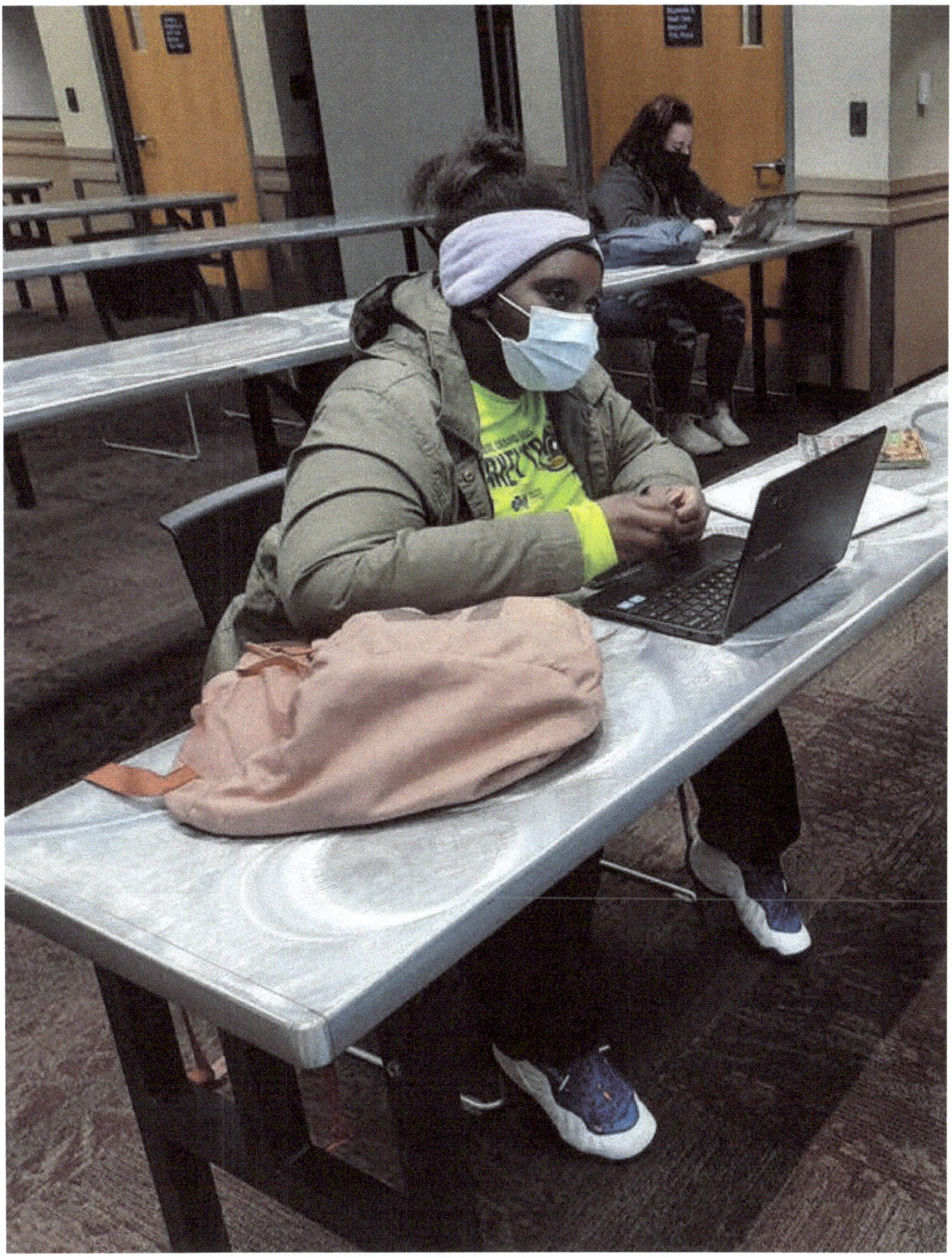

Figure 34. How can composition instructors practice justice with students of color who too often have experienced a lesser preparation for the rigors of college writing? Photo by Author.

Black Lives Matters

In *Race Talk and the Conspiracy of Silence*, Derald Wing Sue writes, "Race talk violates the academic protocol" (25). Since college pursues academic "objectivity, detachment, and rational discourse," the seemingly subjective emotional and visceral experiences of African Americans are sometimes considered inappropriately antagonistic to the sought neutrality of scientific rationalism; however, "race talk on the part of people of color is about bearing witness to their lived realities, their personal and collective experiences of subordination, and their stories of racism" (26). Relegating their lived experiences to subjective, personal, and therefore unempirical, even irrational, subjectivisms unallowed in empirical, legitimized higher discourse and academic composition, writing instructors sometimes suppress black and other minority students' stories and may appear to disqualify their experiences as unworthy of written consideration.

In *Race and Writing Assessment*, Asao B. Inoue adds, "The more a student practices writing, the better she will get … [as] quality is a function of quantity" (81). Inoue further observes that "for African Americans more work did seem to equate to higher quality and more growth in writing, but at the cost of more African Americans not meeting the workload requirements" (90). While insisting on the traditional English usage and standard grammar required by my departments and normally expected in written compositions of higher education institutions—as they are both what we educators know and were trained, and they are generally required for admittance into the subject areas of academia as well as professional careers—I deem it wrong to suppress personal voice in Comp 1, a gateway course to college. Here, African Americans' voices deserve to be heard; in fact, they must be acknowledged and affirmed. One attempt to do so is to ask students to share vernacular dialogue in their first essay, the tour of downtown in which they are required to introduce 3–6 members of their tour group. In addition, since few classmates share their career interests, I suggests that they introduce their second essay, a career exploration research essay, with a personal rationale as to their choice of career to research and a conclusion analyzing why after their findings they are more or less inclined to pursue that career themselves. In the Unsung Hero/Ethnography Research Essay (see below), again I encourage dialogue—though less the student's own questioning voice and more their interviewed Unsung Hero's voice, in an attempt to catch some characteristic phrases or expressions. Recording their hero's voice in dialogue might lead to a deeper understanding of another's language, dialect, or colloquialisms as representative of shoptalk, family or peers' expressions, or ethnic heritage.

Sina Saeedi and Elaine Richardson find that code-switching, distinguishing between formal or standard, and informal or nonstandard, writing,

> … inevitably positions Back Language as inferior to Standardized English by reinforcing blatant racist-segregationist ideologies against Black lives and languages …. Those who are racialized as Black experience the effects of racism regardless of the code they use in their speech and writing. Therefore, granting access to forms of whiteness is an effort to sustain and not to eradicate racialized capitalistic hierarchies. What needs to be disrupted, then, are whiteness and white privilege, and not simply one's lack of access to it. (149)

In light of this fact,

> … teachers with ideological clarity can help students build on Black language resistance traditions, not for appropriateness and survival, but for thriving, rhetorical dexterity, and solidarity. People live their languages and languages live their people, too. Language plays the role of mediator in race relations and negotiations. (Saeedi and Richardson, 158)

In "In Search of Wisdom: Higher Education for a Changing Democracy," Beverly Daniel Tatum states, "We are at an important historical moment with regard to education and our nation's legacy of dealing with race …. We can use our leadership—as educators … to use and value higher education as a location where crucial connections can be forged (107). She continues, writing about "the educational benefits of learning in a diverse community" (110):

> Those students who experienced the most racial and ethnic diversity in and out of their classrooms benefited [from] greater engagement in active thinking processes, growth in intellectual engagement and motivation, … intellectual and academic skills … the most involvement during college in various forms of citizenship, … engagement with people from different races and cultures, and …the interests of the broader community—all outcomes important to the health of our democracy. (110–111)

Ibram X. Kendi asks,

> What if we measured intelligence by how knowledgeable individuals are about their own environments? What if we measured intellect by an individual's desire to know? What if we realized the best way to ensure an effective educational system is not by standardizing our curricula and tests but by standardizing the opportunities available to all students? (103)

That is what we can aspire to in Comp 1. Where better can we encourage students to draw out experiences and draw upon their own environments than through compositions and conversations? Where better can we have students pursue their own interests and observations through exploratory research?

In all our abundant diversity, we need the free participation and independent perspectives of African Americans in order to reform a more perfect union. Undergoing centuries of abuse, blacks alone can provide the singular point of view arising from a legacy of enslavement, forced migrations, insidious institutional racism, perpetual authoritative abuses, and menacing microaggressions. They as much as anyone embody the United States' national conscience.

They deserve amends, and attending to their learning with a welcoming classroom, challenging activities, and engaging assignments is how composition teachers can begin to help them feel valued and welcomed. First-year writing instructors must be noncoercive and nonjudgmental, and must treat every student as an indispensable individual, never a racial representative, acknowledging and applauding all diverse personalities, experiences, and positions with encouragement and insistence.

This is one way we might help heal the hurting during—and after—this pandemic.

Essentials

Watching police officers, fire fighters, and emergency medical technicians applaud nurses and doctors at the end of a 12-hour shift, worldwide all were astounded by the herculean efforts that medical and emergency workers made in treating the breaking waves of people who had suddenly fallen sick, working with limited resources under constrained conditions, ever adjusting to new symptoms and strains of this novel coronavirus flooding communities, cities, states, and nations. From suiting up with personal protective equipment to attending to an in-home emergency call, setting up and servicing drive-thru testing tents and stations, and administering specialized inoculations, their job descriptions evolved and grew to target this unstoppable pathogen passed from person to person.

Besides the technicians, nurses, and doctors, and the police, firefighters, and EMTs, there were so many unacknowledged additional services workers who proved essential to our commonweal. They were all recognized, finally, for their contributions to quell the virus's spread and effects. Supermarket employees, suppliers, truck drivers, farmers, in addition to the manufacturers of cleaners and paper products, flours and cereals—too often overlooked and underappreciated—were realized to be essential to individual and communal sustenance and safety. Food and cleaning products were no longer assumed abundant; the staples and basics of health and life were consumed without a thought or a care no more.

The U.S. Postal Service, United Parcel Service, FedEx, and Amazon delivery workers steered jeeps, parcel trucks, and panel vans around the neighborhoods, ran packages and envelopes to mailboxes, porches, and stoops, and dropped checks, bills, books, and medicines, along with software and hardware, gardening gloves and spring planting tubers, seeds, and bulbs, as well as meat smokers, running sneakers, and home improvement supplies that kept people occupied while whiling away their time at home. Their routes essentially tied communities' fabrics together.

Immigrants and migrants, the regular replenishers and refreshers of our populace and communities, those who cared for children, harvested and planted fruits and vegetables, labored in meat packing plants, cleaned and sterilized hospital and hotel rooms—the U.S. residents who still dreamt, believing the wrinkled promises of America the Generous—were all essential to managing the pandemic. They overcame barriers and borders, divisions and discriminations, to raise and feed generations, supply and support states and nations, and uphold families and faiths.

Educators not only Zoomed and Googled into students' homes, intruded virtual learning into screen-sized activities, but also paraded in cars, attended drive-by stations to return possessions abandoned in vacated lockers and classrooms and dorms, constructed and bedecked temporary graduation stages, and transported lunches and breakfasts by box and bag via bus or van to community centers, parking lots, and front doors. We too gained recognition as essential workers, maybe as much remotely, as when in our classrooms.

Children and the elderly were essential, those stooping who blazed a way before and the ones toddling, who hold our hopes to make a way later. All who suffered from underlying conditions—diabetics, asthmatics, the heavy-hearted and the memory-impaired—they, too, wanting restoration, their healthy selves were essential. And all the overtly healthy who masked up religiously, who stayed at home, praying, waiting, willing their neighbors and communities well—they were essential.

Seeing 2020 through, students weathering all its tidal waves of crises, especially are essential to restore the commonweal of a crippled country in a wounded world.

Writing it acknowledges us. Scribing it documents us. Phrasing it recollects us.

Recalling 2020 and the continuing pandemic seasons of 2021 and 2022 and beyond may help us to heal, and may yet spur us to stitch together the ripped and frayed racial, political, social, and economic fabric to restore all the health and well-being that was torn and wounded by these years of trials.

Works Cited

Inoue, Asao B. "Grading Contracts: Assessing Their Effectiveness on Different Racial Formations." In *Race and Writing Assessment*, edited by Asao B. Inoue, and Mya Poe, Peter Lang, 2012, pp. 79–94.

Kendi, Ibram X. *How to Be an Antiracist*, One World, 2019.

Mulder, Tom. *English Composition Teacher's Guidebook: How to Survive (and Even Thrive) as an Adjunct or Part-time Instructor*, Equinox, 2020.

Palfrey, John. *Safe Spaces, Brave Spaces: Diversity and Free Expression in Education*, MIT P, 2017.

Saeedi, Sina and Elaine Richardson. "A Black Lives Matter and Critical Race Theory-Informed Critique of Code-Switching Pedagogy." In *Race, Justice, and Activism in Literacy Instruction*, edited by Valerie Kinloch, Tanja Burkhard, and Carlotta Penn, Teachers College P, 2020, pp. 147–161.

Stewart, Dafina-Lazarus. "Language of Appeasement," *Inside Higher Ed*. 30 March 2017.

Sue, Derald Wing. *Race Talk and the Conspiracy of Silence: Understanding and Facilitating Difficult Dialogues on Race*, Wiley, 2015.

Tatum, Beverly Daniel. "In Search of Wisdom: Higher Education for a Changing Democracy." *Can We Talk about Race? And Other Conversations in an Era of School Resegregation*. Beacon Press, 2007, pp. 105–126.

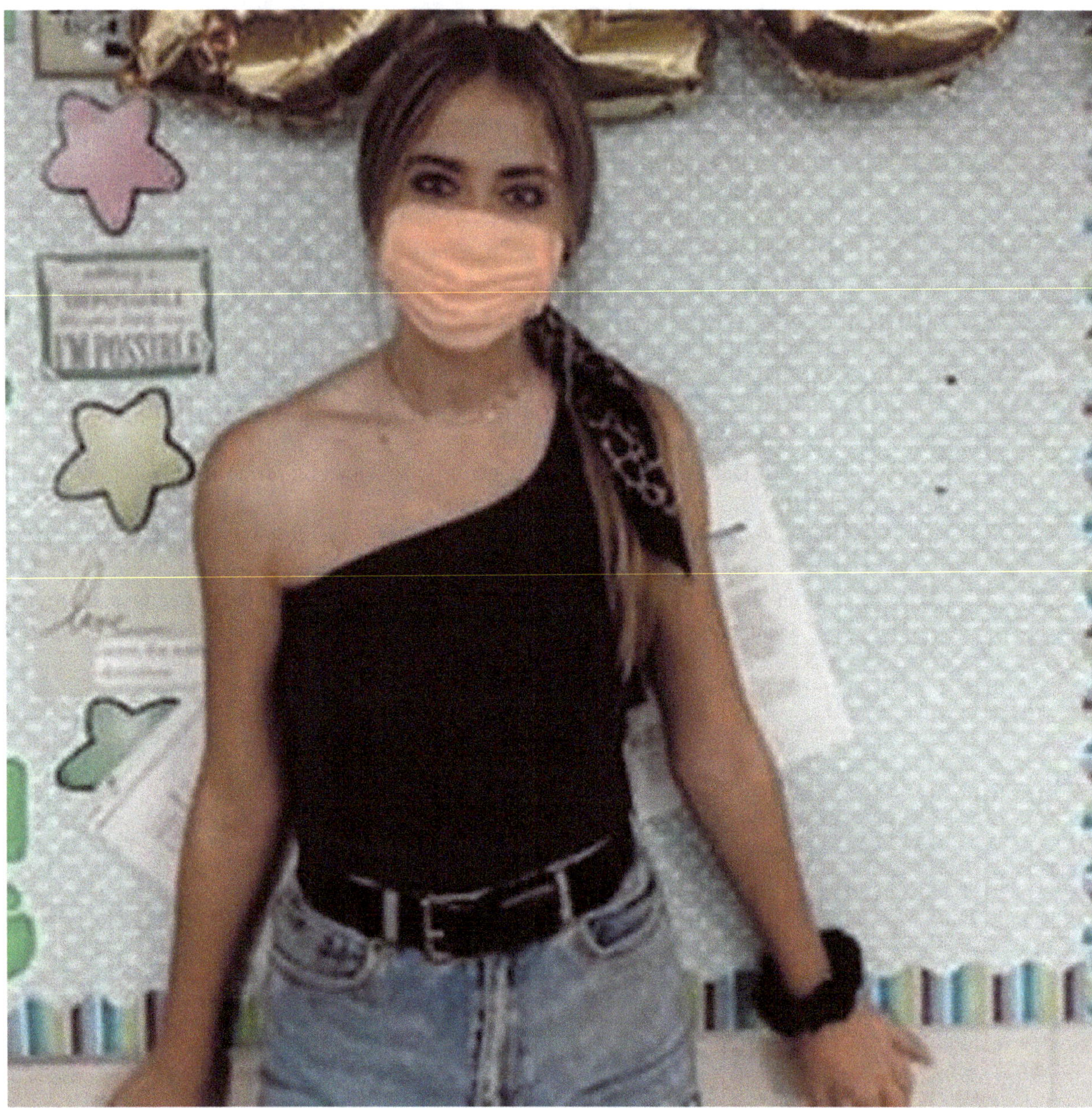

Figure 35. Hadley Mueller, author of "Here." Photo Courtesy of Student.

Student's Story—"Here," by Hadley Mueller

Here we are. I have not been inside with my grandma since last Christmas. I am no longer able to see my grandpa due to his kidney problems. I cannot see my friends unless we are at school with masks on, but now we are not even able to attend.

COVID-19 took over our lives and changed them in insurmountable ways. March 13, 2020, we had a two-week "vacation" to quarantine because the virus was killing people. I just thought of it as a two-week vacation, but then I got a text saying that DECA internationals had been canceled. This trip meant everything to me. I had been looking forward to it for years, and then it was taken away. Little did I know that internationals would not be the only thing taken from me.

I am in a business program at school called SQA where I learn through a college in Scotland. Since 8th grade, I was looking forward to the trip to Scotland to study business. I had never been overseas, and this was most exciting for me. The trip was not until June so I assumed that by that time, the whole quarantine situation would be over, but I was so very wrong.

At first, not being able to go on these trips felt like the end of the world. I often feel let down and robbed of these experiences, but then again, I need to take a step back and realize that I am so fortunate to have my health and be in a position where I can continue to do the right thing to keep those in my community safe as well, through such simple activities as wearing a mask and properly social distancing.

COVID-19 is much bigger than any one individual. People are dying, and others are losing their loved ones. Our selfish acts do nothing to benefit the world. So we must take this time to put others before ourselves, and protect our world and those living in it. It is easy to look at the death counts and say, "Oh well that isn't affecting me" or "There is no way I can die from this, so it doesn't matter what I do." But when people think like this, that is what causes the numbers to continue to grow and we lose more people to this battle against the pandemic. So when completing the actions that we must do to prevent the spread of COVID, we have to think every single day like we are doing it to directly protect ourselves and our families.

BP/DP/AP—Before, During, and After Pandemic Foundations

BP, after a cursory introduction to the class, syllabus, and everything else, I arranged students in groups, often mixing them to assure groups' diversity, so all could benefit from others' topics and perspectives when reading one another's posted discussions, conduct peer reviews, participate in classroom conversations, and connect and contact for any out-of-class questions or clarifications.

DP, although everyone is assigned a diverse group for all of these same functions, it is the out-of-class contacts that most often prove useful when students have to contend with quarantine after exposure to a COVID carrier or isolation having caught the coronavirus themselves. When holding lessons in the physical classroom, instead of my arranging groups, I ask them to rearrange themselves beside others to form a new group, including someone whom they have not yet sat next to. Before, behind, and beside, they are welcome to keep one or two from their former group for comfort or stability as long as they exchange some other group members. This allows the few African Americans and Asian Americans normally enrolled in my classes to keep a companion of like ethnicity, which may free them both to comfortably interact with the usually more numerous white and Latinx students. Always, I am careful now to include an element of choice in the group membership—without its ever becoming completely student-chosen. (For more about my approach to assigning seats and its rationale, see my *English Composition Teacher's Guidebook*.)

AP, in my in-person classes I plan to continue moderating the seat-selection process that I initiated during the pandemic (DP) to include some self-selection within my otherwise randomly assigned seats and groups.

Bottom line: *Variety with harmony* is the watchword: Regularly mix up the seating arrangements to ensure cross-classroom cultural interactions and the concomitant interest and challenge that doing so offers, but allow individuals a modicum of stability and comfort by encouraging them to retain a neighbor from the previous grouping, thereby establishing a new foundation for seating, one of moderated selection.

BP/DP/AP (2)—Before, During, and After Pandemic Discussions

BP, to ensure that all would benefit from others' topics and perspectives when reading one another's posted discussions, conducting peer reviews, participating in classroom conversations, and connecting with each other outside of class to seek clarifications or answers to questions, I nominated group speakers every class period by asking a personal question requiring an additional conversation to answer. For example, "Your group's speaker today is the person who has the most (or fewest, oldest, or youngest) siblings." I have compiled a whole list of such questions that often initiate conversations themselves, such as, "Who has traveled the farthest (or to the most states and provinces, to the most countries, or to an out-of-county destination most recently)"?

DP, except for using my colleges' LMS's to continue Discussion Board posts with responses to posted questions and replies to group members, the group speaker questions were curtailed while classes were online. When classes returned to in-person mode, I returned to the group speaker questions.

AP, I plan to continue assigning daily discussions of both casually light and challengingly deeper issues—such as racial and social justice topics like white privilege as current events may suggest. As I like to remind students periodically, "You don't speak for anybody besides yourself—not your family, your race, your religion, your political party, your community, or your culture. You speak only for yourself. Speak honestly, openly, and often, and always feel free to adjust or change your mind as you talk things out and think things through. Finally, what is said in class stays in class: Don't share anyone else's opinions outside. Play fair."

Bottom line: *Variety with harmony* necessitates insisting that everyone's voice is given a change to be heard. A nonthreatening approach like using icebreaker questions such as the examples above to ensure that everyone contributes to class discussions, and opening with lighter conversation topics before delving into deeper beliefs can help students whose voices are too often silenced to find and free their voices.

COVID-19 Notes: "Turned Purple"

What if [this virus] can allow us to see that we're not as stupid as our political parties want us to be ...? A purple America is a far more interesting one than the red or blue one that some insist on.

—Colum McCann

Most who vote sound as influenced by what they vote against as by whom they vote for—at least to judge by the vociferous sound-offs through the un-social media. Here in the state of Michigan, we have been both blessed and burdened with two brazenly boisterous executives, stuck between a pugnacious Governor G. "Better 6 feet apart than 6 feet under" Whitmer—made famous nationally by a forgetful and/or condescending U.S. Prez's sputtered, "That woman from Michigan"—and that "If I say it, it's true" President D. "It's a hoax" Trump. Paradoxically, it is Whitmer's conservative adherence to Trump's touted criterion to wait through 14 days of demonstrated decline in the count of COVID-19 cases before relaxing lockdown restrictions that had him tweeting in angry caps, "LIBERATE MICHIGAN." It is safe to say, his target was not the overwhelmingly Republican stonewalling Michigan state legislature.

Stay home. Stay safe. That is the MI moniker for one-size-fits-all shelter-in-place, whether in uber-urban Detroit at the southeast corner of the lower peninsula or the ultra-unpopulated Porcupine Mountains at the northwest extreme of Michigan's Upper Peninsula. From 0 cases of coronavirus with no fatalities in some counties up north to 2,000-some deaths and more than 20,000 COVID-19 cases in Detroit-area counties, every one gets locked down. Maybe fair is fair across the board, but could a more situational, surgical treatment, and a region-to-region and county-to-county prognosis have led to better outcomes for both economy and cure? (Beggin and Wilkinson; "Michigan Coronavirus Dashboard").

Michigan's COVID-19 patients exceed 50,000 with fatalities nearing 5,000. Daily tests state-wide have risen to 15,000, and new hospitalizations have shrunk to almost 1,000.
—"Michigan Coronavirus Dashboard"

The United States has almost 1½ million COVID-19 patients with close to 90,000 deaths. Worldwide, 4.7 million have been diagnosed with COVID-19, and more than 300,000 have died.

—"Mortality Analyses"

Whether you color yourself lightly lavender or a deep-dark plum, your shade of purple should permit a chuckle at a President named *Trump* who gambles. He gambles with trade, treaties, economies, and now a pandemic health crisis. He eagerly takes chances and takes sides, playing states in bidding wars against one another and his own federal government for slackened stocks of Personal Protective Equipment (PPE) and medical ventilators. "Not responsible," he rattles trash talk, cajoling and contradicting doctors, cabinet members, feds, reporters, himself, as he spins and re-spins in cycles—airing out, shaking out, and calling out nightly.

The Trump Show, his daily evening airtime infomercials—impromptu, reactionary, accusatory—rolled out bumpily and interminably—sort of a prezzy *Seinfeld* without sets, and only uncertainly humorous or entertaining—as he attempted to personally upstage and perpetually undermine his administration's expert spokespeople. As day by day it devolved into the Prez's staggering, painful efforts at sarcastic humor by inviting his TV audience to ingest hydroxychloroquine, which at best should not harm a patient, or to inject bleach or some counter cleanser—a sinister punchline, as apparently some viewers who mistook his humor for truth discovered.

Its ratings slumping as the *Trump Show* grew more personally vindictive and political and less factual and forthright, the Prez-producer yanked it—only to replace it with regular online tweets and tirades, boosted by in-person rallies with the MAGA faithful, perpetually fueling distrust of the U.S. government and retribution towards all who would not bend to his will, and leading to his infamously consequential January 6 call to action. Aren't we overdue for some straightforward, upright, and forthright leadership in governance?

Maybe this virus can allow us to see that "we're not as stupid as our political parties want us to be," nor as unidirectional as our TV channels and online apps appear to believe we are, nor the cowed consumers and workers that corporate America and big business want us to be. Purple America, made up of nuanced, independent, and multi-faceted consumer-citizens, is far more interesting.

We do not need to simplify views and divide politics. We should instead multiply perspectives, expand purviews, and broaden purposes. We need to be brave enough to reach across the aisles and bold enough to select and solve world-worthy problems. We should choose to confront the most challenging crises of our times—alleviating the climate crisis, rescuing refugees, bringing social justice, healing populations plagued by pandemic viruses—and elect those bold enough to command united action towards their proposed solutions. Haven't we had enough of divisive liars, petty mudslingers, reckless fearmongers, and hate-spewing bullies? The gravity of facing a pandemic has shown us the immediate need to face the nation's and world's critical issues—certainly, more of us should turn purple.

Works Cited

Beggin, Riley and Mike Wilkinson. "When Will Gov. Whitmer Reopen Michigan? It's Complicated. And a Bit Vague." *Bridge Magazine*, 17 May 2020, www.bridgemi.com/michigan-government/ when-will-gov-whitmer-reopen-michigan-its-complicated-and-bit-vague.

McCann, Colum. "What if the Virus Can Teach Us to Change?" *TIME*, 18 May 2020, p. 19.

"Michigan Coronavirus Dashboard: Cases, Deaths and Maps." *Bridge Magazine*, 18 May 2020, www.bridgemi.com/michigan-coronavirus-dashboard-cases-deaths-and-maps.

"Mortality Analyses." *Johns Hopkins Coronavirus Resource Center*, 18 May 2020, coronavirus.jhu.edu/data/mortality.

Mulder, Tom. *English Composition Teacher's Guidebook: How to Survive (and Even Thrive) as an Adjunct or Part-time Instructor*, Equinox, 2020.

—Noted May 18, 2020

Q7.

How do you meet the learning needs of your African American students as well as other students of color? What issues of race could you overtly address in your class? What teaching practices can you use to advance social justice and racial equity?

Figure 36. What allowances should composition instructors grant students given the heightened demands of juggling a college writing class and their other coursework, jobs, and relationships in the context of viral threats and other disruptions? Photo Courtesy of Student.

Chapter 8. Exploring a Person and People

We—of the American Dream—can have ... opportunity to thrive across generations by bolstering within our public discourse democracy's promise of fair participation and assuring that our conversations do not neglect or forget anyone's depiction of their experience.

—Barbara Couture and Patti Wojahn

Essay #3: MLA Unsung Hero/Ethnography Research Essay

"Who is your reader?"

"I am definitely sharing mine with my unsung hero after she shared her family's story with me."

"My boss is going to read mine after all I researched about how other restaurant owner-managers were affected so badly during COVID-19."

"So is my co-worker, a nurse in the hospital who went from getting applauded after every shift to feeling abandoned now that the coronavirus has hit so hard. This essay might even help her feel better."

"Mine is going to my mom because I wonder if she even knows everything about grandma that I learned for the first time in our interview."

"I'm making my friends read it because I don't think any of them know what custodial maintenance workers like my unsung hero have to go through just so they get a clean classroom and cafeteria."

"I might have my roommate read it and possibly my boyfriend. I guess my group members and you are going to read it, too, right?"

"From populist demagogues, we learn the indispensability of democracy; from isolationists, we learn the need for global solidarity; and from tribalists, we learn the beauty of cosmopolitanism," claims author Elif Shafak ("The Revolutionary Power of Diverse Thought"). Shafak asserts that plurality, diversity, and complexity are essentials to a thriving democracy that can stand in the face of the demagoguery and authoritarianism to which even the USA itself may no longer remain immune. Writing instructors can do our part by assigning students outside their tribes to interview others, converse with those from unalike backgrounds, and seek out those who are often overlooked. Focusing on them as essay subjects, and interviewing them as research sources ennobles, entitles, and accepts individuals whose stories and selves may be undervalued or unattended even when they work on a college campus, serving the students and staff who interact around them daily, as Rahema Ellis reported following an interview with student Febin Bellamy for *NBC Nightly News* (Ellis).

Although an anthropologist might take issue with the descriptive and comparative approaches to fieldwork and ethnography taken in this essay assignment, it addresses the need raised by David Westbrook "to talk to marginal people, wherever they may be found ... to rediscover the humanity in the peripheral subject" (11):

> Conversation intuitively seems to be a good way to approach questions about how different sorts of people live now.... From this perspective, there is something appealing about

ethnography, which has long used conversations as data. Why cannot conversations, organized in some academically respectable fashion and branded "ethnography," be used to confront, think through, the chaos of contemporary social life? (23)

As Barbara Dennis maintains,

> … the most ideal image of research is an egalitarian and equitable conversation. A conversation *with* people that seriously honors and defers to the wisdom, value, and ethics of those at the metaphorical table. It is purposeful and dialogic, fallible and action-oriented, ethical and open. (xvi)

In being conversations, and thus dialogic, "[e]thnographic truths are …," as James Clifford and George E. Marcus remind us in their Introduction to *Writing Culture: The Poetics and Politics of Ethnography*, "inherently *partial*—committed and incomplete" (7). Perhaps more like the descriptive and comparative approaches taken by "armchair anthropologists," described by Lynda Mannik and Karen McGarry in "The Roots of Ethnographic Fieldwork," in their *Practicing Ethnography* (18–19), the Unsung Hero/ Ethnography Research Essay gives students an approachable introduction to the interviewing and fieldnotes required for writing ethnography; but for my purposes in English 101, students spend at least as much effort researching the experiences of others to serve as background to their primary research and to compare to their own fieldnotes of a selected "unsung hero."

For their Virtual Tour Essay, many students who know someone working downtown in the service, restaurant, or entertainment industry choose to interview them for recommendations about menu items, best times to visit, or sometimes insider scoops about deals or promotions. For the Career Exploration Essay, some choose to interview individuals whom they know in the field they are researching—usually, a family member, neighbor, fellow employee, or fellow student who is a year or so ahead, and occasionally, a professor in a congruent subject area or possibly a cold-called individual employed in the career of choice. One semester, for example, a student of mine seeking a criminal justice degree visited the local police department to volunteer, hoping to get his foot in the door for a future internship that could lead ultimately to employment there. Already there, he arranged to interview a scheduling sergeant as well as a patrol officer, with both of whom he had retained a rapport that he hoped to advance in his semesters ahead.

Whereas the Virtual Tour and Career Exploration essays allow and may encourage an interview as part of the assignment, the Unsung Hero essay requires one. Students identify and profile someone who otherwise might be overlooked, unappreciated, or taken for granted. During the COVID-19 pandemic, finding a medical care provider, emergency medical treatment worker, commodities stocker, package delivery driver, daycare or childcare employee, teacher, or individual working from home because of either a workplace requirement or a homeplace necessity added poignancy to their writing. Many students had personal connections to colleagues, teammates, classmates, family members, and neighbors who were taking extra precautions or taking on extra responsibilities to contend with the medical and economic demands of 2020. Many more selected telephone interviews, emailed interviews, and texted interviews rather than the face-to-face personal interview; nevertheless, many essential workers and homebound students were able to interview "live" fellow employees and extended family members that they might not otherwise have been able to.

From the Unsung Hero interview, students must select an ethnography theme to research. For this purpose, they need to craft suitable Socratic questions that can reveal background heritage, family history, a hobby or other interest of their Unsung Hero, or some other group-level characteristic of their selected person to research. Again, I provide links to suitable and reputable databases and websites, so that students do not get caught up in Googly goose-chases. I like to suggest that they use databases' options to email themselves sources' links along with their MLA citations; try accessing multiple media: broadcast news, journals, magazine articles, streaming sources, podcasts, infographics, photos, and whatever else they can find; and play with the timelines and Advanced options of electronic sources, narrowing and broadening their searches.

I ask them in writing the essay to introduce their Unsung Hero, preferably using some of the person's own words in quotations, in a way that leads into introducing people who share some characteristic(s) with the Unsung Hero that they have researched, finishing with an introduction-closing robust thesis statement—all written in third person, both singular and plural, without any first- or second-person pronouns. This required structure aims to offset any temptations toward scribing their own Socratic questions and opening in a trite Q & A format. In the essay as a whole, I suggest they write body paragraphs in third person plural, with plural noun subjects, to focus on the Ethnography theme—for example, writing about caterers, raised-bed gardeners, or Bosnian immigrants to western Michigan—then follow with a comparison to their interviewed Unsung Hero written in the third person singular. In the conclusion, I recommend beginning with a refurbished, still robust, restated thesis that summarizes their Ethnography theme's main topics, then finish with a return to the Unsung Hero, preferably giving their interviewee the last word in a final quotation, if feasible.

While this can be a demanding and sometimes intricate essay assignment, involving a variety of research sources along with a comparison and juxtaposition of an ethnographic group study to an individual Unsung Hero's story, students thoroughly invest themselves into this essay's purpose and processes, and they eagerly discuss and read one another's introductions and investigations.

Works Cited

Clifford, James and George E. Marcus. *Writing Culture: The Poetics and Politics of Ethnography*, University of California Press, 1986.

Couture, Barbara and Wojahn, Patti. *Crossing Borders, Drawing Boundaries: The Rhetoric of Lines across America*, Utah State University Press, 2015, p. 24.

Dennis, Barbara. *Walking with Strangers: Critical Ethnography and Educational Promise.* Critical Qualitative Research, Vol. 29, edited by Shirley R. Steinberg, Peter Lang, 2020.

Mannik, Lynda and Karen McGarry. *Practicing Ethnography: A Student Guide to Method and Methodology*, University of Toronto Press, 2017.

"Paying Back the Unsung Heroes of Georgetown University." *NBC Nightly News with Lester Holt*, reported by Rahema Ellis, 21 Oct. 2016.

Shafak, Elif. "The Revolutionary Power of Diverse Thought." TED New York, 27 Oct. 2017, https://www.ted.com/talks/elif_shafak_the_revolutionary_power_of_diverse_thought.

Westbrook, David A. *Navigators of the Contemporary: Why Ethnography Matters*, University of Chicago Press, 2008.

<u>Instruction Sheet 4.1</u>

Unsung Hero/Ethnography Research Essay Assignment

3–6 pp. MLA Essay Comparison: 1→Many

<u>Overview</u>

Select someone who seems underappreciated—like the essential workers during the COVID-19 coronavirus pandemic—those who do not always receive the recognition or acknowledgement they deserve. Ask suitable questions in a telephone, email, or live interview, asking permission to record it or quickly writing notes afterwards. Next, identify one hobby, interest, or background characteristic of your unsung hero to research for statistics, examples, and additional individual stories.

<u>Unsung Hero's Profile Description and Interview</u>

1. Begin by answering these <u>questions</u>:
   a. Who is your **Unsung Hero and where are they from**? _________________
      Campus Community Workplace
   b. How would you **describe** this <u>person</u> and their <u>setting</u> in detail?
   c. What **characteristics** distinguish your Hero? Appearance Mannerisms Speech Actions
   d. What 3–6 Socratic-style, open-ended **interview questions** could you ask this person?
   e. What group **ethnography theme** could you research in relation to your Hero?

<u>Ethnography Research of a Group Theme</u>

2. Include the <u>sources</u> in your background research, and write 3–6 MLA formatted notes including facts, statistics, and similar Unsung Hero's stories to compare and contrast with yours:
   a. **English Composition <u>Library Subject Guide</u>** → Databases—Circle all that apply.
      1) Academic OneFile JSTOR ProQuest Central
      2) Ethnic NewsWatch G. R. Press New York Times Newsbank: Michigan newspapers
         Circle the types of sources you research.
         Newspaper article Magazine article Journal article E-book chapter Streaming video
   b. **Websites—Google Advanced Searches**
      1) **.gov** domain
      2) **.org** domain
3. a. Unsung Hero's profile description & interview   Due: ___/___/___
   b. Ethnography EN Comp. subject guide research   Due: ___/___/___
   c. Rough draft, revised draft, and peer reviews   Due: ___/___/___
   d. MLA final edited copy & Reflection/Analysis form   Due: ___/___/___

<u>**Instruction Sheet 4.2**</u>

Unsung Hero/Ethnography Research Essay Plan and Interview Report

Form questions to Interview an Unsung Hero, someone who is underappreci-ated or unacknowledged—such as an essential worker during the COVID-19 pandemic.

Ask suitable, open ended questions that begin with "How do you …?" "Why did you …?" or "What would you …?" in a telephone, email, or in-person (distanced) interview, with permission to record or quickly writing notes afterwards.

Identify one ethnographic—*group*—characteristic of your Unsung Hero: ethnic or family background, interest, or experience shared by other people that you will research.

Try to take or obtain one or more photos of your Unsung Hero and signed or emailed permission to include it/them with your assignment.

Email your instructor or upload on the class's LMS 3–6 Socratic interview ques-tions asked of your unsung hero and their paragraph-length responses along with an MLA citation of the interview in the form:

Works Cited

Last Name, First Name. Personal [or Telephone, Email, ….] Interview.
      Date Month Year.

Instruction Sheet 4.3

Unsung Hero/Ethnography Research Essay Plan and Interview Report Score

Assessment: 6 Points Possible
(3 pts = C, 4 pts = B, 5 pts = A, 6 pts = A+)

3 pts. 3 questions with paragraph-length responses
3 sentences per paragraph response
Completed MLA citation of the interview

4 pts. 4 questions with paragraph-length responses
4 sentences per paragraph response
Completed MLA citation of the interview

5 pts. 5 questions with paragraph-length responses
5 sentences per paragraph response
Completed MLA citation of the interview

6 pts. 6 questions with paragraph-length responses
6 sentences per paragraph response
Completed MLA citation of the interview
Photo(s) of your interviewed Unsung Hero with MLA caption + signed or
email permission to include it/them in your assignment

Notes

<u>Instruction Sheet 4.4</u>

Unsung Hero/Ethnography Research Essay Rough Draft

Email your instructor or upload on the class's LMS a rough draft of your essay that includes these items:

1. **An MLA-style template** (saved as… from an earlier essay or uploaded new).
   - Running head with your last name and page numbers in top right corners.
   - Name block with your name, instructor's name, course name, and date.
   - Two-part Working Title centered in plain text.
   - Works Cited page with an MLA in-text citation matching every source.

2. **Introduction**
   - Descriptive profile of your interviewed Unsung Hero in a suitable setting.
   - Introduction to the characteristic of your interviewed Unsung Hero selected for Ethnography research.
   - Robust working Thesis statement about your research theme and hero.
   - No definition of or explanation why your Unsung Hero is one.

3. **Body Paragraphs**
   - Variety of researched facts, stories, histories of Ethnography group.
   - Follow-up relating researched information to interviewed Unsung Hero.
   - Optional photo(s) with MLA caption(s).
   - MLA in-text citations in parentheses within every paragraph.

4. **Conclusion**
   - Reworded working Thesis statement to open concluding paragraph.
   - Return to interviewed Unsung Hero to close Conclusion.

Instruction Sheet 4.5

Unsung Hero/Ethnography Research Essay Rough Draft Score

Assessment: 6 Points Possible
(3 pts = C, 4 pts = B, 5 pts = A, 6 pts = A+)

3 pts. 3 pages in all 3rd person perspective—singular for Unsung Hero and plural for Ethnography group
3 MLA Works Cited sources and in-text citations

4 pts. 4 pages in all 3rd person perspective—singular for Unsung Hero and plural for Ethnography group
4 MLA Works Cited sources and in-text citations

5 pts. 5 pages in all 3rd person perspective—singular for Unsung Hero and plural for Ethnography group
5 MLA Works Cited sources and in-text citations

6 pts. 6 pages in all 3rd person perspective—singular for Unsung Hero and plural for Ethnography group
6 MLA Works Cited sources and in-text citations
Photo(s) in "squared" text with MLA caption(s)

Notes

<u>**Instruction Sheet 4.6**</u>

Unsung Hero/Ethnography Research Essay Revised Draft

Email your instructor or upload on the class's LMS a revised draft of your essay that includes these items:

1. **An MLA-style template**
   - Running head matches font and size of essay's text.
   - Name block typed in plain text, doubled-spaced, with no additional spaces.
   - Title has two parts connected with a colon, and is centered in plain text.
   - No additional spaces between paragraphs.
   - MLA in-text citations appropriately match Works Cited sources.

2. **Introduction**
   - Compelling Opening Hook, such as a quotation from Unsung Hero interview.
   - Robust Thesis statement previewing Ethnography research theme.
   - Transitional word or phrase connecting Unsung Hero to Ethnography theme.

3. **Body Paragraphs**
   - Each paragraph addresses one topic about Ethnography group.
   - Paragraphs include abundant researched examples with facts and stories.
   - Follow-up relating researched information to interviewed Unsung Hero.
   - MLA in-text citations included in all and following every direct quotation.
   - Optional photo(s) with MLA caption(s).

4. **Conclusion**
   - Reworded Thesis reiterates Ethnography research theme.
   - Word or phrase transitions from reworded Thesis back to Unsung Hero.
   - Closing statement memorably describes, quotes, or takes leave of Hero.

<u>**Instruction Sheet 4.7**</u>

Unsung Hero/Ethnography Research Essay Revised Draft Score

<u>Assessment: 6 Points Possible</u>
(3 pts = C, 4 pts = B, 5 pts = A, 6 pts = Bonus A+)

> **3 pts.** 3 substantive changes made to essay
>
> **4 pts.** 4 substantive changes made to essay
>
> **5 pts.** 5 substantive changes made to essay
>
> **6 pts.** 6 substantive changes made to essay

Email your instructor or upload on the class's LMS a list of the 3–6 substantive changes you made to your essay for the revised draft.

A *substantive change* may involve rewriting the Introduction, rewriting the Conclusion, adding a body paragraph, rearranging the body paragraphs, adding an introductory transitional word or phrase to every paragraph, or combining and rephrasing the sentences inside a paragraph.

<u>**Notes**</u>

<u>**Instruction Sheet 4.8**</u>

Unsung Hero/Ethnography Research Essay Peer Review

Email your revised draft of the Unsung Hero/Ethnography Review Essay to your group members or upload it on the class's LMS for your classmates to access.

Send or share your replies to the questions to the <u>writer</u>, then email your instructor the names of those whose essays you peer reviewed as well as those who peer reviewed your essay.

Normally, you receive one point for <u>each essay you peer review</u> (limit 3) + the number of group members <u>who reviewed your essay</u> (limit 3) <u>to match</u> the number of sentences inside your <u>resulting changes paragraph</u> = **Peer Review Score (maximum 6)**.

- Write **Unsung Hero/Ethnography Research** with your **First & Last Name** and **Course Name & #** on the <u>email Subject line</u>.
- List the names of students who peer reviewed your essay as well as the names of those whose essays you peer reviewed.
- After reading the peer reviews of your essay, write a 3–6 sentence paragraph explaining what changes you plan to make in your essay.

1. **Y/N: Does the <u>two-part title</u> include Ethnography Group and Unsung Hero?**

2. **Y/N: Are the Introduction and the Conclusion effective?**

3. **What is an additional thing the writer could add about the Ethnography?**

4. **What was described with the most specific details, sensory portrayal, narrative illustration, or historical background?**

5. **What is something the author did that you might like to try writing yourself?**

<u>Instruction Sheet 4.9</u>

Unsung Hero/Ethnography Research Essay Peer Review Score

<u>Assessment: 6 Points Possible</u>
(3 pts = C, 4 pts = B, 5 pts = A, 6 pts = Bonus A+)

Email your instructor a list of the names of your classmates whose essays you peer reviewed as well as those who peer reviewed your essay, as well as a 3–6 sentence paragraph detailing what changes you plan to write as a result.

Normally, you receive one point for <u>each essay you peer review</u> (limit 3) + the number of group members <u>who reviewed your essay</u> (limit 3) <u>to match</u> the number of sentences inside your <u>resulting changes paragraph</u> (3–6) = **Peer Review Score (maximum 6)**.

- Write **Unsung Hero/Ethnography Research** with your **First & Last Name** and **Course Name & #** on the <u>email Subject line</u>.

- List the names of students who peer reviewed your essay as well as the names of those whose essays you peer reviewed.

- After reading the peer reviews of your essay, write a <u>3–6 sentence paragraph</u> explaining what changes you plan to make in your essay.

<u>Notes</u>

Instruction Sheet 4.10

Unsung Hero/Ethnography Research Essay Final Draft with Editing and Formatting

Follow these five final steps before turning in your essay:

1. **Check your <u>MLA formatting</u>**
   - **Running head** with your last name and page numbers in top right corners on all pages.
   - **Name block** with your name, instructor's name, course name, and date written out formally with no punctuation, like 28 May 2023, on separate lines aligned at left margin on first page only.
   - **Two-Part Title** with a colon (:) and centered, plain text, double-spaced with no additional spaces between the name block and Introduction.
   - **MLA in-text citations** with last name of author and page number or web-page's or article's title within parentheses in every body paragraph.
   - **Works Cited** page with complete MLA citations in same font style and font size as essay, double-spaced with no additional spaces, set up in hanging indentation, in alphabetical order.
   - **No bold or underlined** text, **all double-spaced** with no additional spaces between paragraphs or sources.
   - **Any photos** have an **MLA caption** beneath and text wrapped "square" around the picture, so there are no blank gaps on the page.

2. **Run a <u>spell check</u> and double-check words for usage and variety.**

3. **Run a <u>grammar check</u> to ensure clarity and lucidity.**

4. **Check every page for varied <u>sentence styles</u> and <u>paragraph organization</u>.**

5. **<u>Scan</u> to remove plagiarism and <u>turn in</u> your essay. Congratulations!**

<u>**Instruction Sheet 4.11**</u>

Unsung Hero/Ethnography Research Essay Editing and Formatting Score

<u>**Assessment: 6 Points Possible**</u>
(3 pts = C, 4 pts = B, 5 pts = A, 6 pts = Bonus A+)

Email your instructor a total from your tally of the Editing and Formatting score, giving yourself 1 point for each of the 6 items you completed.

- Write **Editing & Formatting Score** with your **First & Last Name** and **Course Name & #** on the <u>email Subject line</u>.

1. **Checked <u>MLA formatting</u>**
   - **Running head**
   - **Name block**
   - **Two-part title**
   - **MLA in-text citations**
   - **Works Cited**
   - **No bold or underlined** text, **all double-spaced**

2. **Ran a <u>spell check</u> and double-checked words for usage and variety.**

3. **Ran a <u>grammar check</u> to ensure clarity and lucidity.**

4. **Checked every page for varied <u>sentence styles</u> and <u>paragraph organization</u>.**

5. **<u>Scanned</u> to remove plagiarism and <u>turn in</u> your essay.**

6. **Optional photo(s) included with MLA caption(s) and "squared" text.**

<u>**Notes**</u>

Instruction Sheet 4.12

Unsung Hero/Ethnography Research Essay Reflection/Analysis Score

Assessment: 6 Points Possible
(3 pts = C, 4 pts = B, 5 pts = A, 6 pts = Bonus A+)

Email your instructor a 3–6 sentence paragraph answering the questions below, including the number of sentences you wrote for each paragraph: (3 pts for each paragraph = C, 4 pts/each ¶ = B, 5 pts each ¶ = A, 6 pts/ each ¶ = A+)

- Write **Essay Reflection/Analysis Score** with your **First & Last Name** and **Course Name & #** on the email Subject line.

1. **What 3–6 things that are new to you did you attempt in this essay?**

2. **What 3–6 things do you like most about your writing?**

<u>Instruction Sheet 4.13</u>

Unsung Hero/Ethnography Research Essay Final Score

<u>Assessment: 6 Points Possible</u>
(3 pts = C, 4 pts = B, 5 pts = A, 6 pts = Bonus A+)

Email your instructor a total of your scores for every step of the Unsung Hero/ Ethnography Research Essay.

- Write **Essay Reflection/Analysis Score** with your **First & Last Name** and **Course Name & #** on the <u>email Subject line</u>.

1. **Essay Plan Score: ____**

2. **Rough Draft Score: ____**

3. **Revised Draft Score: ____**

4. **Peer Review Score: ____**

5. **Editing and Formatting Score: ____**

6. **Essay Reflection/Analysis Score: ____**

= Total Score (1+2+3+4+5+6): ____ divided by 6 = Average Score: ____

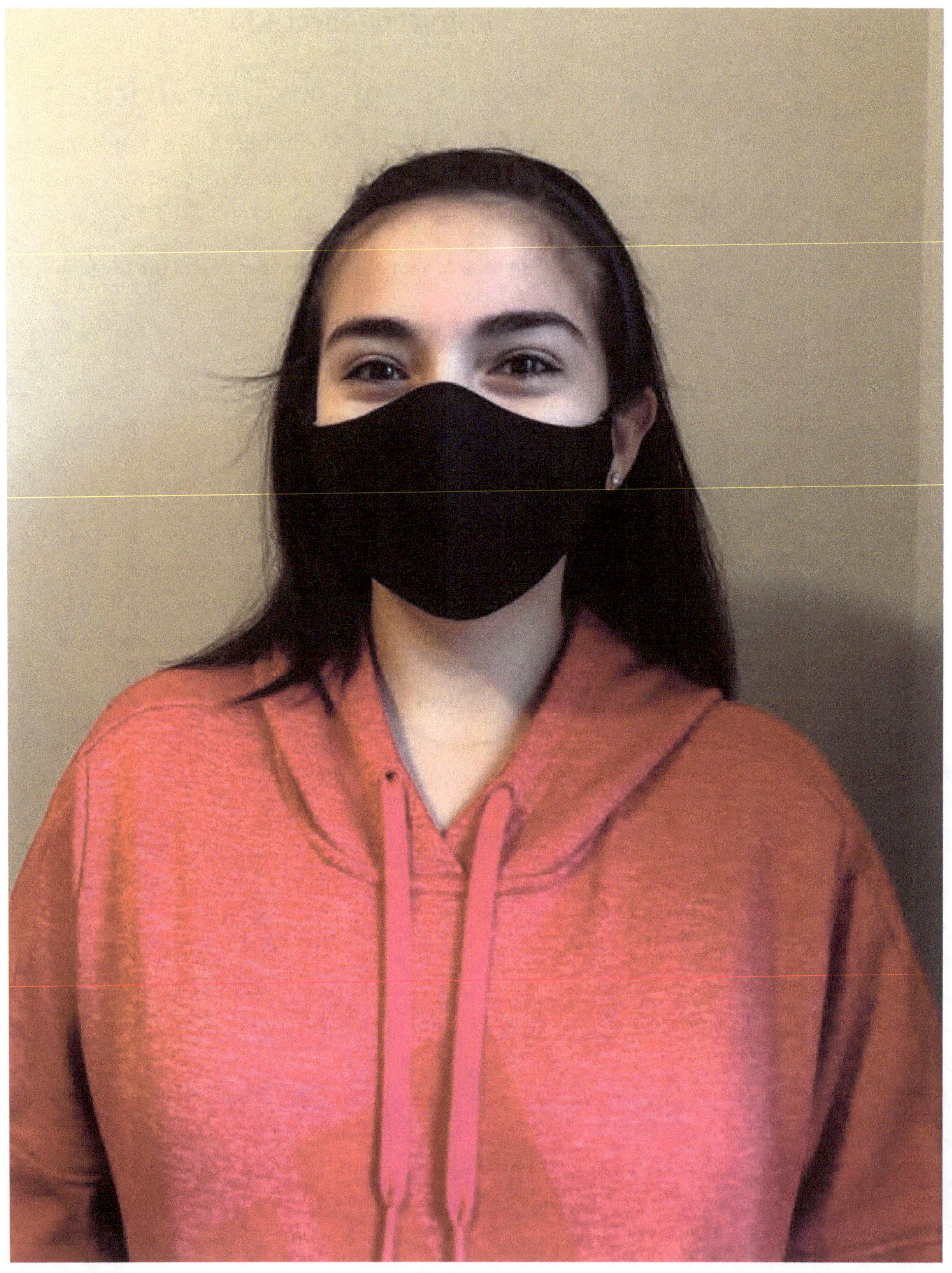

Figure 37. Holly Tovar, author of "K-------- R--------: Hispanic Businessperson." Photo Courtesy of Student.

Unsung Hero/Ethnography Research Sample Student Essay

Holly Tovar
Tom Mulder
EN 101-1051
7 December 2020

K----- R------: Hispanic Businessperson

"Our job never stops no matter the field you work in at the retirement home because they [senior citizens] need care no matter what" (R-----). K----- R----- is a 25-year-old second generation Hispanic born in California, and she is a cook at Sunset Retirement Home in Jenison, Michigan. Her typical day at work starts at 6 am by turning on the ovens, warmers, and flat grill; after that, she checks the menu to see what she needs to cook for breakfast, which consists of 140 people (R-----). After breakfast is cooked, she will begin cooking lunch for 409 residents based on what the menu for the day says. The dining halls of the retirement home are closed due to COVID-19, so for both breakfast and lunch, she'll do what they call "dish up," which is serving the food in to-go boxes that will be taken to the residents' rooms (R-----). Once lunch is finished, she begins prepping for the next day's meals so that everything is ready when she goes in to work the next day. R------ is an unsung hero because cooking for elderly people at a retirement home is something very important, and without people like her senior citizens that cannot cook their own meals would not have food to eat.

R----- received a culinary degree and has loved cooking since she was younger. Often, she would spend time with her mom in the kitchen helping her cook meals (R-----). R----- grew up seeing her mother, who owns her own hairstyling business, and has learned from that. Coming from hardworking immigrant parents, R----- has also had that as an inspiration to start her own business. During an interview she stated that her dream is to start her own business using her culinary degree received at GRCC (Fig. 1.). Hispanic unsung heroes are found everywhere nowadays; in addition, the number of Hispanic businesses is increasing since the Hispanic population in the United States is rising.

In 2013, 4.3% of the general population of West Michigan was of Mexican heritage; out of the entire Hispanic/Latino population Mexicans were about 68% of the population ("Surprises Found in Socioeconomic Characteristics"). This information relates to R----- because she comes from Mexican heritage as both of her parents were born in Mexico. R----- has been living in West Michigan for about 21 years, contributing to the data. This year, in California Hispanics will count for about 41% of the state's population, and in California alone, there are about 700,000 businesses owned by Hispanics (Martinez). From 2000 to 2004, Hispanics counted for 14% of the population in the United States ("Latinos and the Future of the U.S."). Before West Michigan, R----- and her parents lived in California; however, her parents decided to move to Michigan for better job opportunities when R----- was only four years old (R-----). This has made R----- consider moving for better job opportunities.

In 2007, California had about 2.8 million businesses that were owned by Hispanics while in 2012, the estimated number of Hispanic-owned businesses was 4.3 million, yet 88% of those businesses were only small businesses in which the owner was self-employed and had no employees ("California Hispanic Chambers of Commerce"). R----- wishes to one day start her own business where she does employ workers; however, she is planning to start her business as just herself (R-----). R----- has grown up seeing her mother work her own business where she is the only worker and has also used that as inspiration, but she hopes to have a bigger business where she can have other workers to help her out (R-----). With the increase of Hispanics in the country, there is also an increase in Hispanic-owned businesses. Many immigrants want to start their own businesses to have a stable job to provide for their families ("California Hispanic Chambers of Commerce"). For example, during an interview, R----- explained how her mom opened her own business in Kentwood, Michigan: "Seeing my mom work hard to open up her own hairstyling business to provide for my family has acted as an inspiration for me to want to start my own business" (R-----).

An example of a Hispanic-owned business in Michigan is "Lugo's Taco Street" in Huron County, Michigan owned by Andres Lugo (Creenan). Lugo moved from the state of Jalisco in Mexico to South Dakota at the age of four with his family. Then once he was older, he moved to Huron County when the owners of a Mexican restaurant contacted him to offer him a position as the manager of the restaurant. After working there for a while, Lugo realized that he no longer wanted to work at that restaurant; therefore, he decided to follow his dream of opening his own Mexican restaurant (Creenan). R-----'s parents are also from the state of Jalisco (R-----), sharing Andres Lugo's background. She also has the dream of opening her own restaurant like Lugo. This relates to R----- because they both come from Mexican heritage and have the same dream of opening a restaurant where they can tie in their culture's food customs.

Many Hispanic/Latino chefs who have opened their own businesses often start working in other restaurants or as apprentices. Some may receive formal training, and some may have a combination (Salas). An example of a chef that opened her own business is Sylvia Casares Copeland, for she is a Mexican chef and restaurant owner. She received a degree in home economics and was not satisfied with her career, so she decided that she would use her self-taught cooking skills and her education to open a restaurant. Casares now owns a restaurant in Houston, Texas, and cooks Hispanic based food. Casares stated that she began her restaurant in a very small place, but as she grew and became more known she was able to take out a loan to buy a bigger restaurant (Salas). K----- R----- is doing just that with her business, starting small as she becomes more known and gets more clients. Although Casares received no formal culinary training, R----- did, which is a way they differ.

Nevertheless, Hispanic unsung heroes with big dreams are found everywhere; and the Hispanic count in the U.S. is increasing as are Hispanic owned businesses. R----- has a dream of starting her own business; in fact, she wishes to one day own a café where she can sell traditional Hispanic food, pastries, and desserts. During her interview, she stated, "My parents always taught me that if you want something, you need to put in the time and effort and really work for it because nothing is going to fly to your doorstep." Currently, she is starting her business from home, baking cakes, cookies, and many other desserts and selling them to friends and family as well as working over 40 hours a week in her job as a cook at the Sunset Retirement Home (R-----). R----- is also taking some classes at GRCC to get a degree in business, so she can acquire more knowledge of business to reach her goal. She has recently started her own page on Facebook to help advertise her business in hopes of reaching her dream, "My final goal is to open up a café kind of like Starbucks but with homemade goods" (R-----).

Works Cited

Business Organization to Top Online Resource for Hispanic Business Information." *PR Newswire*, 18 Aug. 2008. *ProQuest*, http://grcc.idm.oclc.org/login?url=https://wwwproquest-com.grcc.idm.oclc.org/docview/448589113?accountid=11183.

"California Hispanic Chambers of Commerce Links Up with National Hispanic Business Information Clearinghouse: Agreement Connects Members of Nation's Largest Regional

Creenan, Robert. "Lugo's Provides Quick, Homemade Mexican Food." *Huron Daily Tribune, The (Bad Axe, MI)*, sec. Insider, 19 Nov. 2020. *NewsBank: America's News*, infoweb.newsbank.com/apps/news/documentview?p=NewsBank&docref=news/17EDF8FB2FEA5F68. Accessed 5 Dec. 2020.

Herring, Hubert B. "A Closer Look at the Hispanic Population (Published 2006)." *The New York Times—Breaking News, US News, World News and Videos*, 13 Aug. 2006, www.nytimes.com/2006/08/13/business/a-closer-look-at-the-hispanicpopulation.html?searchResultPosition=1.

"Los Latinos y El Futuro De EE.UU./Latinos and the Future of the U.S." *El Diario La Prensa*, 18 July 2006, p. 24. *ProQuest*, http://grcc.idm.oclc.org/login?url=https://www-proquestcom.grcc.idm.oclc.org/docview/368457048?accountid=11183.

Martinez, Mark. "California's Fast-Growing Job Creator: Latino Businesses." *La Prensa San Diego*, 22 Mar. 2013, p. 6. *ProQuest*, http://grcc.idm.oclc.org/login?url=https://wwwproquest-com.grcc.idm.oclc.org/docview/1353084102?accountid=11183.

R-----, K-----. Personal Interview. 11 Nov 2020.

Salas, Alexandra. "Hispanic Culinary Arts; Spicing Up Americana." *The Hispanic Outlook in Higher Education*, vol. 14, no. 22, 9 Aug. 2004, p. 18. *ProQuest*, http://grcc.idm.oclc.org/login?url=https://www-proquestcom.grcc.idm.oclc.org/docview/219242588?accountid=11183.

"Surprises Found in Socioeconomic Characteristics of West Michigan's Hispanic Communities." *US Fed News Service, Including US State News*, 19 Jan. 2007. *ProQuest*, http://grcc.idm.oclc.org/login?url=https://www-proquestcom.grcc.idm.oclc.org/docview/472353137?accountid=11183.

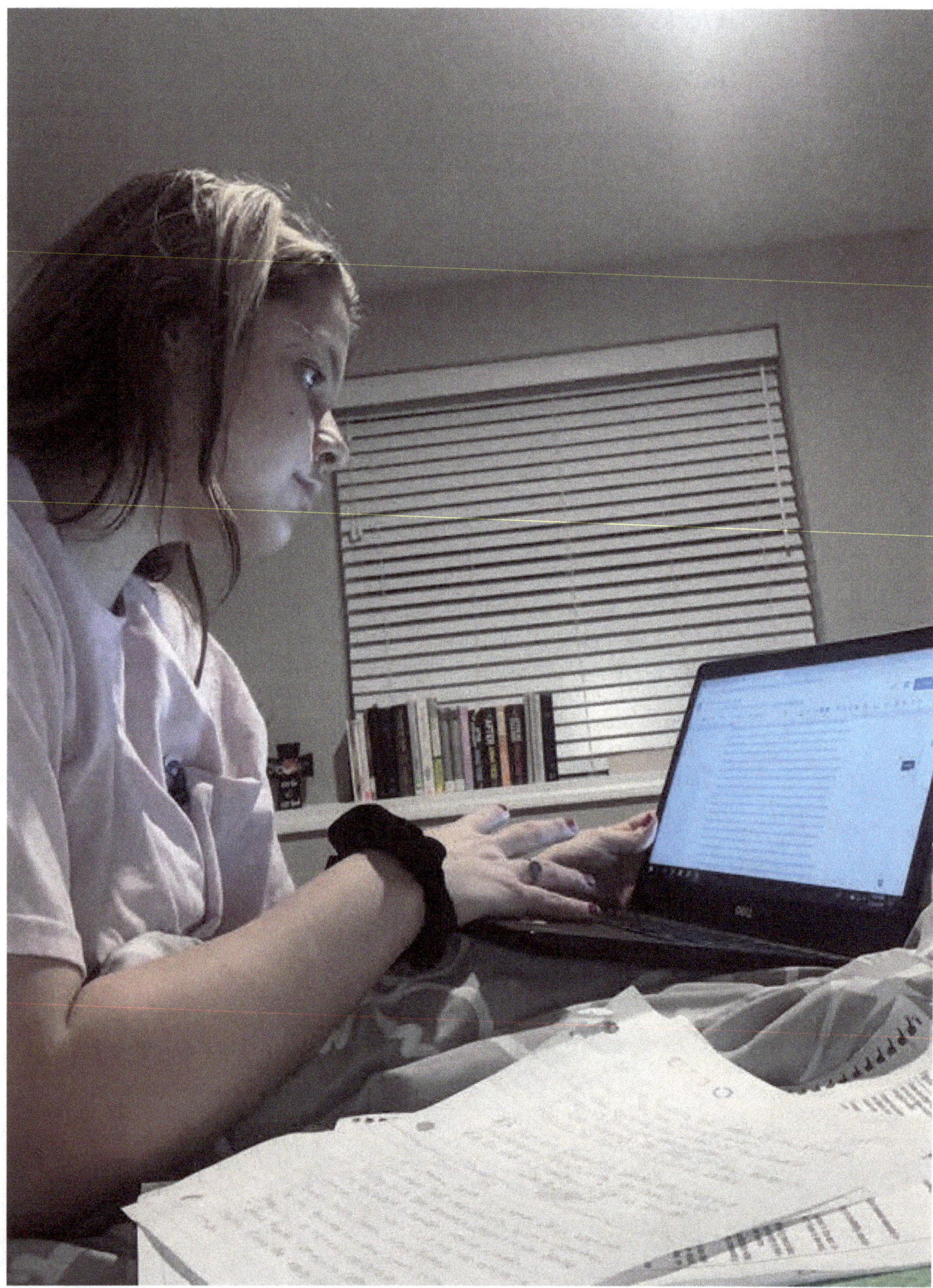

Figure 38. How could identifying, interviewing, and writing about an underappreciated individual help students more than writing an argument or a problem-solution essay? Photo Courtesy of Student.

Unsung Hero/Ethnography Research— Students' Reflections

From commentary on using databases to research, overcoming the fear of interviewing someone, and reading groupmates' ethnographies for peer reviews, this is what several had to say about the Unsung Hero/Ethnography Research Essay in their semesters' end reflections:

- The recent Ethnographic essay, the last one for the course, designed a great way to end. I was introduced to many research databases that I have been paying for as a college student while not realizing. These have assured me that there is more to research than a Google or Yahoo search.
- What made this essay a little easier than the rest was that it was a combination of multiple different techniques we had learned throughout the semester. It included MLA, research, and uploading a picture with the proper title. What did make this one a little different and difficult was interviewing people and asking them some personal questions. Being the nosy person that I am I really enjoyed that part of the research, but with COVID going on much of my interview was over the phone. This paper was a unique way for us students to take a step back and appreciate those we might not necessarily take time to appreciate. One thing that really expanded my knowledge was the fact that we had to research a story about someone else who had a similar life story in the same ethnography group. I thought this was a cool way to compare people's lives and realize that so many people are traveling the same road.
- Writing about my unsung hero, I learned a lot of life lessons when interviewing my hero as well as how to incorporate an interview with my essay. This interview took a lot of courage to do since I did not know S----- K----- too well, and I went out of my comfort zone. To become a great writer, you must go outside your comfort zone, try new things, and take risks to challenge yourself.
- By writing about my unsung hero, I was able to do a lot of research into my ethnography group, which was small business owners during COVID-19. Through this, I learned a lot of information about the business side of COVID-19, and it helped me gain a new stance on the situation. I also was able to learn about others' ethnography groups through peer reviews on my classmates' essays. For example, one of my classmates wrote about fostering, which is something that I knew very little about.

Figure 39. Drew Gommesen, author of "Workout." Photo Courtesy of Student.

Student's Story—"Workout," by Drew Gommesen

During the lockdown period, weeks felt like months, and months felt like years. I got so angry, and it seemed as if every time I went into work, I heard someone talk about how ridiculous it was to lock everyone in their houses. Since I worked at a grocery store during the lockdown, I was not worried about contracting the Coronavirus. I had been interacting with tons of people every day and never got the virus. Also, they gave us hazard pay, which was a $2.00 raise for everyone.

Many good things came from my Coronavirus experience. I started to work out in my basement very consistently. During my time, I gained a fair amount of muscle, and was super happy with my results. I also found my way outside while following lockdown rules. I began to ride my bike. I contacted one of my friends, and we started to ride together. We would bike almost 5 miles away from our houses. I had always driven my car along the paths that we went on, but riding my bike allowed me to see nature in greater detail. We rode our bikes so often a couple of miles was nothing.

Overall, I made the best of my Coronavirus experience, and I was fortunate not to have been negatively affected mentally. However, I would not ever want to live through it again. Now, it seems almost like a joke. Recently, cases have been skyrocketing, and it seems as if we are not taking it as seriously as when it was not as bad.

COVID-19 Notes: "Abundance"

Just three days after students and instructors returned from spring break, my colleges both closed on March 12 in "an abundance of caution" allowing instructors four days to translate our courses to remote, online delivery. Watching the closures-banners scroll like a Snow Day Announcement across the TV, I checked the college websites to confirm. I toggled from one to the next. Alarming red-band mastheads scrolled atop both home pages. I sent an Announcement email to my students hoping to head off their commutes to class.

Whether from TV, website, or email, almost all of my students received the news. Fortunately, since my students were grouped into quartets to peer review essays and collaborate on assignments, they had one another's contact numbers. Their hotlines must have been humming warmly that morning. Only two—one of whom came to class immediately after clocking out from the third shift—had driven in, missing all messages until arriving on campus and exiting the elevator on the fourth floor and encountering our locked classroom before its silence and emptiness registered.

Some of the students called their employers to boost work hours, taking advantage of a closure to increase income. Soon, several students were instructed by bosses to increase work hours, whether they wanted to or not. One informed me that his shipping distribution center doubled his hours to meet a burgeoning public demand for household staples that were flying off stores' shelves. "You won't believe this," he wrote, "but we can't keep the toilet paper stocked. Not sanitizers or soap, it's tp." I could imagine his silent chuckle while typing.

Another, one of at least five of my students who were employed by area hospitals, emailed me that she had been mandated to work 70 hours per week until further notice. Studying to become an RN, she received financial aid from her employer, but her scholarship required her to earn a minimum 3.00 GPA. She herself was satisfied with nothing less than an A, promptly rewriting every essay to excellence and reworking every assignment to meet her self-imposed, stellar expectations. When her kids' school closed on March 16, so students could not gather in numbers exceeding 100 out of "an abundance of caution," she added daycare and homeschooling to her days' demands. She told me she could not keep up, but she had to finish.

Now, I am no gatekeeper, guarding a golden realm of academic excellence from errant efforts of first-year writing rookies, but I strive not to be a slouch, either. *Give it the old college try* is my watchword, and I like nothing better than to see students sustaining focused reading and researching, writing and revising. When we switched from onsite workshops to remote online classes, I promised students they would not miss any content or rigor while we were apart, and I planned to pull the full package back together when we returned to the classroom again in a couple of weeks. I suggested she skip the assignments in favor of the essays, which were grade-weighted heavier. Grateful, she also sounded somewhat disappointed.

Students residing on campus were advised to move home until the end of March. Some called it a "coronavacation," and one preliminary newscast suggested that there may have been a resuscitated "down-south spring-break" celebration uptown. Rapidly afterwards, the campuses vacated. Belongings were left behind, ostensibly provisionally, as students expected to return and resume studies shortly.

My colleagues and I hunkered down on computers, rushing to reform and post course contents online, vacating campuses to custodians and cleaning services.

—Noted April 5, 2020

COVID Quote–2020

For the U.S. to find the same curve-flattening spirit it harnessed this spring, public-health and elected officials must help a tired and skeptical population dig deep and accept that it's still crucial, and possible, to make changes that will keep the virus from spreading further. Quarantine fatigue is real, and so is misinformation. As of June, 25% of American respondents to a Pew Research Center poll thought there was some truth to the conspiracy theory that powerful people planned the coronavirus pandemic. Others have latched on to the incorrect idea, promoted by Trump and others in his orbit, that COVID-19 is "just the flu." Some don't think the pandemic is real at all—some patients have called the coronavirus a hoax until the moment they stop breathing, according to reports from a South Dakota nurse that have attracted widespread news coverage.

—Ducharme

Q8.

With COVID-19's economic disruptions causing closures, unemployment, and severe demands on medical providers, first responders, caregivers, and other frontline workers, how might you help students to honor and ennoble those who too often do not receive the acknowledgement they deserve?

Figure 40. What are some ways that first-year writing classes could engender hope and healing to counter the isolation and hurt caused by COVID or other traumatic events? Photo Courtesy of Student.

Chapter 9. Cyclic

I'd imagined the weight of teaching during a pandemic and thought I had a pretty good sense of how hard it must be, but I didn't feel the weight of it in my body until I returned to the building. It made me wonder what we'd feel if we were able to slip into each other's worlds for even a morning.

—Rebekah Taussig

Will the Circle

Whenever I feel lured into thinking that each new wave of the latest COVID variant looks like the end of the pandemic disruption, when the peaks of the initial outbreak and then alpha, delta, and now omicron variants' crests have plunged down to seemingly manageable, low levels, I pull myself back down to earth, pondering the not-so-hypothetical future: "What new height might its next manifestation reach? How many would a new variant infect? Whom will it kill?"

Christmas 2020—The End, Take 1

With the COVID-19 pandemic-filled year of 2020 staggering to its end, I sat at my computer cloistered at home, glancing out the second-story study's window at the snow flaking the neighbors' houses. Whether because of the cold, the dread of illness, or the many lures hooking people online, nobody has ventured out. Shopping, studying, working, teaching, gaming—we have all become technology intermediaries, orphaned of democratic discourses, collegial camaraderies, campus and classroom communities. I feel fortunate, this advent to Christmastide: I am healthy, mostly employed, sheltered and fed, and connected via machine to family and students. Still, I feel restless, unsettled.

All remains remote. Exiting a Zoom, all of the participants' boxed faces and bust-portraits clicked away, diminished and divided, no one wholly present in the two-dimensional confines, I worry what would bridge the distances. Emails, texts, and calls to colleagues mostly go unheeded, no one granted the time or drive to take on anything past coping with the immediacy of necessities, harried by kids, students, kids who are students, spouses, parents, administrators, and the constant inner nag that keeps interrupting: *You probably are not doing it right. There must be a better, faster, safer, kinder way to communicate, teach, parent, care-give, cook, connect ....*

In more buoyant moments, I recognize that the year was an aberration of polemic politics—the culmination of four years' fulmination from an inciting president and others of his ilk, the alternately craven or cruel race-based cultural conflicts, the far-flung fringes flinging hatred via social media platforms, the misinformed fears fanning further pandemic spreads, as well as all of their attendant mental struggles, emotional isolations, retreatist defeatism, willful ignorance, and rampant rage. Rosily, I wish the doomsayers, deniers, and denigrators would stand down and make way for a long sought, calmly virtuous wisdom and grace. A safe return to campuses and classrooms may allow us educators and writers to assist with the restoration and rebuilding—hopefully, soon.

May a New Year of growth, hope, and resolve redeem the use of our technologies from baleful, deceitful, and racist divisions into renewed roles for support, enlightenment, connection. May 2020's politically and culturally deviant empowerers and enablers be defeated by a New Year's resolve to care and heal by seeking substantiated truth, restoring relational trust, and appreciating others' differences without sowing fear-mongering distrust and division.

Maybe we can vaccinate ourselves out of this COVID-19 miasma we have been bellicosely backed into. Possibly we will convince enough naysayers to mask up, distance up, and wash up to flatten the pandemic down to some manageable plateau. New leaders may yet legislate and adjudicate universities and communities, states and nations forward to safety and sense. In the meantime, let's resolve to care for ourselves, students, and colleagues, as well as all who instigate growth, hope, and encouragement to mitigate the pall of harm and assault from the far-flung effects of the pandemic. For the year 2021 and New Year's hereafter, let's pledge to grant grace generously and regularly.

Now as much as ever, our students, communities, states, and nations need teaching to discern truth, to uncover deceit, to empower, and to affirm all whose voices are unjustly suppressed, and to create a forum for diverse peoples to speak and listen candidly and caringly, so that we can act together to confront viral pandemics and other debilitating and killing ills of this world, all so blatantly on display in 2020. This is what teachers of writing do. We teach *for* these transitions, these major changes of course. We teach *in* these transitions, and we teach *through* the transitions to help one another make them make sense. We assist in making the meaning—*of* and *in* these transitions. Writing instructors are the essential workers who sew the seams of society, stitching its meaning together. Our craft and expertise remain essential, especially in such a time as the relentlessly regrettable and remarkable year of 2020.

Halloween 2021—The End, Take 2

At the end of October 2021, I am back at my desk looking out at surprisingly still verdant green leaves covering neighborhood maples, oaks, and beeches, some of which have leaves blistered with brown spots from a late summer's drought, still stubbornly refusing to change their colors and drop for the fall. Even trees this season seem unnaturally heated. Fiery and fiendishly antagonist, vaccination- and mask-averse protestors persist hell-bent to stymie efforts to control and quell the pandemic spread and proliferation: picketing healthcare providers, shouting at emergency first responders, and disparaging frontline workers—even us educators for prioritizing students' safety by insisting on masks and vaccinations. Incendiaries, bewitched with counter truths, contest their lost election and demonize the victors. My niece the nurse contends that many of them also clog her hospital's corridors. "Still, there is no satisfaction in telling them it's too late for prevention when they seek a deathbed conversion and beg for an inoculation."

With all the societal illnesses bared and exacerbated by inundating waves of COVID-19—social injustices inflicted on peoples of color, immigrants and refugees, women and LGBTQ individuals, impoverished and homeless people, incarcerated and addicted persons, the unemployed and underemployed, as well as indebted students and graduates, overburdened professors and teachers, and all the undercompensated and underappreciated adjunct and contingent instructors—we see so many injured and trace the extent of their wounds and wrongs. Because we see it, we educators should say it: we need to call it out. Already beleaguered, we teachers must rise and aim to reform a world of sickened nations and places by teaching truth, exposing falsehood, and revealing deceivers who twist fact. Rhetors, writers, and teachers, we hold and bestow the tools to truth—of language, of logic, of argument—and our expertise is exceptionally vital now.

Fortunately, hereabouts, colleges and universities are taking precautions to keep campuses safe from viral spreads, resolutely insisting on following local, state, and federal health guidelines: "This year, outbreaks have dropped precipitously and college campuses in Michigan are often safer from COVID than their surrounding communities," reports *Bridge Michigan* (French and Wilkinson). My local university requires that all students and staff be vaccinated or submit to regular testing for the virus; in addition, everyone must mask up on campus. The community college here also requires masking, but it does not require immunization or tests for the coronavirus. Instead, it offers frequent immunization clinics on campus and rewards students who have been vaccinated with a $200 stipend added to their college accounts. Stopping short of any FERPA or HIPPA violations, I share my own vaccination experiences, encourage students to get vaccinated, and support their advocacy for their peers', families', and coworkers' immunizations as they are made available; moreover, when they travel to visit relatives or resorts, I remind them to sojourn safely and return responsibly, looking out for one another and all our significant others as well.

Teaching three Middle College English 101 classes in separate high schools this semester, I am negotiating a mixed bag of responses. One of the three requires all students and staff to wear masks even though the state no longer requires it of secondary schools, but the other two do not mandate mask wearing, merely *strongly encouraging* or *recommending* it, instead. I do, however, insist that all students in my classes mask up: "Welcome to college where wearing a mask is a requirement in our classroom." And I intone at practically every class session the mantra, "Pull that mask up over your nose, please." It proves especially challenging when students who already met maskless in the same classroom earlier in the day must return for my class with faces covered. In this way, I am the gatekeeper, guardian of health and wholeness for our class and our families and all whose airwaves we and they and theirs share.

Last summer, I wore a mask simply to show solidarity with the two classes of high school students who were bused to campus for college introduction classes, all fully masked as they were not as yet eligible for injections in Michigan. My evening summer class of college students, unmasked, required no masks, nor did I wear one myself—until the final two weeks of the summer session when the college, following the local county's health edict reinstating a mask mandate in all classrooms as the Delta variant inundated Michigan and tsunamied across the northern Midwest states. Raiding neighboring classrooms for leftover facemasks from the spring semester, I gathered what few remaining disposables I could forage as no new summer stockpiles were delivered to the few classes meeting in person on that satellite campus. Students, unprepared for the suddenly renewed mask mandate, frequently arrived unmasked, reliant in those last days on my purloined supply. Apparently, others needed them, too, as my classroom mask-stash always emptied on the days between classes, requiring my pilfering from ever farther classrooms reaching distant areas of the building until I had exhausted the remaining supplies of every single room of every last floor by our final class meeting.

Still, I'm fortunate, doubly immunized and booster-shot. I continue to mask face and cleanse hands just as during fall term 2020 right through the fall of 2021. Students learn to abide by classroom safety protocols—mostly amenably albeit resignedly—and all invariably appreciate their opportunity to gather at school, especially after sitting sequestered or testily trudging through the seemingly endless succession of trials during these relentlessly regrettable and remarkable years, 2020 and 2021. We learners and teachers emerge wiser every term, despite the fiendish virus now swirling with deadly spreads and spikes. We who lead and educate others steadfastly continue carving out places of refuge, creating the safe havens for truth-seekers and truth-tellers in our classrooms, through streaming airwaves and on our campuses, continually teaching and learning alongside our students. We fervently pray that our invocations to this generation of writers and learners will lead to an upsurge of truth and justice in addition to an upswell of healing.

Epiphany 2022—The End, Take 3

Epiphany, the weeks between Christmas and Lent, are traditionally a time prescribed for self-reflection, hope, and joy. On January 6, 2022, the day of Epiphany—which commemorates the Three Kings, eastern Magi who followed the star to deliver their gifts for the Christ child and which falls exactly one year after a failed president's cry for insurrection—we see the vulnerabilities of a democracy to the despotic desires of a defeated chief executive surrounded with self-serving sycophants and unchecked by shortsighted and craven legislators. Glances backwards grant us clarity of vision at a global economic supply chain critically harmed as shortages of product—medical facemasks and other PPE, ventilators, semiconductor chips, and Christmas toys—and personnel, whether caring for ill family members or taken ill themselves; homeschooling children whose schools and childcare centers have closed; or laid off, resigned, career-changing, or retired—cause stoppages in the systems of manufacture and mobility. Peering over our shoulders, we view the shortfalls in healthcare that is dependent on full employment as screened through the micro-filters of cost-conscious insurance companies, behemoth medical corporations, and mega-pharma. We can see clearly the social and racial injustices; the macro- and microaggressions; the police, environmental, and xenophobic malpractices; as well as the reformed guidelines on masking, distancing, cleansing, and gatherings while scientists race to chase the variant alphas, deltas, omicrons, and expected other future Greek-letter variants washing across cities, states, nations, and the globe.

America, for all its medical and scientific prowess and despite the remarkable development and mass production of messenger RNA immunizations and their amazing levels of protection, has not jabbed the virus into submission. Herd immunity won't come about as a result of any adherence to community leaders' pleas or a collective concern for the community's well-being. Instead, citing rights and slights, spinning and recycling the slop of pods and pundits, many continue to plot and conspire, dig foxholes, unfurl flags, and hurl bromides. On a winter's walk, I was told resignedly by a neighbor, and have been regaled resolutely by others, who doggedly refuses the COVID vaccination, "I guess I've just made up my mind that if I catch this thing, when it's my time to go it's time to go." Recalcitrancy trumps his reason, unwilling to risk reprisals from his particular political tribe.

Epiphany brings the Winter 2022 term with additional classes on campus, in person with continued mask mandates and a modicum of distancing. One of my two schools offers about one third of its course offerings in person, three-foot distancing of single-sized tabletop desks, and filtered and cycled air circulation in all classrooms, with the remainder online or partially online. The other campus has neared its pre-COVID arrangements with a majority of its classes back in person, little effort at distancing students within classrooms, and minimal attempts at increasing air-circulation capacity in classrooms. Both have abandoned the ineffective, often too-little-too-late contact tracing efforts of past semesters. One college requires immunizations or frequent, regular testing for coronavirus while the other recommends them and offers immunization and testing clinics but stops short of requiring either. Both are now remarkably adept at rapidly relaying students' reports of infection to instructors with specific, clear instructions about confidentiality and follow-up. Neither buries us any longer with avalanches of emailed health updates and evolving policies from sundry offices and administrators. The prevalent homemade cloth masks and gaiters of last year have been mostly replaced by blue-pleated medical masks, or N-95 and KN-95 masks, now that an abundant supply of manufactured ones is readily available. The community college stations mask dispensaries inside every campus building entrance. Each college continues to provide cleansing supplies inside classrooms as well as hand sanitizers scattered among classrooms, hallways, and office areas. I admit to rarely cleaning my workstations these days, and I no longer ask students to do theirs either, now that the risks of transmission through surface contact is minimal. Or maybe I am experiencing some COVID fatigue myself.

One day in February 2022, my students and I were standing in the hallway, locked out of our 8:00 am class until the facilities department could send someone from north campus to open the door, causing a 15-minute delay to the start of class. They were short-staffed. As many as ten students were absent from my classes that day due to COVID-19 sickness, exposure, or the need to provide caregiving attention to another family member. Another four were out due to emotional or mental struggles or self-ascribed exhaustion for several reasons, all of which were exacerbated by the coronavirus's unpredictability and ubiquity. The return to in-person classes has struck some with fears of catching or carrying COVID or with anxieties about interactions they had lost the ability to negotiate while remote. In addition, some who are new to West Michigan can be especially vulnerable to seasonal affective disorder, when the cloudbanks well up above Lake Michigan, blocking the sun for days at a time; and several students in my classes this semester have been regularly taking well-being absences to cope. A few, too, were involved in auto accidents on the frequently slippery roadways. Several students commute from distant counties, many lured back to college with frontline scholarships offering free tuition to those employed in "frontline" medical and supply chain jobs, to complete their degrees. Often they arrive with harrowing winter tales of unseen black ice; blowing and drifting whiteouts caused by lake-effect snow bursts; and weather-induced slide-offs, rollovers, rear-enders, and pileups. Five times already this term a student of mine has declared, "I'm OK, but my car was totaled."

It can be a struggle for teachers to remember from class to class who missed what. "Before leaving class, please email or text your group members to make sure all keep up to speed with today's assignments. Thank-you for looking out for one another." Occasionally, I get a question in reply through a group member as intermediary via a phone communique from an absent groupmate: I remind them: "Be kind to one another. Let's help one another along, eh?" When asked how long they should wait to hear back from an absent peer, I usually suggest waiting through a weekend, then arranging with others who are experiencing the same predicament to peer review each other's essays so as to have enough responses to complete the assignment. Oftentimes with a few extra days, a missing student can get caught up with group tasks as well as individual responsibilities. Always, I accord both students full credit, regardless of how late they turn in an assignment. Seasons of sorrow and suffering warrant bountiful grace and mercy even to those for whom it seems unmerited, for who can say with what unspoken trials they may be contending?

Teaching writing, these relentlessly regrettable and remarkable years, 2020, 2021, and 2022, have required radical rethinking and revising. Composition instruction always has, of course, but in this time of pandemic, every process appears particularly pronounced. All seems a hybrid. In-person learning remains distanced, and students come and go as illnesses and obligations pull them into and out of classes. Virtual learning is up-close, sometimes too up-close, and it demands individualization, although simultaneously compartmentalized and shrunk onto an electronic monitor. Finally, maybe the worst of this viral pestilence has passed, undulating ever diminishing waves of successively lesser variants that are wider in scope but shallower in consequence—at least for those vaccinated, boosted, or already infected, and for the communities and caregivers charged with their healing.

The End(emic)

Returning from spring break at the beginning of March 2022, two years into the pandemic, students, staff, and faculty at my community college were no longer required to wear masks on campus since the Centers for Disease Control, using county statistics on the incidence of COVID and on hospital admissions and capacity, had designated West Michigan counties as "Low" or "Medium" ("COVID by County"). The state university, noting the same criteria, retained its mask mandates inside classrooms and classroom buildings, easing them in some offices and across the campus. All buses and transportation hubs continue to require mask wearing. The omicron spike in Michigan has ebbed to fewer than 1,000 new cases, the lowest number in a year, but the BA.2 variant, apparently a greater spreader but lesser debilitator, was rising hereabouts.

Comparing different models that project how the COVID-19 pandemic might end, *Time* magazine's *How COVID Ends* issue reported an admittedly optimistic possibility:

> … by the time Omicron works its way through the global population, up to half of the world will have been infected, and presumably be immune to the variant. With fewer unprotected hosts to infect, viruses generally begin to peter out …. If so, then COVID-19 would shift from a pandemic to an endemic disease, confined to pockets of outbreaks … that are manageable and containable because most people would be protected from its worst effects. (Park)

Historically, the flu pandemic that began in 1918, which resulted in 50 million fatalities worldwide and 675 thousand in the U.S, spiked again in 1919 and 1920, but essentially stopped spiking after that, sinking to endemic scale, only now and again turning up since then (Mack A1–A5). Maybe this is COVID-19's trajectory, too: three years of spiky decimations followed by endemic flatlines with some regional blips now and again. Well beyond its initial outbreak, maybe the virus will settle into the background by the fall term of 2023, and college communities, campuses, and classes can collectively breathe a sigh of relief while returning to their crowded cafeterias and corridors, maxed class sizes, and closely clustered classroom groups gathered at common tables.

The first article in my local newspaper's annual *College Guide 2022* insert recommends that students pack a "Quarantine Bag" for the Fall term with two weeks' extra clothing, foodstuffs, utensils, facemasks, toiletries, and a backup phone charger to prepare for the possibility of testing positive themselves or having a roommate contract COVID, resulting in their becoming isolated on campus ("Items to Include" 2). It appears that we have wisely resigned ourselves to live with the vestiges of pandemic, now endemic, on our campuses and in our communities. Instead of the blowing with the winds of raging reactionary political polarities and battering one another across the tribal divides as in these past couple of years, we have reconciled to rationally balancing the risks and logically responding to each new wave's threat with measured levels of defense and intervention—immunizing, masking, cleansing, testing, quarantining, and isolating proportionate to the episodic conditions on campuses and in communities—and then communicating and practicing those defenses and interventions with consistency and clarity in the classrooms.

Weighing the relative merits and perils of returning to campuses or classrooms, of remotely e-learning, and of variegated hybrids, and with enough resources to weather the latest viral ebbs and flows, we can continually educate ourselves to a COVID mindfulness and adroitly pivot to meet the needs of every locale as they arise—state-by-state, community-by-community, school-by-school, and class-by-class. May such actions, finally, break the cycles and speed the end of this virus-driven period in our history—if not eradicate the virus itself. And may we be a part of the intervening healing changes through our classes, at our colleges, and in our communities.

Winter completes an age.
—W. H. Auden

Works Cited

"A Timeline of COVID-19 Developments in 2020." *American Journal of Managed Care*, 3 July 2020, www.ajmc.com/view/a-timeline-of-covid19-developments-in-2020.

Auden, W. H. "For the Time Being: A Christmas Oratorio." *For the Time Being.* Random House, 1944.

"COVID by County." *Centers for Disease Control and Prevention*, 25 Feb. 2022, www.cdc.gov/coronavirus/2019-ncov/your-health/covid-by-county.html.

Ducharme, Jamie. "The U.S. COVID-19 Outbreak Is Worse Than It's Ever Been. Why Aren't We Acting Like It?" *Time*, 19 Nov. 2020, time.com/5913620/covid-third-wave/.

French, Ron and Mike Wilkinson. "Michigan College COVID Outbreaks Plummet as Students Vaccinate and Mask Up." *Michigan News, State, Politics, Jobs, Education | Bridge Michigan*, 12 Oct. 2021, www.bridgemi.com/talent-education/michigan-college-covid-outbreaks-plummet-students-vaccinate-and-mask?utm_source=Bridge+Michigan&utm_campaign=76b115d371--73895517.

"Items to Include in College Students' Quarantine Bags." *College Guide, MLive*, Mar. 2022. p. 2.

Mack, Julie. "Nearly Two Years In, Many Wonder: How Do Pandemics End?" *The Grand Rapids Press*, A1–A5, 21 Dec. 2021.

Park, Alice. "The Beginning of the End?" TIME. Vol. 199, Nos. 5–6, 14–21 Feb. 2022. 39–42.

Taussig, Rebekah. "Age of Uncertainty." TIME. Vol. 199, Nos. 7–8, 28 Feb./7 Mar. 2022. 70–73.

Q9.

Having traversed the peaks and valleys of this historic coronavirus pandemic, how have your thoughts and reflections about teaching writing changed? What changes would you like to see reinforced or accelerated to benefit yourself and your students?

Figure 41. What are some ways that teachers can guide a student to supplant a "go-it-alone" mindset with one of collaboration, camaraderie, and community? Photo Courtesy of Student.

Timeline of Selected Events from Christmas 2019 to Easter 2022

<u>Michigan</u>	<u>USA</u>	<u>World</u>	Academia	Related News

Dec. 31, 2019—China reports viral outbreak in Wuhan (Knowles).

--**2020**

Jan. 10, 2020—Chinese scientists post COVID-19 DNA Sequence (Knowles).

Jan. 11—First death of COVID-19 is reported in China (Knowles).

Jan. 20—First confirmed COVID-19 case in USA (Knowles).

Feb. 4—13,700 quarantined on Diamond Princess ship (Muccari et al.).

Feb. 11—The WHO names the coronavirus COVID-19 ("Listings").

Mar. 8—500 cases of COVID-19 confirmed in U.S. (Muccari et al.).

Mar. 13—Michigan is one of three states closing all schools (Muccari et al.).

Mar. 13—The COVID epicenter moves from China to Europe ("Listings").

Mar. 23—Michigan Governor Whitmer signs "Stay Home. Stay Safe" order (Muccari et al.).

Mar. 23—The U.K. begins a nationwide lockdown (Muccari et al.).

Mar. 24—New York exceeds 25,000 cases becoming the U.S. epicenter (Muccari et al.).

Mar. 24—Prime Minister Narendra Modi declares shutdown of India (Muccari et al.).

Mar. 25—Britain's parliament closed, Prince Charles tests positive (Muccari et al.).

Mar. 26—The U.S. becomes the world epicenter of COVID-19 (McNeil).

Mar. 27—U.S. cases top 100,000 (Muccari et al.).

Apr. 2—World cases exceed 1 million; more than 51,000 died (Muccari et al.).

Apr. 3—The CDC and White House recommend wearing cloth face masks (Muccari et al.).

Apr. 5—Prime Minister Boris Johnson hospitalized for COVID-19 ("Coronavirus: Boris Johnson").

Apr. 4—Michigan's first COVID-19 wave crests at 1670 new cases; 585 total deaths ("Have We Flattened the Curve?")

Apr. 6—U.S. deaths pass 10,000 (Muccari et al.).

Apr. 7—The U.K. reports more than 55,000 COVID-19 cases and 6,000 deaths (Muccari et al.)

Apr. 9—New York reports 151,598 COVID cases, more than any nation besides the U.S. (Muccari et al.)

Apr. 10—World deaths pass 100,000 (Muccari et al.).

<u>Michigan</u>	<u>USA</u>	<u>World</u>	Academia	Related News

Apr. 15—Over 3,000 protest the Michigan governor's lockdown by clogging capital's roads (Smith, Allan).

Apr. 15—President Trump stops U.S. funding of the World Health Organization (Clark).

Apr. 16—Seventeen COVID-19 fatalities discovered hidden in New Jersey nursing home (Muccari et al.).

Apr. 17—Trump calls on anti-lockdown protestors to "Liberate Michigan" and two other states (Fritze and Jackson).

Apr. 19—More than 100,000 Europeans died of COVID-19 (Suliman).

Apr. 30—Armed militia members threaten Michigan legislators in state capitol (Oosting).

May 1—New York Governor Andrew Cuomo keeps state schools closed through school year (Burke).

May 3—Canada's worst week of deaths: 1,295 ("COVID-19 Map").

May 15—President Trump introduces "Operation Warp Speed" to develop a COVID vaccine (Muccari et al.).

May 19—India's cases exceed 100,000 with over 3,000 deaths (Muccari et al.).

May 20—In Michigan, hundreds protest the lockdown with a free haircut outside capitol (Gregorian).

May 20—More than 5 million worldwide sickened by COVID-19 (Muccari et al.).

May 25—George Floyd's murder by a Minneapolis policeman spurs nationwide protests (Edwards).

May 27—U.S. passes 100,000 deaths (Muccari et al.).

June 2—Public Health English reports blacks and Asian ethnic minorities nearly twice as likely to die of COVID-19 as whites (Muccari et al.).

June 5—Governor Whitmer eases lockdown restrictions in Michigan (Muccari et al.).

June 8—Imperial College London reports lockdowns averted 3 million European deaths of COVID (Muccari et al.).

Aug. 8—The U.S. passes 5 million COVID cases (Muccari et al.).

Aug. 11—The world surpasses 20 million cases (Muccari et al.).

Fall, 2020—US college/university enrollments drop over 3% from 2019; faculty fall almost 4% (Weissman. "New Federal Data Confirm Enrollment Declines").

Fall 2020—Low-income college enrollees in Michigan plunge nearly 10% from 2019 (French).

Sept. 29—More than 40 million have contracted COVID worldwide (Muccari et al.).

Oct. 1—44% of 3000 colleges mostly or all online; 27% in-person; 21% hybrid (Davidson College).

Oct. 2—President Trump hospitalized for COVID-19 (Gringlas and Sprunt).

<u>Michigan</u>   <u>USA</u>   <u>World</u>   Academia   Related News

Oct. 8—FBI uncovers militia plot to kidnap Michigan Governor Gretchen Whitmer (Burns).

Oct. 19—COVID tops 40 million cases and 1.1 million deaths ("A Timeline").

> *As the year ended, the United States surpassed 20 million infections from SARS-CoV-2, and more than 346,000 deaths. Globally, cases rose to 83,832,334 and 1,824,590 deaths ….*
>
> *Cases in some parts of the country began surging again in the weeks after Thanksgiving; the same effect may be seen in January as health officials are gravely concerned about the extent of travel for the Christmas and winter holidays. The Transportation Security Administration said it screened the most passengers (1.3 million) on the Sunday before Christmas, the most since March 15 ….*
>
> **—"A Timeline of COVID-19 Developments in 2020"**

Nov. 20—The CDC warns against foreign travel as US tops 11 million cases ("A Timeline").

Nov. 30—Michigan's second COVID-19 wave crests at 8344 new cases; 9,564 total deaths ("Have We Flattened…?")

Dec. 8—A British 90-year-old receives the first COVID inoculation (Smith, Alexander).

Dec. 9—Canada approves Pfizer/BioNTech vaccine for emergency use (Gillies).

Dec. 11—Pfizer/BioNTech releases COVID-19 two-dose vaccine for emergency use in the US ("Pfizer and BioNTech").

Dec. 18—Moderna releases its COVID-19 two-dose vaccine for emergency use in US.

Dec. 30—The U.K. approves Oxford/AstraZeneca vaccine (Gallagher and Triggle).

--**2021**

Jan. 3—India OK's Oxford/AstraZeneca, Bharat Biotech vaccines ("Coronavirus: India").

Jan. 6—Trump incites insurrection attack on U.S. Capitol (Wise).

Jan. 10—US's worst week of new cases: 1,734,000 ("COVID-19 Map").

Jan. 10—UK's worst week of new cases: 418,669 ("COVID-19 Map").

Jan. 11—Michigan community college enrollment down 10% from 2020; national enrollment down 9.4% (Dodge B1).

Jan. 17—US's worst week of deaths: 23,752 ("COVID-19 Map").

Jan. 24—Worst week worldwide with 100,993 deaths of COVID-19 ("COVID-19 Map").

<u>Michigan</u>	<u>USA</u>	<u>World</u>	Academia	Related News

Jan. 24—UK's worst week of deaths: 8,700 (COVID-19 Map").

Feb. 22—U.S. COVID-19 deaths reach 500,000 (Woodruff and Brangham).

Mar. 21—Nearly 90% of U.S. Blacks and Latinos experienced hardship on the pandemic misery index measurement (Thomas).

Apr. 10—Michigan's 3rd wave of COVID-19 crests at 7,873 new cases; 17,563 total deaths ("Have We Flattened…?")

COVID Quote—2021

One out of every 100 Michigan residents was hospitalized with COVID-19 in 2021.

—Julie Mack, *The Grand Rapids Press*

Apr. 18—Canada's worst week of new cases: 60,965 ("COVID-19 Map").

May 9—India's worst week of new cases: 2,737,000 ("COVID-19 Map").

May 23—India's worst week of deaths: 29, 330 ("COVID-19 Map").

Aug. 9—The Russell Group, representing 24 UK universities, announces return to in-person classes with blended learning in autumn (Russell Group).

Apr. 25—Worst week Worldwide at 5,785,000 new COVID cases ("COVID-19 Map").

Fall, 2021—Beginning College Survey of Student Engagement reports 53% claim increased "mental and emotional exhaustion" (Carrasco).

Sept. 14—1 in 500 Americans has died of COVID-19 (*NBC*).

Sept. 21—Over 1,000 US colleges mandate vaccines of students, staff, or both in fall (Thomason and O'Leary).

Sept. 21—First Lady Jill Biden returns to teaching both in-person and hybrid writing classes at Northern Virginia Community College (Weissman. "Community College Leaders Celebrate First Lady's Return").

Sept. 22—Michigan passes 1 million COVID cases (Wilkinson).

Oct. 9—Michigan's fourth wave crests at 4230 new cases; 22,702 total deaths ("Have We Flattened the Curve?").

Oct. 20—At-risk elderly, those with underlying conditions, and essential workers that include educators qualify for a booster shot ("Coronavirus (COVID-19) Update").

Michigan   USA   World   Academia   Related News

> # COVID Quote—2021
>
> *Michigan is now the epicenter of COVID-19 pandemic again.*
>
> —**Julia Dragos**, *WZZM-13*

Nov. 30—Michigan reports the highest week of new cases per day, 7,654 on Nov. 19, highest per capita infections in the U.S., and highest number of COVID hospitalizations in the nation (Salisbury and Hicks A1–A3).

---2022

Jan 13—The National Student Clearinghouse reports a greater than 5% drop in U.S. college student enrollment since Fall of 2019, and incoming first year students have declined more than 9% ("Current Term").

Jan. 29—Canadian truckers begin a two-week blockade of the capitol, Ottawa, that later expands to the Ambassador Bridge and several other Canada-U.S. crossings to protest required immunizations for cross-border truckers (Levinson-King).

Feb. 8—Michigan exceeds 2 million cases of COVID since the virus arrived in 2020 (Salisbury B1).

Feb. 20—Queen Elizabeth contracts COVID-19 ("Queen Elizabeth").

Mar. 8—The World Health Organization reports more than 6 million have died of COVID-19 worldwide ("Coronavirus Disease").

Mar. 18—Masks no longer required in most Michigan colleges and universities (Salisbury and Levin A1, A7).

Apr. 4—Patrick Lyoya, an immigrant from Congo, is shot dead by a Grand Rapids Police Officer (Huffman and Roelofs).

> # COVID Quote—2022
>
> *On Easter Monday, April 18, 2022, the World Health Organization reported 507,354,499 confirmed cases of COVID-19 worldwide, and 6,222,186 deaths from COVID-19. In the USA, 983,914 died of 80,178,549 COVID cases; India had 30,338,697 cases with 522,193 deaths; and the United Kingdom experienced 21,959,933 cases and 174,170 deaths.*
>
> —*WHO Coronavirus (COVID-19) Dashboard*

Works Cited

"A Timeline of COVID-19 Developments in 2020." *American Journal of Managed Care*, 20 November 2020, www.ajmc.com/view/a-timeline-of-covid19-developments-in-2020.

Burke, Minyvonne. "New York State Will Keep Schools, Colleges Closed for Rest of Academic Year." *NBC News*, 1 May 2020, www.nbcnews.com/news/us-news/new-york-state-will-keep-schools-colleges-closed-rest-academic-n1197791.

Burns, Gus. "Plot to Kidnap Michigan Gov. Gretchen Whitmer, Kill 'tyrants,' Revealed in Court Filing." *Mlive*, 9 Oct. 2020, www.mlive.com/public-interest/2020/10/plot-to-kidnap-michigan-gov-gretchen-whitmer-kill-tyrants-revealed-in-court-filing.html.

Carrasco, Maria. "Most Incoming Freshmen Are Mentally Exhausted." *Inside Higher Ed | Higher Education News, Career Advice, Jobs*, 17 Aug. 2021, www.insidehighered.com/news/2021/08/17/most-incoming-freshmen-are-mentally-exhausted.

Clark, Dartunorro. "Trump Halts Funding for the World Health Organization." *NBC News*, 15 Apr. 2020, www.nbcnews.com/politics/white-house/trump-says-he-halting-funding-world-health-organization-n1183941.

"Coronavirus: Boris Johnson Moved to Intensive Care as Symptoms Worsen." *BBC News*, 7 Apr. 2020, www.bbc.com/news/uk-52192604.

"Coronavirus (COVID-19) Update: FDA Takes Additional Actions on the Use of a Booster Dose for COVID-19 Vaccines." *U.S. Food and Drug Administration*, 20 Oct. 2021, www.fda.gov/news-events/press-announcements/coronavirus-covid-19-update-fda-takes-additional-actions-use-booster-dose-covid-19-vaccines.

"Coronavirus Disease (COVID-19)—World Health Organization." *WHO | World Health Organization*, www.who.int/emergencies/diseases/novel-coronavirus-2019.

"Coronavirus: India Approves Vaccines from Bharat Biotech and Oxford/AstraZeneca." *BBC News*, 3 Jan. 2021, www.bbc.com/news/world-asia-india-55520658.

"COVID-19 Map." *Johns Hopkins Coronavirus Resource Center*, coronavirus.jhu.edu/map.html.

"Current Term Enrollment Estimates." *National Student Clearinghouse Research Center*, 10 June 2021, nscresearchcenter.org/current-term-enrollment-estimates/.

Davidson College's College Crisis Initiative. "Here's Our List of Colleges' Reopening Models." *The Chronicle of Higher Education*, 1 Oct. 2020, www.chronicle.com/article/heres-a-list-of-colleges-plans-for-reopening-in-the-fall/.

Dodge, Samuel. "Community Colleges Hit Hard by Enrollment Declines." *The Grand Rapids Press*, 16 Nov. 2021, p. B1.

Dragos, Julia, News Anchor. *WZZM 13 News*. ABC-TV, 18 Nov. 2021.

Edwards, Erika. "May 31 George Floyd Protests and Nationwide Unrest." *NBC News*, 1 June 2020, www.nbcnews.com/news/us-news/live-blog/nationwide-protests-over-george-floyd-s-death-live-updates-n1220126.

French, Ron. "Even As COVID Wanes, Fewer Low-income Students Enroll in Michigan Colleges." *Michigan News, State, Politics, Jobs, Education | Bridge Michigan*, 19 July 2021, www.bridgemi.com/talent-education/even-covid-wanes-fewer-low-income-students-enroll-michigan-colleges. Accessed 23 Aug. 2021.

Fritze, John and David Jackson. "Trump Calls to 'liberate' States Where Protesters Have Demanded Easing Coronavirus Lockdowns." *USA TODAY*, 17 Apr. 2020, www.usatoday.com/story/news/politics/2020/04/17/coronavirus-trump-calls-liberate-virginia-michigan-minnesota/5152120002/.

Gallagher, James and Nick Triggle. "COVID-19: Oxford-AstraZeneca Vaccine Approved for Use in UK." *BBC News*, 30 Dec. 2020, www.bbc.com/news/health-55280671.

Gillies, Rob. "Canada Health Regulator Approves Pfizer's COVID-19 Vaccine." *AP NEWS*, 9 Dec. 2020, apnews.com/article/Canada-coronavirus-pandemic-9cde42d f20e80c50752768b6696d45d5.

Gregorian, Dareh. "Anti-lockdown Demonstrators Trade Guns for Scissors at Michigan 'haircut' Protest." *NBC News*, 20 May 2020, www.nbcnews.com/politics/ politics-news/anti-lockdown-demonstrators-trade-guns-scissors-michigan-haircut-protest-n1211366.

Gringlas, Sam and Barbara Sprunt. "Timeline: What We Know of President Trump's COVID-19 Diagnosis, Treatment." *NPR.org*, 5 Oct. 2020, www.npr. org/sections/latest-updates-trump-covid-19-results/2020/10/03/919898777/ timeline-what-we-know-of-president-trumps-covid-19-diagnosis.

Huffman, Bryce and Ted Roelofs. "Patrick Lyoya's Parents: Our Hearts Are Broken. Grand Rapids Mourns as Well." *Michigan News, State, Politics, Jobs, Education | Bridge Michigan*, 14 Apr. 2022, www.bridgemi.com/michigan-government/ patrick-lyoyas-parents-our-hearts-are-broken-grand-rapids-mourns-well?utm_ source=Bridge+Michigan&utm_campaign=183ed14383-Bridge+Newsletter+04 %2F14%2F2022_COPY_01&utm_medium=email&utm_term=0_c64a28dd5a-183ed14383-73895517.

Knowles, David. "A Timeline of Trump's Missed Opportunities on Coronavirus." *Yahoo*, 8 Apr. 2020, www.yahoo.com/news/a-timeline-of-trumps-missed-opportunities-on-coronavirus-193202249.html?.tsrc=jtc_news_index.

Levinson-King, Robin. "Trucker Protests: Ontario Calls State of Emergency." *BBC News*, 11 Feb. 2022, www.bbc.com/news/world-us-canada-60352980.

"Listings of WHO's Response to COVID-19." *WHO: World Health Organization*, 29 June 2020, www.who.int/news/item/29-06-2020-covidtimeline.

Mack, Julie. "Virus Has Put 1 of Every 100 Michiganders in the Hospital." *The Grand Rapids Press*, 10 Feb. 2022, pp. A1–A3.

McNeil Jr., Donald G. "The U.S. Now Leads the World in Confirmed Coronavirus Cases." *The New York Times—Breaking News, US News, World News and Videos*, 28 May 2020, www.nytimes.com/2020/03/26/health/usa-coronavirus-cases.html.

Muccari, Robin, Denise Chow and Joe Murphy. "Coronavirus Timeline: Tracking the Critical Moments of Covid-19." *NBC News*, 1 Jan. 2021.

NBC Nightly News with Lester Holt. 15 Sept. 2021, NBC Universal News Group.

Oosting, Jonathan. "Maybe It's Time to Rethink Allowing Guns in Michigan Capitol, Officials Say." *Michigan News, State, Politics, Jobs, Education | Bridge Michigan*, 1 May 2020, www.bridgemi.com/michigan-government/ maybe-its-time-rethink-allowing-guns-michigan-capitol-officials-say.

"Pfizer and BioNTech Celebrate Historic First Authorization in the U.S. of Vaccine to Prevent COVID-19." *Pfizer: One of the World's Premier Biopharmaceutical Companies*, 11 Dec. 2020, www.pfizer.com/news/press-release/press-release-detail/ pfizer-and-biontech-celebrate-historic-first-authorization.

"Queen Elizabeth Tests Positive for COVID." *BBC*, 20 Feb. 2022, www.bbc.co.uk/ programmes/p0bq6spw.

"Russell Group Comment on Plans for Autumn Term Teaching." *The Russell Group*, 9 Aug. 2021, russellgroup.ac.uk/news/russell-group-comment-on-plans-for-autumn-term-teaching/.

Salisbury, Danielle. "State Surpasses 2 Million Cases Since Start of the Pandemic." *The Grand Rapids Press*, 8 Feb. 2022, p. B1.

Salisbury, Danielle and Justin P. Hicks. "What Made Michigan the Worst in Country Is Unclear." *The Grand Rapids Press*, 30 Nov. 2021, pp. A1–A3.

Salisbury, Danielle and Scott Levin. "Most Michiganders Can Dump the Masks." *The Grand Rapids Press*, 1 Mar. 2022, pp. A1–A7.

Smith, Alexander. "Britain Becomes First to Roll out Clinically Approved Vaccine." *NBC News*, 8 Dec. 2020, www.nbcnews.com/news/world/britain-becomes-first-roll-out-clinically-approved-biontech-pfizer-vaccine-n1250330.

Smith, Allan. "'Lock Her Up!': Anti-Whitmer Coronavirus Lockdown Protestors Swarm Michigan Capitol." *NBC News*, 16 Apr. 2020, www.nbcnews.com/politics/politics-news/lock-her-anti-whitmer-coronavirus-lockdown-protestors-swarm-michigan-capitol-n1184426.

Suliman, Adela. "Europe Reaches Grim Milestone, Surpasses 100,000 Coronavirus Deaths." *NBC News*, 19 Apr. 2020, www.nbcnews.com/news/world/europe-reaches-grim-milestone-surpassing-100-000-coronavirus-deaths-n1187376.

Thomas, Kyla. "Pandemic Misery Index Reveals Far-reaching Impact of COVID-19 on American Lives, Especially on Blacks and Latinos." *The Conversation*, 1 June 2021, www.theconversation.com/pandemic-misery-index-reveals-far-reaching-impact-of-covid-19-on-american-lives-especially-on-blacks-and-latinos-159902.

Thomason, Andy and Brian O'Leary. "Here's a List of Colleges That Require Students or Employees to Be Vaccinated Against COVID-19." *The Chronicle of Higher Education*, 21 Sept. 2021, www.chronicle.com/blogs/live-coronavirus-updates/heres-a-list-of-colleges-that-will-require-students-to-be-vaccinated-against-covid-19.

Weissman, Sara. "New Federal Data Confirm Enrollment Declines." *Inside Higher Ed | Higher Education News, Career Advice, Jobs*, 15 Sept. 2021, www.insidehighered.com/news/2021/09/15/new-federal-data-confirm-enrollment-declines.

Weissman, Sara. "Community College Leaders Celebrate First Lady's Return." *Inside Higher Ed | Higher Education News, Career Advice, Jobs*, 21 Sept. 2021, www.insidehighered.com/news/2021/09/21/community-college-leaders-celebrate-first-ladys-return?utm_source=Inside+Higher+Ed.

WHO Coronavirus (COVID-19) Dashboard, World Health Organization, 18 Apr. 2022, covid19.who.int/.

Wilkinson, Mike. "Coronavirus Tracker | CDC Panel Recommends Pfizer Booster; Total Cases Surpass 1 Million in Michigan | Bridge Michigan." *Michigan News, State, Politics, Jobs, Education | Bridge Michigan*, 22 Sept. 2021, www.bridgemi.com/michigan-health-watch/coronavirus-tracker-what-michigan-needs-know-now.

Wise, Alana. "Trump Condemns Capitol Hill Violence, Ignores His Role in Inciting the Mob." *NPR.org*, 7 Jan. 2021, www.npr.org/sections/insurrection-at-the-capitol/2021/01/07/954587997/white-house-condemns-violence-on-capitol-hill-without-addressing-trumps-role.

Woodruff, Judy and William Brangham. "February 22, 2021—PBS NewsHour Full Episode." *PBS NewsHour*, 22 Feb. 2021, www.pbs.org/newshour/show/february-22-2021-pbs-newshour-full-episode.

Figure 42. In a time fraught with insecurity and endemic, what can we teachers of composition do to enable, encourage, and enlighten our students? Photo Courtesy of Student.

References

"A Timeline of COVID-19 Developments in 2020." *American Journal of Managed Care*, 3 July 2020, www.ajmc.com/view/a-timeline-of-covid19-developments-in-2020.

"A Timeline of COVID-19 Developments in 2020." *American Journal of Managed Care*, 20 November 2020, www.ajmc.com/view/a-timeline-of-covid19-developments-in-2020.

"About Black Lives Matter." *Black Lives Matter Global Network Foundation*, https://blacklivesmatter.com/about/.

Anderson, Greta. "Did Students in Campus Housing Learn Better?" *Inside Higher Ed: Higher Education News*, 3 Dec. 2020, www.insidehighered.com/news/2020/12/03/survey-students-campus-housing-had-better-social-and-learning-outcomes?

Auden, W. H. "For the Time Being: A Christmas Oratorio." *For the Time Being.* Random House, 1944.

Barlett, Peggy F. and Geoffrey W. Chase. "Introduction," pp. 1–26. *Sustainability on Campus: Stories and Strategies for Change*, edited by Peggy F. Barlett and Geoffrey W. Chase, MIT Press, 2004.

Barlett, Peggy F. and Geoffrey W. Chase, editors. *Sustainability on Campus: Stories and Strategies for Change*. MIT Press, 2004.

Beggin, Riley and Mike Wilkinson. "When Will Gov. Whitmer Reopen Michigan? It's Complicated. And a Bit Vague." *Bridge Magazine*, 17 May 2020, www.bridgemi.com/michigan-government/when-will-gov-whitmer-reopen-michigan-its-complicated-and-bit-vague.

Burke, Minyvonne. "New York State Will Keep Schools, Colleges Closed for Rest of Academic Year." *NBC News*, 1 May 2020, www.nbcnews.com/news/us-news/new-york-state-will-keep-schools-colleges-closed-rest-academic-n1197791.

Burns, Gus. "Plot to Kidnap Michigan Gov. Gretchen Whitmer, Kill 'tyrants,' Revealed in Court Filing." *Mlive*, 9 Oct. 2020, www.mlive.com/public-interest/2020/10/plot-to-kidnap-michigan-gov-gretchen-whitmer-kill-tyrants-revealed-in-court-filing.html.

Carlo, Rosanne. *Transforming Ethos: Place and the Material in Rhetoric and Writing.* Utah State University Press, 2020, p. 138.

Carrasco, Maria. "Most Incoming Freshmen Are Mentally Exhausted." *Inside Higher Ed | Higher Education News, Career Advice, Jobs*, 17 Aug. 2021, www.insidehighered.com/news/2021/08/17/most-incoming-freshmen-are-mentally-exhausted.

Clark, Dartunorro. "Trump Halts Funding for the World Health Organization." *NBC News*, 15 Apr. 2020, www.nbcnews.com/politics/white-house/trump-says-he-halting-funding-world-health-organization-n1183941.

Clifford, James and George E. Marcus. *Writing Culture: The Poetics and Politics of Ethnography*, University of California Press, 1986.

"Coronavirus: Boris Johnson Moved to Intensive Care as Symptoms Worsen." *BBC News*, 7 Apr. 2020, www.bbc.com/news/uk-52192604.

"Coronavirus (COVID-19) Update: FDA Takes Additional Actions on the Use of a Booster Dose for COVID-19 Vaccines." *U.S. Food and Drug Administration*, 20 Oct. 2021, www.fda.gov/news-events/press-announcements/coronavirus-covid-19-update-fda-takes-additional-actions-use-booster-dose-covid-19-vaccines.

"Coronavirus Disease (COVID-19)—World Health Organization." *WHO | World Health Organization*, www.who.int/emergencies/diseases/novel-coronavirus-2019.

"Coronavirus Disease 2019 (COVID-19) Test for Current Infection—Viral Test." *Centers for Disease Control and Prevention*, 2 Sept. 2020, www.cdc.gov/coronavirus/2019-ncov/testing/diagnostic-testing.html.

"Coronavirus: India Approves Vaccines from Bharat Biotech and Oxford/AstraZeneca." *BBC News*, 3 Jan. 2021, www.bbc.com/news/world-asia-india-55520658.

Couture, Barbara and Wojahn, Patti. *Crossing Borders, Drawing Boundaries: The Rhetoric of Lines across America*, Utah State University Press, 2015, p. 24.

"COVID by County." *Centers for Disease Control and Prevention*, 25 Feb. 2022, www.cdc.gov/coronavirus/2019-ncov/your-health/covid-by-county.html.

"COVID-19 Map." *Johns Hopkins Coronavirus Resource Center*, coronavirus.jhu.edu/map.html.

Crick, Nathan. "Rhetoric and Dewey's Experimental Pedagogy." In *Trained Capacities: John Dewey, Rhetoric, and Democratic Practice*, Edited by Brian Jackson and Gregory Clark, University of South Carolina Press, 2014, p. 186.

"Current Term Enrollment Estimates." *National Student Clearinghouse Research Center*, 10 June 2021, nscresearchcenter.org/current-term-enrollment-estimates/.

Davidson College's College Crisis Initiative. "Here's Our List of Colleges' Reopening Models." *The Chronicle of Higher Education*, 1 Oct. 2020, www.chronicle.com/article/heres-a-list-of-colleges-plans-for-reopening-in-the-fall/.

Davidson, Cathy N. *The New Education: How to Revolutionize the University to Prepare Students for a World in Flux*, Basic Books, 2017.

DeLind, Laura B. and Terry Link. "Place as the Nexus of a Sustainable Future: A Course for All of Us," pp. 121–137. *Sustainability on Campus: Stories and Strategies for Change*, edited by Peggy F. Barlett and Geoffrey W. Chase, MIT Press, 2004.

Dennis, Barbara. *Walking with Strangers: Critical Ethnography and Educational Promise.* Critical Qualitative Research, Vol. 29, edited by Shirley R. Steinberg, Peter Lang, 2020.

Denworth, Lydia. "Why Zoom Fatigue is Real and What You Can Do About It." *Psychology Today*, 31 July 2020, www.psychologytoday.com/us/blog/brain-waves/202007/why-zoom-fatigue-is-real-and-what-you-can-do-about-it.

Dodge, Samuel. "Community Colleges Hit Hard by Enrollment Declines." *The Grand Rapids Press*, 16 Nov. 2021, p. B1.

Dragos, Julia, News Anchor. *WZZM 13 News*. ABC-TV, 18 Nov. 2021.

Ducharme, Jamie. "The U.S. COVID-19 Outbreak Is Worse Than It's Ever Been. Why Aren't We Acting Like It?" *Time*, 19 Nov. 2020, time.com/5913620/covid-third-wave/.

Editorial Board. "Opinion—America's Protests Won't Stop Until Police Brutality Does." *New York Times*, 1 June 2020, https://www.nytimes.com/2020/06/01/opinion/george-floyd-protest-police.html.

Edwards, Erika. "May 31 George Floyd Protests and Nationwide Unrest." *NBC News*, 1 June 2020, www.nbcnews.com/news/us-news/live-blog/nationwide-protests-over-george-floyd-s-death-live-updates-n1220126.

"Employment Projections: 2019–2029 Summary." *U.S. Bureau of Labor Statistics*, 1 Sept. 2020, www.bls.gov/news.release/ecopro.nr0.htm.

Farooqui, Salmaan. "Online Classes Put Post-Secondary Students in Hard Place: Many Consider Deferring Courses as Institutions Limit in-Person Learning." *Toronto

Star, 18 Jan. 2021. *Press Reader Digital Newspaper.* Available by subscription at https://www.pressreader.com/.

Feiler, Bruce. *Life Is in the Transitions: Mastering Change at Any Age.* New York: Penguin, 2020.

French, Ron and Mike Wilkinson. "Michigan College COVID Outbreaks Plummet as Students Vaccinate and Mask Up." *Michigan News, State, Politics, Jobs, Education | Bridge Michigan*, 12 Oct. 2021, www.bridgemi.com/talent-education/ michigan-college-covid-outbreaks-plummet-students-vaccinate-and-mask?utm_ source=Bridge+Michigan&utm_campaign=76b115d371--73895517.

French, Ron. "Even As COVID Wanes, Fewer Low-income Students Enroll in Michigan Colleges." *Michigan News, State, Politics, Jobs, Education | Bridge Michigan*, 19 July 2021, www.bridgemi.com/talent-education/even-covid-wanes-fewer-low-income-students-enroll-michigan-colleges. Accessed 23 Aug. 2021.

Fritze, John and David Jackson. "Trump Calls to 'liberate' States Where Protesters Have Demanded Easing Coronavirus Lockdowns." *USA TODAY*, 17 Apr. 2020, www.usatoday.com/story/news/politics/2020/04/17/ coronavirus-trump-calls-liberate-virginia-michigan-minnesota/5152120002/.

Gallagher, James and Nick Triggle. "COVID-19: Oxford-AstraZeneca Vaccine Approved for Use in UK." *BBC News*, 30 Dec. 2020, www.bbc.com/news/health-55280671.

Gannon, Kevin M. *Radical Hope: A Teaching Manifesto.* West Virginia University Press 2020, p. 5.

Garcia, Antero and Cindy O'Donnell-Allen. *Pose Wobble Flow: A Culturally Proactive Approach to Literacy Instruction*, Teachers College Press and National Writing Project, 2015, p. 63.

Garvelink, William. "The Future with Pandemics." Presentation, January Series, 8 Jan. 2021, Calvin University, Grand Rapids, Michigan.

Gillies, Rob. "Canada Health Regulator Approves Pfizer's COVID-19 Vaccine." *AP NEWS*, 9 Dec. 2020, apnews.com/article/Canada-coronavirus-pandemic-9cde42d f20e80c50752768b6696d45d5.

Goldrick-Rab, Sara. *Paying the Price: College Costs, Financial Aid, and the Betrayal of the American Dream*, University of Chicago Press, 2017.

Gregorian, Dareh. "Anti-lockdown Demonstrators Trade Guns for Scissors at Michigan 'haircut' Protest." *NBC News*, 20 May 2020, www.nbcnews.com/politics/ politics-news/anti-lockdown-demonstrators-trade-guns-scissors-michigan-haircut-protest-n1211366.

Gringlas, Sam and Barbara Sprunt. "Timeline: What We Know of President Trump's COVID-19 Diagnosis, Treatment." *NPR.org*, 5 Oct. 2020, www.npr. org/sections/latest-updates-trump-covid-19-results/2020/10/03/919898777/ timeline-what-we-know-of-president-trumps-covid-19-diagnosis.

Huffman, Bryce and Ted Roelofs. "Patrick Lyoya's Parents: Our Hearts Are Broken. Grand Rapids Mourns as Well." *Michigan News, State, Politics, Jobs, Education | Bridge Michigan*, 14 Apr. 2022, www.bridgemi.com/michigan-government/ patrick-lyoyas-parents-our-hearts-are-broken-grand-rapids-mourns-well?utm_ source=Bridge+Michigan&utm_campaign=183ed14383-Bridge+Newsletter+04 %2F14%2F2022_COPY_01&utm_medium=email&utm_term=0_c64a28dd5a-183ed14383-73895517.

Inoue, Asao B. "Grading Contracts: Assessing Their Effectiveness on Different Racial Formations." In *Race and Writing Assessment*, edited by Asao B. Inoue, and Mya Poe, Peter Lang, 2012, pp. 79–94.

"Items to Include in College Students' Quarantine Bags." *College Guide, MLive*, Mar. 2022. p. 2.

Jenlink, Patrick M. "Transforming the School into a Democratically Practiced Place: Dewey's Democracy as Spatial Practice," pp. 274–296. *Dewey's Democracy and Education Revisited: Contemporary Discourses for Democratic Education and Leadership*, edited by Patrick M. Jenlink, Rowman & Littlefield Education, 2009.

"June 1, 2020—PBS NewsHour Full Episode." https://www.pbs.org/newshour/show/june-1-2020-pbs-newshour-full-episode.

Kendi, Ibram X. *How to Be an Antiracist*, One World, 2019.

Knowles, David. "A Timeline of Trump's Missed Opportunities on Coronavirus." *Yahoo*, 8 Apr. 2020, www.yahoo.com/news/a-timeline-of-trumps-missed-opportunities-on-coronavirus-193202249.html?.tsrc=jtc_news_index.

Koshhar, Rakesh. "Unemployment Rose Higher in Three Months of COVID-19 Than It Did in Two Years of the Great Recession." *Pew Research Center*, 26 Aug. 2020, www.pewresearch.org/fact-tank/2020/06/11/unemployment-rose-higher-in-three-months-of-covid-19-than-it-did-in-two-years-of-the-great-recession/.

Kransz, Michael. "Kent County Sees 'Sharp Decline' in People Seeking COVID-19 Tests." *Mlive*, 21 Sept. 2020, www.mlive.com/news/grand-rapids/2020/09/kent-county-sees-sharp-decline-in-people-seeking-covid-19-tests.html.

Lee, Jena. "A Neuropsychological Exploration of Zoom Fatigue." *Psychiatric Times*, 17 Nov. 2020, www.psychiatrictimes.com/view/psychological-exploration-zoom-fatigue.

Levinson-King, Robin. "Trucker Protests: Ontario Calls State of Emergency." *BBC News*, 11 Feb. 2022, www.bbc.com/news/world-us-canada-60352980.

"Listings of WHO's Response to COVID-19." *WHO: World Health Organization*, 29 June 2020, www.who.int/news/item/29-06-2020-covidtimeline.

Loepp, Eric. "What Students Want: A Simple, Navigable LMS Course Design." *Faculty Focus: Higher Ed Teaching Strategies from Magna Publications*, 1 Feb. 2021, www.facultyfocus.com/articles/online-education/online-course-design-and-preparation/what-students-want-a-simple-navigable-lms-course-design/.

Mack, Julie. "Nearly Two Years In, Many Wonder: How Do Pandemics End?" *The Grand Rapids Press*, A1–A5, 21 Dec. 2021.

Mack, Julie. "Virus Has Put 1 of Every 100 Michiganders in the Hospital." *The Grand Rapids Press*, 10 Feb. 2022, pp. A1–A3.

Mack, Julie. "Why Did It Get So Bad Here?" *The Grand Rapids Press.* 19 Apr. 2020. pp. A.1, 6.

Mannik, Lynda and Karen McGarry. *Practicing Ethnography: A Student Guide to Method and Methodology*, University of Toronto Press, 2017.

Marsicano, Christopher R. "Embracing Break-and-Bake Cookies." *Inside Higher Ed: Career Advice, Teaching Today*, 10 Apr. 2020, www.insidehighered.com/advice/2020/04/10/professor-inexperienced-zoom-teaching-shares-lessons-learned-his-first-weeks-it.

Massey, Mike. "Encountering Nature: Outdoor Walks to Reduce Stress and Increase Focus in Students." *Faculty Focus: Higher Ed Teaching Strategies from Magna Publications*, 23 Sept. 2020, www.facultyfocus.com/articles/teaching-and-learning/encountering-nature-outdoor-walks-to-reduce-stress-and-increase-focus-in-students/.

Mazur, Eric and Bob Kerrey. "Higher Ed's Coronavirus Opportunity." *Wall Street Journal*, 11 May 2020. ProQuest, http://grcc.idm.oclc.org/login?url=https://www.proquest.com/newspapers/higher-eds-coronavirus-opportunity/docview/2400255906/se-2?accountid=11183.

McCann, Colum. "What if the Virus Can Teach Us to Change?" *TIME*, 18 May 2020, p. 19.

McNeil Jr., Donald G. "The U.S. Now Leads the World in Confirmed Coronavirus Cases." *The New York Times—Breaking News, US News, World News and Videos*, 28 May 2020, www.nytimes.com/2020/03/26/health/usa-coronavirus-cases.html. https://doi.org/10.4324/9781003138976-2.

"Michigan Coronavirus Dashboard: Cases, Deaths and Maps." *Bridge Magazine*, 18 May 2020, www.bridgemi.com/michigan-coronavirus-dashboard-cases-deaths-and-maps.

"Mortality Analyses." *Johns Hopkins Coronavirus Resource Center*, 18 May 2020, coronavirus.jhu.edu/data/mortality.

Muccari, Robin, Denise Chow and Joe Murphy. "Coronavirus Timeline: Tracking the Critical Moments of Covid-19." *NBC News*, 1 Jan. 2021, www.nbcnews.com/health/health-news/coronavirus-timeline-tracking-critical-moments-covid-19-n1154341.

Mulder, Tom. *English Composition Teacher's Guidebook: How to Survive (and Even Thrive) as an Adjunct or Part-time Instructor*, Equinox, 2020.

NBC Nightly News with Lester Holt. 15 Sept. 2021, NBC Universal News Group.

O'Mara, Shane. *In Praise of Walking: A New Scientific Exploration*, W.W. Norton, 2020.

Obama, Barack. "How to Make This Moment the Turning Point for Real Change." *Medium*, 1 June 2020, https://barackobama.medium.com/how-to-make-this-moment-the-turning-point-for-real-change-9fa209806067.

Oosting, Jonathan. "Maybe It's Time to Rethink Allowing Guns in Michigan Capitol, Officials Say." *Michigan News, State, Politics, Jobs, Education | Bridge Michigan*, 1 May 2020, www.bridgemi.com/michigan-government/maybe-its-time-rethink-allowing-guns-michigan-capitol-officials-say.

Palfrey, John. *Safe Spaces, Brave Spaces: Diversity and Free Expression in Education*, MIT P, 2017.

Park, Alice. "The Beginning of the End?" TIME. Vol. 199, Nos. 5–6, 14–21 Feb. 2022. 39–42.

Palmer, Parker, and Zajonc, Arthur. *The Heart of Higher Education: A Call to Renewal: Transforming the Academy through Collegial Conversations.* San Francisco: Jossey-Bass, 2010, p. 36.

Patton, Laurie L. "A Surprising Fruit of Our Pandemic Fall Semester." *Inside Higher Ed: Higher Education News*, 7 Dec. 2020, www.insidehighered.com/views/2020/12/07/pandemic-has-revealed-academe-dynamism-place-based-learning-opinion?

"Paying Back the Unsung Heroes of Georgetown University." *NBC Nightly News with Lester Holt*, reported by Rahema Ellis, 21 Oct. 2016.

Peterson-Ahmad, Maria B. and Randa G. Keeley. "Five Ways to Engage Students in an Online Learning Environment." *Faculty Focus: Higher Ed Teaching Strategies from Magna Publications* 27 Jan. 2021, www.facultyfocus.com/articles/online-education/online-course-delivery-and-instruction/five-ways-to-engage-students-in-an-online-learning-environment/.

"Pfizer and BioNTech Celebrate Historic First Authorization in the U.S. of Vaccine to Prevent COVID-19." *Pfizer: One of the World's Premier Biopharmaceutical*

Companies, 11 Dec. 2020, www.pfizer.com/news/press-release/press-release-detail/pfizer-and-biontech-celebrate-historic-first-authorization.

Pretty, Jules and Peggy F. Barlett. "Concluding Remarks: Nature and Health in the Urban Environment," pp. 298–319. *Urban Place: Reconnecting with the Natural World*, edited by Peggy F. Barlett, MIT Press, 2005.

"Queen Elizabeth Tests Positive for COVID." *BBC*, 20 Feb. 2022, www.bbc.co.uk/programmes/p0bq6spw.

"Remote Work by the Numbers." *Time*, Vol. 195, Nos. 12–13, 6–13 April 2020, p. 47.

Roelofs, Ted. "Michigan Nursing Homes, Where Information on Coronavirus Goes to Die." *Michigan Healthwatch, Bridge Magazine*, 21 Apr. 2020 www.bridgemi.com/michigan-health-watch/michigan-nursing-homes-where-information-coronavirus-goes-die.

"Russell Group Comment on Plans for Autumn Term Teaching." *The Russell Group*, 9 Aug. 2021, russellgroup.ac.uk/news/russell-group-comment-on-plans-for-autumn-term-teaching/.

Saeedi, Sina and Elaine Richardson. "A Black Lives Matter and Critical Race Theory-Informed Critique of Code-Switching Pedagogy." In *Race, Justice, and Activism in Literacy Instruction*, edited by Valerie Kinloch, Tanja Burkhard, and Carlotta Penn, Teachers College P, 2020, pp. 147–161.

Salisbury, Danielle and Justin P. Hicks. "What Made Michigan the Worst in Country Is Unclear." *The Grand Rapids Press*, 30 Nov. 2021, pp. A1–A3.

Salisbury, Danielle and Scott Levin. "Most Michiganders Can Dump the Masks." *The Grand Rapids Press*, 1 Mar. 2022, pp. A1–A7.

Salisbury, Danielle. "State Surpasses 2 Million Cases Since Start of the Pandemic." *The Grand Rapids Press*, 8 Feb. 2022, p. B1.

Schroeder, Ray. "Zoom Fatigue: What We Have Learned." *Inside Higher Ed: Higher Education News*, 20 Jan. 2021, www.insidehighered.com/digital-learning/blogs/online-trending-now/zoom-fatigue-what-we-have-learned.

Shafak, Elif. "The Revolutionary Power of Diverse Thought." TED New York, 27 Oct. 2017, https://www.ted.com/talks/elif_shafak_the_revolutionary_power_of_diverse_thought.

Smalley, Andrew. "Higher Education Responses to Coronavirus (COVID-19)." *National Conference of State Legislatures*, 22 March 2021, www.ncsl.org/research/education/higher-education-responses-to-coronavirus-covid-19.aspx.

Smith, Alexander. "Britain Becomes First to Roll out Clinically Approved Vaccine." *NBC News*, 8 Dec. 2020, www.nbcnews.com/news/world/britain-becomes-first-roll-out-clinically-approved-biontech-pfizer-vaccine-n1250330.

Smith, Allan. "'Lock Her Up!': Anti-Whitmer Coronavirus Lockdown Protestors Swarm Michigan Capitol." *NBC News*, 16 Apr. 2020, www.nbcnews.com/politics/politics-news/lock-her-anti-whitmer-coronavirus-lockdown-protestors-swarm-michigan-capitol-n1184426.

Smith, Gregory A. and David Sobel. *Place- and Community-based Education in Schools*, Routledge, 2010, p. viii.

St. Amour, Madeline. "Report: Fewer High School Students Went Straight to College." *Inside Higher Ed: Higher Education News*, 10 Dec. 2020, www.insidehighered.com/quicktakes/2020/12/10/report-fewer-high-school-students-went-straight-college?

Stewart, Dafina-Lazarus. "Language of Appeasement," *Inside Higher Ed*. 30 March 2017.

Sue, Derald Wing. *Race Talk and the Conspiracy of Silence: Understanding and Facilitating Difficult Dialogues on Race*, Wiley, 2015.

Suliman, Adela. "Europe Reaches Grim Milestone, Surpasses 100,000 Coronavirus Deaths." *NBC News*, 19 Apr. 2020, www.nbcnews.com/news/world/europe-reaches-grim-milestone-surpassing-100-000-coronavirus-deaths-n1187376.

Sullivan, Patrick M. "'A Lifelong Aversion to Writing': What if Writing Courses Emphasized Motivation?" *Teaching Composition at the Two-Year College: Background Readings*, edited by Patrick M. Sullivan and Christie Toth, Bedford/St. Martin's, 2017, p. 169.

Tatum, Beverly Daniel. "In Search of Wisdom: Higher Education for a Changing Democracy." *Can We Talk about Race? And Other Conversations in an Era of School Resegregation.* Beacon Press, 2007, pp. 105–126.

Taussig, Rebekah. "Age of Uncertainty." TIME. Vol. 199, Nos. 7–8, 28 Feb./7 Mar. 2022. 70–73.

Thomas, Kyla. "Pandemic Misery Index Reveals Far-reaching Impact of COVID-19 on American Lives, Especially on Blacks and Latinos." *The Conversation*, 1 June 2021, www.theconversation.com/pandemic-misery-index-reveals-far-reaching-impact-of-covid-19-on-american-lives-especially-on-blacks-and-latinos-159902.

Thomason, Andy, and Brian O'Leary. "Here's a List of Colleges That Require Students or Employees to Be Vaccinated Against COVID-19." *The Chronicle of Higher Education*, 21 Sept. 2021, www.chronicle.com/blogs/live-coronavirus-updates/heres-a-list-of-colleges-that-will-require-students-to-be-vaccinated-against-covid-19.

Tunison, John. "West Michigan Nursing Home Now Reporting 6 Coronavirus Deaths of Residents." MLive. 10 Apr. 10, 2020, https://www.mlive.com/news/grand-rapids/2020/04/west-michigan-nursing-home-now-reporting-6-resident-coronavirus-deaths.html.

Weissman, Sara. "Community College Leaders Celebrate First Lady's Return." *Inside Higher Ed | Higher Education News, Career Advice, Jobs*, 21 Sept. 2021, www.insidehighered.com/news/2021/09/21/community-college-leaders-celebrate-first-ladys-return?utm_source=Inside+Higher+Ed.

Weissman, Sara. "New Federal Data Confirm Enrollment Declines." *Inside Higher Ed | Higher Education News, Career Advice, Jobs*, 15 Sept. 2021, www.insidehighered.com/news/2021/09/15/new-federal-data-confirm-enrollment-declines.

Westbrook, David A. *Navigators of the Contemporary: Why Ethnography Matters*, University of Chicago Press, 2008.

WHO Coronavirus (COVID-19) Dashboard, World Health Organization, 18 Apr. 2022, covid19.who.int/.

Wilkinson, Mike. "Coronavirus Tracker | CDC Panel Recommends Pfizer Booster; Total Cases Surpass 1 Million in Michigan | Bridge Michigan." *Michigan News, State, Politics, Jobs, Education | Bridge Michigan*, 22 Sept. 2021, www.bridgemi.com/michigan-health-watch/coronavirus-tracker-what-michigan-needs-know-now.

Wilkinson, Mike. "Michigan May Be Past Coronavirus Peak, but Cases Grow Outstate." *Bridge Magazine*, 19 Apr. 2020, www.bridgemi.com/michigan-health-watch/michigan-may-be-past-coronavirus-peak-cases-grow-outstate.

Wise, Alana. "Trump Condemns Capitol Hill Violence, Ignores His Role in Inciting the Mob." *NPR.org*, 7 Jan. 2021, www.npr.org/sections/insurrection-at-the-capitol/2021/01/07/954587997/white-house-condemns-violence-on-capitol-hill-without-addressing-trumps-role.

Woodruff, Judy and William Brangham. "February 22, 2021—PBS NewsHour Full Episode." *PBS NewsHour*, 22 Feb. 2021, www.pbs.org/newshour/show/february-22-2021-pbs-newshour-full-episode.

Zee, Ginger. "Earth Day Boasts Beautiful Before and After Photos in Nature." *Good Morning America*, 22 April 2020, www.goodmorningamerica.com/news/video/earth-day-boasts-beautiful-photos-nature-70283163.

Index

CPSIA information can be obtained
at www.ICGtesting.com
Printed in the USA
JSHW060857280623
43761JS00002B/4